real life

Make your mark!

SARAH CUNNINGHAM   JONATHAN BYGRAVE

PEARSON
Longman

Grammar	Present tenses
	Past tenses
Vocabulary	Success and achievements
	Extreme adjectives and intensifiers
	Adverbials in narrative
Phrases	Talking about photographs
	Expressing an opinion

Listening & Vocabulary

1 In pairs, read the questions and discuss your answers. Use the prompts to help you.

- What are your most important achievements and skills?
- What goals do you have, outside schoolwork?

❝ *I've been in three plays.*
I know how to ride a motorbike.
I've played for the school basketball team.
I want to pass my driving test.
I would like to learn how to ski.

2 Read about the three people in the photos. What are their goals or achievements?

3 **a** (1.3) What kind of practice and preparation do you think PJ, Amy and Carolina do? Listen and check.

b Describe each person's training routine briefly.

4 Words **2** know (1.4) Check the words in blue. Then listen again and answer the questions.

Which speaker

1 particularly impresses the interviewer with his or her **motivation** and **dedication**?

PJ

2 enjoys the **challenge** and **satisfaction** of doing difficult things?

3 gained **inspiration** from one of his or her parents?

4 compares the **discipline** of his or her daily routine with that of the army?

5 feels that his or her **achievements** will gain the **respect** of other people in his or her community?

6 feels under **pressure** because there is so much **competition** from other people?

7 made **sacrifices** when he or she was a young child, in order to improve?

5 SPEAKING Read the questions and tick (✓) three that you would like to answer. Discuss your answers in pairs.

1 ☐ Do you think that PJ, Amy and Carolina's hard work and sacrifices are worthwhile?

2 ☐ Do you know a dedicated sportsperson or musician? How does this affect his or her life?

3 ☐ Do you find doing difficult things motivating? Give some examples.

4 ☐ Are you motivated by competition? Why? Why not?

5 ☐ Are you disciplined? In what ways?

❝ *My friend Marin is a dedicated swimmer. He practises every morning for two hours before school and …*

MINI WORKBOOK exercise 8 page 106

(1.2)

Dedicated!

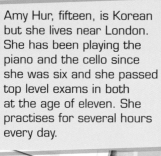

1 Philip (PJ) Foster, eighteen, has wanted to compete in the Ironman event in his home state of Hawaii since he was thirteen. Competitors swim four kilometres, cycle 180 kilometres and run forty-two kilometres, all without a break. PJ is currently training for this year's race and hopes to become one of the youngest competitors ever to cross the finishing line.

2 Amy Hur, fifteen, is Korean but she lives near London. She has been playing the piano and the cello since she was six and she passed top level exams in both at the age of eleven. She practises for several hours every day.

Grammar Focus

Present tenses

6 Read the texts about PJ, Amy and Carolina again. Find an example of:
- the present simple
- the present continuous
- the present perfect simple
- the present perfect continuous

7 Read *Grammar2know* and match the sentences 1–9 to the rules a–f. There is more than one example for some rules.

1 When someone crosses the finishing line everyone shouts.
rule a

2 I'm doing exams so I'm not practising so much.

3 I've been coming to events for years.

4 I've always been musical.

5 I've just done a twenty-five kilometre run.

6 I'm taking a break from my studies to do Miss Venezuela.

7 I'm speaking to Carolina Carrizo.

8 I'm getting fitter and fitter.

9 I've been practising seriously since I was nine.

3 Some people say that beauty is in the eye of the beholder but for Carolina Carrizo, nineteen, from Venezuela, it is all about hard work. Beauty queen Carolina has recently won a place at the Miss Venezuela School in Caracas, where they 'aim to make every girl perfect'.

Present simple and present continuous

a Use the present simple to describe repeated actions, habits, routines and general truths:
*Amy **practises** for several hours every day.*
*She **lives** near London.*

b Use the present continuous to describe actions in progress either at the moment of speaking or during the present period:
*PJ **is** currently **training** for this year's race.*

c Use the present continuous to describe gradual changes that are happening in the present period:
*It's **getting** more interesting.*

Remember that we do not use the present continuous with state verbs (*know, want, like,* etc.).

Present perfect simple and present perfect continuous

d Use the present perfect to describe actions that happened in the past but are still important in the present:
*Carolina's recently **won** a place at the Miss Venezuela School.* (this affects her life now)

e Use the present perfect to describe actions that started in the past but continue into the present:
*PJ **has wanted** to compete in the race since he was thirteen.*

f Use the present perfect continuous to emphasise that the action is repeated or has continued for a long time:
*Amy's **been playing** the piano since she was small.*

Remember that we do not use the present perfect continuous with state verbs.

8 Underline the correct verb form.

Our national hockey team ¹*play/are playing* really well this season. They ²*are doing/have been doing* a lot of extra training recently and they ³*have just found/have just been finding* a fantastic new coach. Their results ⁴*are really improve/are really improving* – they ⁵*have won/have been winning* an important international match this week. But unfortunately the normal goalkeeper ⁶*doesn't play/isn't playing* with them because he ⁷*recovers/is recovering* from an injury.

9 a In pairs, tell your partner the name of someone you know who plays a sport or musical instrument well or has another skill. It can be yourself!

b Use the prompts to make questions in the correct tense about the person you chose in exercise 9a. Then ask and answer.

1 Which sport or musical instrument/play?
Which sport does she play?

2 How long/do it?

3 practise or train/a lot?

4 prepare/for anything special/at the moment?

5 win/any competitions or pass/any exams?

6 improve/much/recently?

MINI WORKBOOK exercises 1–3 page 104

going to extremes

5

Grammar Focus

Past tenses

1 Discuss the questions in pairs.

- Who do you think are the best actors at the moment?
- Which have been their best roles?
- Read the caption. Have you seen Daniel Day-Lewis in any films?

2 Read the text and answer the questions.

1 Which four films are mentioned? What roles did Day-Lewis play in them?

2 Which films are in the photos?

3 How did he prepare for each role?

4 In what ways was his behaviour strange during filming?

5 Do you know any other actors who prepare like this?

3 **a** Read the text again. Find an example of:

- the past simple
- the past continuous
- the past perfect simple
- the past perfect continuous

b Read *Grammar2know* and find another example of each rule a–c in the text.

Grammar 2 know

Past simple and past continuous

a Use the past simple to describe completed actions and events in the past and the past continuous to describe actions in progress (continuing) at that time:

*Day-Lewis **annoyed** Neeson when they were **making** 'Gangs of New York' together.* (action in progress at that time)

Past perfect simple and past perfect continuous

b Use the past perfect to describe what happened before an action in the past:

*Gerry Conlon **went** to prison for a crime he **hadn't committed**.* (before he went to prison)

c Use the past perfect continuous (***had + been + verb + -ing***) to emphasise that the earlier action continued for a long time or was repeated:

*By the time filming **started** (main event), he **had been training** for two years.* (a period of time before that)

DANIEL DAY-LEWIS
Does he take acting
TOO FAR?

Daniel Day-Lewis is one of the outstanding actors of his generation. He has won two Oscars for Best Actor and a number of other awards.

1.5

1   Like Robert De Niro and Christian Bale, the actor Daniel Day-Lewis believes that to play a role really well you have to live the way the character lived. But sometimes his preparations can be extreme! For example, when he was
5   playing a disabled artist in the film *My Left Foot*, Day-Lewis refused to leave his wheelchair. The crew carried him everywhere and fed him with a spoon ... even when he wasn't acting!

In *In the Name of the Father*, he played Gerry Conlon, who
10 went to prison for a crime that he hadn't committed. Day-Lewis prepared for the role by spending several nights alone in a freezing prison cell. He told crew members to throw cold water at him, even when they weren't filming, because this had happened to Gerry Conlon. In 1997,
15 Day-Lewis played the lead role in the film *The Boxer*. By the time filming started, he had been training for two years, seven days a week! He was as good as a professional boxer.

Other actors don't always like his approach. Day-Lewis annoyed co-star Liam Neeson when they were making
20 *Gangs of New York* together. He addressed Neeson by his character's name, even when they were chatting in the hotel after work. 'I've never known anyone like him,' said one crew member. 'Daniel was playing a gangster called Bill the Butcher and when he was doing a violent scene
25 he got really furious. He was absolutely terrifying.' He discovered later that Day-Lewis had been working as a butcher for months before filming started!

4 (1.6) Complete the text below with a past tense (there may be more than one correct possibility). Listen and check.

MINI WORKBOOK exercises 4–7 pages 104–105

★ ★ ★ ★ ★ ★
OSCAR
WINNING ACTORS
TOP FACTS!

1 Robert De Niro ¹*also played* (also play) a boxer in his Oscar-winning role in the 1980 classic *Raging Bull*. When filming ²___ (start), he ³___ (train) so intensively that he ⁴___ (become) one of the top boxers in the world. While he ⁵___ (make) the film, De Niro ⁶___ (put) on thirty kilos, in order to play the boxer as an old man. He ⁷___ (previously lose) twenty-five kilos so that he ⁸___ (can) play the young boxer.

2 Heath Ledger ⁹___ (win) an Oscar for his role in *The Dark Knight*. The twenty-eight-year-old actor ¹⁰___ (finish) filming the movie just months before his death in 2008. Ledger ¹¹___ (sleep) very badly in the weeks before he ¹²___ (die), and friends say that he ¹³___ (suffer) from exhaustion at the time of his death.

3 James Dean, the iconic 1950s actor, ¹⁴___ (receive) *two* Oscar nominations after his death. He ¹⁵___ (film) the movie *Giant* until a couple of days before his death in a car crash and he ¹⁶___ (not finish) all the voice work on the movie so another actor ¹⁷___ (have to) imitate his voice.

4 Top Hollywood couple Brad Pitt and Angelina Jolie *both* ¹⁸___ (receive) Oscar nominations in 2009. The two stars ¹⁹___ (first meet) in 2004, while they ²⁰___ (film) *Mr and Mrs Smith* together.

★ ★ ★ ★ ★

Vocabulary & Speaking
Extreme adjectives and intensifiers

5 Find an adjective in the text about Daniel Day-Lewis that means:
1 very good *outstanding*
2 very cold
3 very angry
4 very frightening

6 Read *Active Study*.

ACTIVE STUDY

Notice intensifiers
a With extreme adjectives, use an 'extreme' intensifier instead of *very* :
absolutely terrifying   NOT: ~~*very terrifying*~~
b Do not use extreme intensifiers with ordinary adjectives:
very surprising   NOT: ~~*absolutely surprising*~~
c Use *really* with both types of adjective:
really tired   **really** furious

7 Match the extreme adjectives 1–10 to the ordinary adjectives a–j. Use a dictionary to help you.

1 terrible	a very worried
2 amazed	b very clever
3 exhausted	c very wet
4 huge	d very surprised
5 desperate	e very funny
6 soaked	f very tired
7 starving	g very hot
8 brilliant	h very bad
9 hilarious	i very hungry
10 boiling	j very big

8 Say how you would feel in the situations, using an extreme adjective and an intensifier.

1 Someone has deliberately broken your new mp3 player.
   I'd be absolutely furious!
2 It's -10°C and the central heating has broken.
3 You have just finished a ten-mile run.
4 You haven't eaten for two days.
5 You have been out in the pouring rain all day.
6 Your favourite footballer has just joined your local team.
7 You have just got a grade 'A' in your worst subject at school.
8 You have just seen a ghost!

MINI WORKBOOK exercises 9–10 page 106

Reading & Speaking

1 Read the quotations about success. Which do you think are true? Can you think of anyone who illustrates these points?

> 'Success is often about being in the right place at the right time.'

> 'It's not what you know in life that makes you successful, it's who you know.'

> 'If you believe in yourself, you can achieve anything.'

> 'Genius is one percent inspiration and ninety-nine percent perspiration.'

> 'Behind every great man there's a great woman.'

2 Check the *Words2know* and match them with the quotations in exercise 1. Which two qualities are not mentioned?

Words 2 know (1.7)

self-confidence	luck	natural talent
skill	determination and hard work	
support from other people	your social network	

" *I think the first quotation emphasises the importance of luck.*

3 Read the text quickly. Which idea in exercise 2 does the author Malcolm Gladwell think is the most important ingredient of success?

4 Read the text again and choose the correct answer.

1 According to one study, if you have a lot of friends at school you will
   a have a bigger social network later in life.
   b earn more money when you grow up.
   c grow taller.
   d be an exception when you are older.

2 At Mel Gibson's audition, he
   a was unlucky because some drunks had attacked him.
   b was lucky because the drunks hadn't hurt him.
   c was lucky because he was what the film director was looking for.
   d got the role of Napoleon's general.

3 Malcolm Gladwell claims that to reach the top
   a musicians have to practise for 10,000 hours.
   b you have to do 10,000 hours of hard work.
   c talent is not important.
   d dedication is not important.

4 Gladwell says that Mozart
   a was an exception to his theory.
   b had already practised for 10,000 hours when he was four.
   c was only successful because he had a strict father.
   d didn't produce work of true genius until he had done a lot of practice.

(1.8)

Reaching the top

Have you got what it takes?

5 What is the secret X factor that you need in order to be as successful as Rafael Nadal, Bill Gates or Madonna? And why don't equally talented people make it?

10 Many social scientists have studied the phenomenon of success. One American study claims that your social network is the key to success. Apparently, every extra friend that you have at school adds two 15 percent to your salary later in life! Perhaps this boosts your self-confidence or perhaps you have more people to support you. Another study links height and success: every extra centimetre is worth another 20 $300 per year. The trouble is that for every person who conforms to these theories, there is an exception.

So is success just down to luck? Napoleon was once thinking about promoting a 25 general in his army. After he had heard about all the general's talents, he said 'Yes, yes, I realise he's brilliant but is he lucky?' And when you think about it, what use is talent without luck? In 1979, an unknown 30 Australian actor arrived at a film audition looking bruised and exhausted. He had been partying the night before and three drunks had attacked him. The director was looking for a tough, battle-scarred actor to 35 star in his film and immediately offered the actor the part. That actor was Mel Gibson and he went on to become a Hollywood superstar. Talent has kept him famous but it was luck that gave him his first break.

40 However, in his book *Outliers – The Story of Success*, author, Malcolm Gladwell, has come up with a theory that he claims is true in every case. He says that the secret of success is simply many hours of hard work. 45 He has calculated exactly how many hours work you need to do in order to become 'the best' in your field: 10,000 hours apparently or about four hours a day for ten years. Without this kind of determination and 50 hard work you probably won't reach the top, regardless of your talent.

Researchers looked at violin players in a music school to test this theory. Teachers put the players into three groups: average players in group C, good players in group B and outstanding players in group A. It turned out that all the players in group A had done around 10,000 hours of practice in their lifetime. The good players had done around 6,000 hours and the average players only 4,000 hours. However, all the players had entered the school with similar levels of ability.

But surely there are exceptions to this rule? Mozart, for example, is always considered a 'born genius'. He performed in public at the age of four and by six, he had composed several pieces. Surely his success was down to natural talent, not hard work? In fact, Gladwell argues, Mozart had a very strict father who made him practise for hours each day from an early age. And the music that Mozart composed when he was six wasn't outstanding. Mozart wrote his first real masterpiece when he was twenty-one. By that time, he'd done at least 10,000 hours of practice and had 'become' a genius.

Talent, argues Gladwell, is nothing without hard work. So next time you dream of scoring the winning goal in the World Cup or winning an Oscar, ask yourself this question: are you really prepared to put in the hours necessary to achieve your goal?

5 NOTICE IDIOMS Rewrite the sentences using an idiom from the text that means the same as the <u>underlined</u> words.

1 (line 3) Have you got <u>the necessary characteristics</u>?

Have you got what it takes?

2 (line 8) Why don't equally talented people <u>become successful</u>?

3 (line 13)… <u>the most important element of</u> success.

4 (line 23) Is success <u>just a matter of</u> luck?

5 (line 39) It was luck that gave him his <u>first opportunity</u>.

6 (line 50) You probably won't <u>become one of the best in your field</u>.

6 Discuss the questions.

• Do you think Malcolm Gladwell's theory is generally true or not?

• Can you think of any exceptions?

• Are there any goals that you would work this hard for?

❝ *I'd play football for 10,000 hours if I could be a top professional footballer!*

7 (1.9) Listen to two students talking about a highly successful person whose achievements they really admire. Answer the questions about each person.

• Who is the person and what is he or she famous for?

• What are or were this person's main achievements?

• What is interesting or admirable about this person?

• Does this person fit Malcolm Gladwell's theory or not?

8 **a** Think of a highly successful person, dead or alive, who you admire. It could be a sports person, actor, musician, writer or leader.

CAN YOU DO IT IN ENGLISH?

b Spend a few minutes preparing a short talk about him or her. Think about the questions in exercise 7 and use the phrases on the back cover to help you.

9 Take turns to give your talk. Discuss whether you think each person fits Gladwell's theory.

❝ *A person I really admire is …*

… has been playing … since … and has won many …

I (don't) think … fits this theory because …

MINI WORKBOOK exercise 11 page 106

going to extremes

9

Writing & Vocabulary

A narrative

1 Look at the picture and read the caption. Discuss the questions in pairs.

- Where is Chute Canyon and what is it like?
- Would you like to go hiking there? Why? Why not?

2 **a** Use the picture and words in the box to predict what happened to James during the hike.

> a rock   a boulder   a pool   to slip

b How do you think the story ended?

3 **a** Read Alex's account of what happened. Compare your answer to question 2 with the real story.

b Answer the questions.

1 Why did the brothers go hiking in Chute Canyon?

2 What did Alex decide to do after his brother's accident?

3 Why was the canyon full of water?

4 How long did James wait for rescue?

4 STRUCTURE Read the story again and match the instructions a–f to the paragraphs 1–4.

a Describe how the story ends.

b Introduce the time, the place and the main characters.

c Describe the important part of the story in detail.

d Hint that something exciting will happen.

e Describe the consequences of events or people's reactions.

f Describe the 'turning point' where something unexpected happens.

Paragraph 1: Background information	• *b – Introduce the time, the place and the main characters.* •
Paragraph 2: The lead up to the main events	•
Paragraph 3: Main events	•
Paragraph 4: The ending	• •

In November 2008, Alex and James Harrison, aged twenty-one and eighteen, went hiking in Chute Canyon, one of the most difficult routes in the mountains in Utah, in the US.

1.10 # A challenge too far

1 Two years ago, my brother James and I set out on a hike through Chute Canyon, Utah. We were hiking fanatics and had dreamt of doing this route for a long time. However, we had no idea of the terrible adventure that was waiting for us.

2 We completed the first part without problems. Then it started to snow and the rocks became slippery. All of a sudden, as I was helping my brother down a huge boulder, he slipped and fell into a pool. Unfortunately, he had landed on a rock just below the surface and his leg shattered.

3 I climbed down and gradually pulled him out of the water. Night was coming and the temperature was falling but my brother couldn't move. Feeling desperate, I decided to head for the nearest camp for help so I left James with some warm clothing and the rest of the food. It had been raining and to my horror, I discovered that the canyon was flooded. But I had no choice, I had to struggle on, soaked and freezing, unable even to think clearly. At one point I got lost, wasting precious hours.

4 At two-thirty the following afternoon, I eventually arrived at the camp. The journey had taken twenty-two hours and I was exhausted and starving. However, I managed to call for help and twelve hours later rescuers reached James. Thankfully, he was still alive and his leg was not permanently damaged. We were hiking again a year later, amazingly – though we've never been back to Chute Canyon!

5 LANGUAGE Read *Language4writing*. <u>Underline</u> seven of these adverbials in the story. Why does the writer use them?

6 ~~Cross out~~ the adverbials that are inappropriate to link the sentences below. One, two or three of them may be correct.

1 We had been searching for the missing child for hours. *Eventually,/Sadly,/Thankfully,* we found her playing safely in the park.

2 We had to drive home through a terrible snowstorm. *Eventually,/Fortunately,/Sadly,* we got home safely.

3 We went camping last month. The weather was absolutely awful, *unfortunately/thankfully/gradually.*

4 Everyone was sleeping peacefully. *All of a sudden,/Fortunately,/Suddenly,* there was a terrible noise.

5 There was a bad earthquake here last summer. No one was killed, *amazingly/sadly/thankfully.*

6 Louisa and Vanessa are cousins. *Surprisingly,/Sadly,/Strangely,* they've never met.

7 **a** Look at the picture story about Ellen Kelman. Match what she said from the box below to the pictures 1–4. Which idea is not illustrated?

> I was just paddling out to sea on my board …
> I saw a shark's fin.
> I just kicked and kicked.
> I've still got a scar.
> I had a big cut down my leg.
> Something hit me.
> The paramedics were there in ten minutes.

b (1.11) In pairs, put the pictures in the correct order. Then listen and check.

8 (1.11) Make notes about the questions. Listen again to check and complete your notes.

1 What do you learn about Ellen's background?

2 Where and when did the story happen?

3 What was the first sign that something was going wrong?

4 Can you describe exactly what happened next? (list the events)

5 How did the story end?

6 Did Ellen's attitude towards surfing change after this?

9 Look again at the table in exercise 4. Match the information in exercise 8 to the correct paragraph. Do you need to add any more details?

10 You are going to write a story. Choose one of the options below and plan your story. Make notes about what happened using the table in exercise 4 to structure your story.

• The story of Ellen Kelman's attack by a shark.

• The story of the hike in Chute Canyon from James's point of view.

• Your own story about an adventure or trip that went wrong.

11 **a** Write the first draft of your story. Then read it through yourself or swap with a partner. Work through the checklist for writing on the back cover.

b Write the final draft of your story.

REAL TIME

Jake, Ella and Ikram are students in Brighton. They also do a two-hour radio show, once a week, for a local radio station.

TALKING ABOUT PHOTOGRAPHS

1 a Look at the photo of Jake, Ella and Ikram and answer the questions.

1 Who do you think are the DJs and who is the producer of the show?

2 Why might they be looking at photos?

b (1.12) Listen and check your answers.

2 (1.12) Listen again and answer the questions.

1 When is the radio show?

2 Which of the photos A–C is Ella describing?

3 What topic connects Ella's photos?

3 a (1.12) Complete Ella's description with the *Phrases2know*. Then listen again and check.

Phrases 2 know

Talking about photographs

These photos are related to the topic of …
They seem … (+ adjective)
I think it's … I think they're …
It looks as though … (+ clause)
They look like … (+ noun)
It makes you think of …
… in the foreground … in the background …
What they have in common is …

Ella: Right, as you can see, ¹_____ music and having fun with music. ²_____ the radio ³_____ of each photo. The photo on the right is black and white and it shows some teenage couples dancing. ⁴_____ from the 1950s. ⁵_____ the early days of pop music.

In this photo, two teenage girls are listening to a portable radio and ⁶_____ they're singing along with it. ⁷_____ very relaxed and they ⁸_____ they're having a good time.

So these photos illustrate different ways of having fun with music. Which one do you think would be best?

b Write the order in which Ella does these things when she describes a photograph.

☐ interpret the photos
☐ describe what's in the photos
☐ state the general theme or topic

A

B

C

4 a In pairs, answer the questions about photo C.

1 Where are the people and what are they doing?

2 How do you think they are feeling?

3 What does the photo make you think about?

4 What does it suggest about having fun with music?

b In groups, describe the photos using the *Phrases2know*.

EXPRESSING AN OPINION

5 Look at photos A and B again. Do you think either (or both) would make a good advert? Why?

6 a (1.13) Listen to the rest of the conversation and answer the questions.

1 Why does the station manager, Mr Douglas, ask questions?

2 Which photo does he prefer in the end?

b Summarise Ikram and Ella's answers to Mr Douglas' questions.

1 How is life different for teenagers now compared to the past?

2 How do teenagers have fun nowadays?

3 How are teenagers now different from teenagers in the past?

4 Does advertising work on teenagers?

7 a Look at the *Phrases2know*. Write (E) if they express an opinion and (J) if they justify an opinion.

Phrases 2know

Expressing and justifying your opinions

- [E] **In my opinion,** teenagers do the same things that they have always done.
- [ ] **If you ask me,** the internet has changed life for teenagers.
- [ ] **To my mind,** teenagers have to cope with more pressure these days.
- [ ] **The way I see it,** teenagers like funny and interesting adverts.
- [ ] **Don't forget that** teenagers are naturally curious.
- [ ] **You have to bear in mind that** it's difficult to find a job these days.
- [ ] **The main reason is** it's interesting and funny

b Use the words in brackets and the *Phrases2know* to express the opinions. If necessary, change the ideas to reflect your opinion and try to justify it.

1 (ask) listening to live music is better than listening to music on the radio

If you ask me, listening to live music is better than listening to music on the radio. The main reason is that it's exciting to see the band.

2 (opinion) life is much easier for teenagers than it was in the past

3 (mind) social networking sites are a good way to keep in touch with your friends

8 Give your own answers to questions 1–4 in exercise 6b. Use the *Phrases2know*.

9 In pairs, read the advert and look at the photos.

Student A: Choose the best photo for the advert. Describe it and explain your choice. Then answer Student B's questions.

Student B: Choose two questions from the list. Listen to Student A's description and ask your questions.

- Why do teenagers use social networking websites?
- What does success mean to teenagers?
- How can a good social network help you achieve success?
- How important is luck in achieving success?

What will help you be successful in life?

Talent, ability, determination and a good social network! Join our school's social network today!

www.schoolsocialnetwork.org

2 living together

Grammar	Present perfect simple and continuous
	Present and past habits
Vocabulary	Behaviour and relationships
Phrases	A formal phone conversation

Boomerang Kids

(1.14) Young people who leave home ... then go back!

As it gets harder for young people to find jobs, a new phenomenon is changing British families. 'Boomerang kids' leave home to go to university but then return to the nest in their twenties. A third of men aged twenty-one to twenty-five now live with their parents. Previous generations moved into shared flats after they left university and started work. But with fewer jobs around, twenty-somethings find it's cheaper to live at home with mum and dad.

Listening & Vocabulary

1 Discuss the questions in pairs.
- When and why do you think you'll leave home?
- In what ways, positive (+) and negative (−), will your life change?

+ I'll have more freedom.
− I'll have to pay rent.

2 Read the text about 'boomerang kids' and discuss the questions.
- What are 'boomerang kids' and why are there more of them?
- Do people in their twenties often live with their parents in your country?
- What problems might families experience when adult children live with their parents?

3 (1.15) Listen to a radio programme about 'boomerang kids'. Tick (✓) true and cross (✗) false. Explain your answers.

The psychologist thinks that

1 ✗ most parents expect their children to live with them after university.

2 ☐ adult children expect to be able to do what they want in their parents' home.

3 ☐ adult children don't expect any help from their parents.

4 ☐ families need written rules about what adult children can and cannot do.

5 ☐ it is wrong for adult children to pay their parents rent.

The listener says that

6 ☐ she is finding it difficult to get on with her parents.

7 ☐ it's reasonable for her parents to expect her to help with household jobs.

4 a **Words 2 know** (1.16) Check the words in blue. Who mentions these things, the psychologist (P), the listener (L) or both (B)?

- P setting clear household rules
- ☐ treating each other with respect
- ☐ sharing adult chores and responsibilities
- ☐ behaving reasonably
- ☐ avoiding rows and conflict
- ☐ having a chat and a laugh together
- ☐ enjoying each other's company
- ☐ communicating about important issues

b (1.15) Listen again and check.

5 SPEAKING In pairs, decide which three things in exercise 4 are important for parents and children to live together happily. What would your parents say?

❝ For me, the most important thing is behaving reasonably.

MINI WORKBOOK exercise 9 page 109

Grammar Focus

Present perfect simple and continuous

6 Read the article on page 15 and answer the questions.

1 Where was Damien living before he graduated and who with?

2 What's the situation now and how does he feel about it?

3 Which issue causes conflict with his parents?

4 Does Damien have a job at the moment?

5 What are his aims?

"It feels like a backward step."

(1.17)

1 Damien Morris, 21, left home over three years ago to study Graphic Design at university. He graduated in June and this summer he has moved back into his parents' home.

'Before I graduated I lived with five other students and I did
5 what I liked, really. I've been living with my parents again for about three months now and it feels like a backward step, like being a child again. **Generally, my parents have been quite reasonable, I suppose.**

They haven't set any "household rules" and they haven't
10 been charging me rent, which is good of them. The main problem is that I get up and go to bed much later than they do and that annoys them. **We've had one or two big rows about it.**

Basically, I'm desperate to move into a place of my own
15 but first I need a job and that's difficult at the moment. **I've been working part-time in a bar this month** so at least I've got a bit of money but I need a proper job – I want to start my career. I've been sending off application forms all summer. In total, I think I've sent off about forty
20 applications but most companies haven't even replied – it's depressing. I'm especially fed up today. One of my friends has just phoned me this morning because **he's found me a room to rent.** It's in a house with some of his mates and they're really cool people, he's known them for years. But
25 I'll have to say no ... it's so frustrating.'

---

7 Read *Grammar2know* and match the four sentences in **bold** in the article to rules a–d.

Grammar 2know

Present perfect simple and continuous

a Use the present perfect simple to describe single complete actions in the period leading up to the present:

This summer he's moved back to his parents' home. (one completed action)

b Use the present perfect continuous to describe continuing or repeated actions in the period leading up to the present. These actions are often incomplete:

I've been living with my parents for three months. (a continuing action that is not finished)

I've been filling in application forms all summer. (a repeated action that he will probably do again)

Compare these examples:

*He has just **phoned** me this morning.* (one phone call)

*He has **been phoning** me this morning.* (many calls)

c Notice that we use the present perfect simple if we say the number of actions:

I've filled in about forty application forms.

d Do not use the continuous form if you use a state verb, even though you are describing a continuing action:

He's known them for years. NOT: ~~He's been knowing them for years.~~

---

8 Circle the correct answer.

1 Which person has sent me more emails?
   a Suzi's emailed me this week.
   b Ali's been emailing me this week.

2 Whose essay is definitely finished?
   a Jonny's written his essay.
   b Callum's been writing his essay.

3 Who has probably done the most exercise?
   a Ben has been to the gym this week.
   b Alex has been going to the gym this week.

4 Whose room is finished?
   a Jade has painted her room.
   b Grace has been painting her room.

9 a Underline the correct tense, present perfect simple or continuous.

1 Have you *had/been having* breakfast today?
2 How many texts have you *sent/been sending* today?
3 How long have you *studied/been studying* English?
4 Have you *gone/been going* out much recently?
5 Have you *passed/been passing* your driving test?
6 How long have you *known/been knowing* your best friend?

b In pairs, ask and answer the questions in exercise 9a.

10 WRITING Write a short description of your life in the last few weeks or months using the present perfect tenses where appropriate.

In the last few weeks I've been going out a lot because I've finished my exams.

MINI WORKBOOK exercises 1–3 page 107

living together

15

Vocabulary & Listening

Behaviour and relationships

1 In pairs, think of three 'stereotypical complaints' that men make about women or that women make about men. Compare answers with the class.

" *According to men, women always spend hours on the phone. Women say that men never …*

2 a Read about Jennifer and Dylan and look at the photo.

> Jennifer and Dylan got married at nineteen while they were still at university. They're happy but they sometimes find each other's habits annoying.

b Words **2 know** (1.18) Check the words in blue. Guess who is making the complaint, Dylan (D), Jennifer (J) or both (B).

3 (1.19) Listen to Dylan and Jennifer complaining about each other's annoying habits. Which habits in exercise 2b does each one mention?

4 (1.19) Listen again and answer the questions.

1 Which habits does each person find particularly annoying and why?
2 Do they know how the other person feels about their annoying habits?
3 Who do you sympathise with most?
4 What do you think Dylan and Jennifer should do to make their relationship better?
5 Do you think Dylan and Jennifer got married too young?

5 Discuss the questions in pairs.

- Which habits in exercise 2b do you find most annoying?
- Do you know anyone who does these things?
- Are there any other habits that you find particularly annoying?

" *It drives me mad when people don't listen to me.*

My friend Anna takes ages to get ready and that really winds me up!

It really gets on my nerves when …

MINI WORKBOOK exercise 10 page 109

He …   She …

- ☑ takes ages to get ready.
- ☐ is always nagging me.
- ☐ spends hours gossiping to his/her mates.
- ☐ is always making a drama out of tiny things.
- ☐ is always showing off in front of his/her mates.
- ☐ keeps interrupting me when I'm trying to concentrate.
- ☐ often ignores what I'm saying or doesn't listen to me.
- ☐ is always leaving a mess and then expects me to clear up.
- ☐ keeps forgetting arrangements.
- ☐ keeps mislaying things.

Grammar **Focus**
Present and past habits

6 **a** **Read the magazine article that Jennifer wrote later and answer the questions.**

1 What are the similarities between the way that Max trained the dolphin and the way that Jennifer 'trained' Dylan?

2 Choose the best ending for the article. He …
  a was going to fix my computer!
  b was training me!
  c wasn't angry with me!

b **Do you know anyone who you would like to 'train' in this way? Why?**

7 **a** **Find five verbs in the text that describe habits or repeated actions. Then read *Grammar2know*.**

b **Find another example of rules b and c in exercise 2b. Find another example of rules d and e in the text.**

Grammar **2** know

Habits in the present and past

a Generally, use the present simple and past simple to talk about habits:

  *He often **ignores** me.*

  *I **nagged** him all the time.*

b Use the present or past continuous + *always* or *constantly* when a habit is annoying or surprising:

  *He's **always forgetting** arrangements.*

  *My computer **was constantly crashing**.*

c Use *keep* + verb + *-ing* to emphasise that something happens very often (especially a bad habit):

  *He **keeps** interrupt**ing** me.*

  *I **kept** think**ing** about it.*

d Use *would* to describe habits and repeated actions in the past:

  *The trainer **would ignore** it.*

e Use ***used to*** for habits and states in the past that have now stopped or changed:

  *It **didn't use to** worry me.*

Notice that we use *would* only for actions but we use *used to* for actions and states.

HOW AN ANIMAL TRAINER CHANGED OUR RELATIONSHIP

(1.20)

1 A few months ago, I interviewed Max Lungren, an animal trainer. He was teaching a dolphin to do a back flip. Every time the dolphin jumped out of the water, even a little, Max would reward it with some food. When the dolphin
5 did something else, Max would just ignore it. At first the dolphin kept swimming round the pool and having fun. But slowly, it learned that when it jumped, it got a reward. After a few days the dolphin was jumping high enough to do a somersault. It had learned the first part of the trick.

10 I was fascinated. I kept thinking about how Max had trained that dolphin … and then I began to wonder if the same techniques might work with my husband, Dylan. He was always leaving dirty washing on the floor and he often used to forget arrangements that we'd made. I
15 nagged him but he ignored me. The piles of washing just got bigger and he would forget even more arrangements. His bad habits didn't use to bother me but now they were driving me mad!

So I decided to copy the dolphin trainer. I praised
20 Dylan when he put anything in the washing basket, even if it was just one sock or when he remembered any arrangement, even if he got the wrong day. Slowly, the piles of dirty washing became smaller and his memory got better. I was so pleased that I told Dylan
25 about my 'training'. He looked thoughtful.

A few days later my computer crashed again. It was constantly crashing and I called Dylan in a panic. The first thing he said was, 'Well done, Jen, you haven't
30 made a drama out of this.' Suddenly, I felt calm. I liked his praise. Then I realised what was happening. He …

8 **a** **Write five sentences about the annoying habits of people you know, including yourself. Use the ideas in the box or your own ideas.**

> complain   nag   interrupt me
> borrow my stuff   lose things   break things
> leave a mess everywhere

I keep losing things.

My aunt is always complaining.

b **Write five sentences about habits you had when you were a child. Use the ideas in the box or your own ideas.**

> bite my nails   suck my thumb   chat non-stop
> eat too many sweets   not eat vegetables
> have nightmares

I was always having nightmares.

I used to chat non-stop.

9 **In pairs, compare your answers to exercises 8a and 8b.**

MINI WORKBOOK exercises 4–8 page 108

living together

Reading & Vocabulary

1 In pairs, look at the photos. Take it in turns to describe a photo and guess which one your partner is describing.

2 Read the text about relationships. Match the headings 1–6 to the sections A–D. There are two extra headings.

   1 When do most people tie the knot*?

   2 Who does what in the house?

   3 How are finances arranged between couples?

   4 How and at what age do couples start dating?

   5 Who's the head of the family?

   6 Who pays for what on a date?

* an idiomatic expression that means 'get married'

3 a **Words 2 know** (1.22) Check the words in blue.

   1 In Australia, _women_ often **ask** _men_ **out**.

   2 Most young Britons start **dating** at the age of about ___ .

   3 In ___ people often only **have** one **relationship** before they get married.

   4 In the UK, most people get married and **settle down** at the age of about ___ .

   5 Many ___ women become **full-time housewives** when they get married.

   6 Many ___ fathers stay at home to **bring up** their children because the mother is the main **breadwinner**.

   7 Japanese ___ are **in charge of** the family finances.

   8 Among the Mosuo, ___ are the **head of the household** and **inherit** all family **property**.

   9 The **divorce rate** among ___ is very high.

   10 ___ percent of marriages in the world are **arranged marriages**.

b Read the text again. In pairs, complete the sentences above with information from the text.

4 a Read the text again and find:
- a custom or fact that is similar in your country
- a custom or fact that is different in your country
- a custom that surprises you
- a custom that you think is wrong

b Compare answers in groups.

Happily ever after? (1.21)

1 How the sexes meet, marry and share domestic life around the world.

A _____

Dating customs around the world vary enormously. In the UK, for example, most people go on their first date at the age of thirteen or fourteen and have a number of relationships before they eventually settle down. In Korea, on the other hand, many young people don't start dating until they are in their twenties and they often only date the person that they eventually marry. In Australia, it is common for women to ask men out and to pay the bill but in the US, men still tend to pay for their partner.

Did you know? In the UK, the most common way to meet a new partner is online.

5 Read *Active Study*.

ACTIVE STUDY

Phrasal verbs (1)

Phrasal verbs consist of a verb and a particle.

1 Sometimes you can work out the meaning of the phrasal verb from the two words:

*The average age for marriage is **going up**.*

But sometimes you can't:

*People have several relationships before they **settle down**.*

2 Some phrasal verbs cannot be separated:

*They **look after the children**.*
NOT: ~~They look the children after.~~

But some are separable:

*Many women **give up** their careers.*

OR: *Many women **give** their careers **up**.*

You can find this information in a good dictionary.

MINI WORKBOOK exercise 12 page 109

B _____

15 The average age at which people get married has been going up steadily in recent years. In the UK, it is now around thirty and in the US, it's around twenty-seven. In Russia, on the other hand, couples tend to marry straight after school or
20 university. However, Russia has one of the highest divorce rates in the world.

Did you know?

Sixty percent of all marriages worldwide
25 are arranged marriages.

C _____

A recent international survey has shown that Swedish men do the most around the house: six times more than Japanese
30 men, who did the least housework in the survey. Japanese husbands do only four hours' housework a week on average, compared with their wives, who do around thirty hours a week. However, in Sweden both partners normally work but in Japan, it is usual for women to give their careers up when
35 they get married in order to become full-time housewives. But it's not all bad news for Japanese wives: the typical Japanese husband hands over his entire salary to his wife, who gives him back pocket money in return!

Did you know?

200,000 men in the UK are
40 househusbands and around twenty percent of under-fives in the US are brought up by stay-at-home-dads, while the mother is the breadwinner.

45 **D** _____

In modern marriages, working out who's in charge of what can be tricky but not among the Mosuo people from South East China. They have one of the last matriarchal societies left on earth: women are the head of the household, look
50 after the children and make all business decisions. The family name passes from mother to daughter and daughters inherit the family property. Children
55 belong to their mother's family and it is not acceptable for fathers to live with their children – they remain part of their own mother's household!

Did you know?

60 Around twenty-five percent of children in the UK and US live in one-parent families, the majority of them
65 with their mother.

6 Match the phrasal verbs 1–9 to the meanings a–i, using the text or a dictionary to help you. Tick (✓) if the phrasal verb is separable and cross (✗) if not.

1	✗ settle down (line 7)	**a** ask on a date
2	☐ ask out (line 11)	**b** calculate
3	☐ go up (line 16)	**c** give completely
4	☐ give up (line 34)	**d** increase
5	☐ hand over (line 37)	**e** raise a child
6	☐ give back (line 38)	**f** return
7	☐ bring up (line 42)	**g** stay in a relationship or place permanently
8	☐ work out (line 46)	**h** stop doing something
9	☐ look after (line 49)	**i** take care of

7 a Read five teenagers' opinions about dating. Do you think the speaker is male (M) or female (F)?

A [M] 'I think it's fine for a girl to ask a guy out – why not? I'd be perfectly happy if a girl asked me out!'

B ☐ *'Personally, I would always expect the guy to pay if we go out on a date. I just think it shows that he cares.'*

C ☐ 'You shouldn't seem too keen when you first start going out with someone. I think you should always wait for them to call you and wait a day or two to answer their texts … you shouldn't be too available.'

D ☐ *'One of the nastiest things that someone can do is to finish with you by text. A girl did that to me once and I was really upset.'*

E ☐ 'If someone stands me up or arrives really late for the date, then it's the end of the relationship … unless they've got a really good reason. If someone treats you like that once, they'll do it again.'

b Rank the opinions A–E from 1 (completely agree) to 5 (completely disagree). Discuss your opinions in pairs.

8 a In groups, make a list of 'Five Golden Rules for Dating' using the ideas in exercise 7, your own ideas and the phrases on the back cover to help you. Give brief reasons for your rules.

CAN YOU DO IT IN ENGLISH?

❝ *Never arrive late for a date because it's rude. Men should always pay the bill.*

b Discuss your list with the class.

MINI WORKBOOK exercises 11–12 page 109

living together

A FORMAL PHONE CONVERSATION

1 a Look at the photo. Read the caption and answer the questions.

1 Where are Ella and Ikram?

2 What do you think is going to happen there?

3 How do you think they feel about it? Why?

b (1.23) Listen and check your answers. What plan do Ella and Ikram make?

2 a Read the phone conversation between Ella (E) and the receptionist (R). <u>Underline</u> the correct phrases. Explain why the other phrases are inappropriate.

> R: Hello. ComfortBreak Hotels.
>
> E: Hello. ¹*Could I speak to your PR manager, please?*/Is your PR manager there?
>
> R: Yes, of course. ²*Who's that?/Who's calling, please?*
>
> E: ³*My name is Ella Campbell./It's Ella.* I'm calling from Bright Lights Radio.
>
> R: And ⁴*what do you want to talk to him about?/can I ask what your call is concerning?*
>
> E: Yes, it's about the new hotel your company is building next to the beach huts in Brighton.
>
> R: Okay. The PR manager is Mr Nash. ⁵*I'll put you through./I'll pass you over to him.*
>
> E: Thank you.
>
> R: ⁶*Hold the line please./Hang on a minute.* … I'm afraid Mr Nash ⁷*has just popped out somewhere/is not available right now.* Can I take a message?
>
> E: Yes. ⁸*Tell him to give me a ring./Could you ask him to call me?* It's quite urgent.

b (1.24) Listen and check. What is the problem and what is Ikram's advice?

c (1.24) Listen again. Write down the phrases from exercise 2a that Ella and Ikram use in their conversation. Explain why they use those phrases.

> Ella and Ikram are walking on Brighton beach when they see a new development …

3 Look at the *Phrases2know* and mark them as formal (F) or informal (I). The neutral phrases have already been marked (N).

Phrases **2** know

Phone conversations

Getting through

Caller:

☐ Could I speak to …, please?   ☐ Is … there?

☐ It's …   ☐ My name is …

☒ I'm calling about …

Other person:

☐ Who's calling, please?   ☐ Who's that?

☐ What do you want to talk to him/her about?

☐ Can I ask what your call is concerning?

☐ I'll put you through.   ☐ I'll pass you over.

☒ I'll see if he's/she's in.

☐ Hold the line, please.   ☐ Hang on a minute.

Giving and taking messages

Other person:

☐ I'm afraid he's/she's not available right now.

☐ He's/She's just popped out somewhere.

Caller:

☒ Could you ask him/her to call me?

☐ Tell him/her to give me a ring.

4 a Complete the phone conversations using *Phrases2know*.

1
A: Hello. Mr Conway's office.
B: Hello. _____ Mr Conway, please?
A: _____ ?
B: Yes, _____ the job vacancy.
A: Okay, I'll _____ . _____ , please.
B: Thank you.
A: Hello. I'm afraid _____ .
B: Oh! _____ ? It's quite urgent.

2
A: Hi, Annie. _____ Dave.
B: Hi, Dave. Do you want to talk to Mark?
A: Yes, please.
B: _____ a minute, I'll _____ .
A: Thanks.
B: I think _____ .
A: Oh, okay. _____ .
B: Sure.

b (1.25) Listen and check. In pairs, discuss the clues that told you whether each conversation was formal or informal.

5 In pairs, act out a formal telephone conversation. Student A look at page 134, Student B look at page 142.

A FORMAL LETTER

6 Read the letter from Ella to Mr Nash at ComfortBreak Hotels. Write down the three questions she asks him.

7 STRUCTURE Match 1–8 to the places in Ella's letter A–H.

1. ☐ say you are waiting for a reply
2. ☐ explain why you are writing
3. ☐ close the letter
4. ☐ ask questions and explain why you are asking them
5. ☐ put the name and address you are writing to
6. ☐ write the date
7. ☐ write your address
8. ☐ begin with *Dear Mr/Mrs/Miss/Ms* + surname

(A) 19 Station Rd
Brighton
BN1 H5P
01273 987 445

(B) Mr Nash
Public Relations Manager
ComfortBreak Hotels
55 Old Hall Way
Blakely
BA7 UT8

(C) 8 April 20XX

(D) Dear Mr Nash,

(E) I am writing to invite you to appear on The Ikram and Ella Student Special, a radio show aimed at teenagers and students on Bright Lights Radio. We are planning a report on your new hotel near the beach huts on Brighton beach and we would like to offer ComfortBreak Hotels the opportunity to answer our listeners' questions.

(F) There are two major areas of concern. Firstly, we would like to know why you have decided to build a new hotel in this particular location. This area is a popular beauty spot and a new hotel will make it much uglier. Secondly, we are interested to know why you have decided to build such a tall hotel. A six-storey building will dominate the beach huts and ruin the pleasure of staying there for many families.

Obviously, your appearance on our show will ensure that the report is fair and balanced. It is due to be broadcast on Thursday 14 April and we very much hope that you can take part. Please let me know if you are available.

(G) I look forward to hearing from you very soon.

(H) Kind regards,

[signature]

Ella Campbell

---

8 Look at *Language4writing* on the back cover and find phrases to match 1–4 in exercise 7.

9 a Look at the advert for a flat-share. Imagine you are interested in the advert. Think of two more questions to ask.

CAN YOU DO IT IN ENGLISH?

how much exactly?

WANTED Housemate to share large house in Brighton with three other students. Cheap rent, friendly housemates. You must be willing to share responsibilities and not leave a mess. If you are interested, send a letter to Graham, 15 Lexmont Close, Brighton, BG1 J5Y

b Write the first draft of your letter. Ask for at least two pieces of information.

10 Swap letters with your partner. Work through the checklist for writing on the back cover. Comment on your partner's letter and write your final draft.

activestudy1

Grammar

1 Complete the sentences with the present simple, present continuous, present perfect simple or present perfect continuous form of the verb in brackets.

1 I *'ve been doing* (do) household chores all weekend and I still *haven't finished* (not finish).

2 Do you think our society ___ (become) more and more competitive?

3 Jessica ___ (date) a different boy every month.

4 Kyung Ju ___ (currently/practise) for a concert.

5 We ___ (know) each other since primary school.

6 I ___ (phone) companies all morning. I think I ___ (make) about twenty calls.

7 My flatmate's so annoying! He ___ (always/nag) me about unimportant things!

2 Complete the sentences with the past simple, past continuous, past perfect simple or past perfect continuous form of the verb in brackets.

I [1] *was sitting* (sit) at my desk last night, trying to finish an essay. I was very tired because I [2] ___ (work) on it all day. Suddenly the phone [3] ___ (ring). My friends [4] ___ (want) me to go out with them. We [5] ___ (go) to a small local club. While we [6] ___ (sit) there talking, my ex-boyfriend Dave [7] ___ (come) in and [8] ___ (join) us. My friend Zoe suddenly remembered she [9] ___ (not lock) the door to her flat and Julie thought she [10] ___ (leave) the iron on. They both [11] ___ (rush) out, leaving me alone with Dave. We [12] ___ (talk) for three hours and … tomorrow I'm going to see him again. But I suspect my friends [13] ___ (plan) it all!

EXAM PRACTICE | Multiple choice

3 Choose the correct word or phrase to complete Millie's blog.

Millie's blog

Last weekend my grandma, Helen, told me some family stories. Her parents got married during the Second World War, after they [1] *c* each other for about six months. After the war they settled [2] ___ in a little village. They were a very traditional family. My great-grandfather was the breadwinner. He [3] ___ home from work, sit down and read a newspaper – really! My great-grandma [4] ___ to do all the housework and look after the children.

They were a good family in a way but Helen knew she wanted her life to be different. She wanted the [5] ___ and satisfaction of an interesting job and she wanted to see the world.

She and my granddad, Tom, met while they [6] ___ Medicine at university. Tom thought Helen was absolutely [7] ___ and she thought the same about him. After they'd graduated, they got married and went to live and work in Africa. Their first child was born in Nigeria after they [8] ___ there for three years.

Now my grandparents [9] ___ together for forty-five years. They have lived in eight countries, they have three children and seven grandchildren and they still enjoy each other's [10] ___ more than anything else.

1	a knew		c	had known ✓
	b have known		d	had been known
2	a down		c	up
	b to		d	back
3	a was coming		c	would come
	b had come		d	had been coming
4	a used		c	was used
	b was		d	had used
5	a motivation		c	achievement
	b dedication		d	challenge
6	a would study		c	had been studying
	b were studying		d	had studied
7	a pretty		c	nice
	b clever		d	brilliant
8	a were working		c	had been working
	b have been working		d	used to work
9	a are living		c	had lived
	b have been living		d	were living
10	a company		c	relationship
	b chat		d	respect

Vocabulary

ACTIVE STUDY | Learn collocations

4 Match the words to make collocations.

1	social		a	talent
2	divorce		b	marriage
3	arranged		c	network
4	natural		d	rate

5 Complete the sentences with the verbs below.

[make ✓   feel   have   leave
  make   take   treat]

1 Please don't _make_ a drama out of this situation. Everything will be okay.

2 I'd never stay in a relationship with someone who didn't ___ me with respect.

3 I like going out with Greg. We always ___ a laugh together.

4 She always used to ___ a mess in the kitchen after she'd been cooking.

5 Young people sometimes ___ under a lot of pressure to succeed.

6 It can ___ ages to train your dog – you have to be patient.

7 Success doesn't come easily. Sometimes you have to ___ sacrifices.

ACTIVE STUDY | Word formation

6 **a** Complete the sentences with the correct form of the word in brackets.

1 Martin Luther King has been a source of _inspiration_ (inspire) for human rights activists around the world.

2 What has been your greatest ___ (achieve) so far?

3 Please behave ___ (reasonable). Don't start a row.

4 Mike could achieve much more but he lacks ___ (self-confident).

5 If you don't share chores and ___ (responsible) fairly, you'll have problems!

6 Laura is the main breadwinner in her ___ (relation); she earns more than her husband.

b (1.26) Listen and check. Repeat the sentences.

Listening skills

ACTIVE STUDY | Listen for gist

7 (1.27) Listen to four young people talking about living on their own for the first time. Match the statements a–e to the speakers 1–4. There is one extra statement.

a ☐ I didn't realise I'd have such problems with money.

b ☐ I miss my family some of the time.

c ☐ I regret moving out because life is more difficult now.

d ☐ Making my own decisions is really important to me.

e ☐ My attitude was not very responsible at the beginning.

Speaking skills

8 Compare and contrast the two photos of people who have achieved success.

Grammar	Future forms
	Second conditional
Vocabulary	Technology
	Linking words
Phrases	Giving a speech (1)
	Answering simple questions
	about a speech

Listening & Speaking

1
a (2.1) Listen and write the pairs of numbers in the order you hear them.

b (2.1) Listen again and check. Then say the numbers.

2
a Read the facts and figures below about how communication technology has changed. Guess which three figures are incorrect.

b (2.2) Listen to part 1 of a TV programme and correct the figures in exercise 2a that are wrong.

3
a (2.3) Listen to part 2 and tick (✓) the technology the expert mentions.
1 ☐ wind-up laptops
2 ☐ laptops with flexible screens
3 ☐ 3D laptops
4 ☐ internet-enabled TVs
5 ☐ 3D TVs
6 ☐ mobile phones with flexible screens

b (2.3) Listen again. What, if any, will be the advantages of each piece of technology?

4
a Which gadgets do you think will exist in the future? Make a list of ideas with the class.

b Do you know anyone who is addicted to any form of technology? What are their symptoms?

Grammar Focus

Future forms

5 Look at the messages on page 25. Which one is
a an arrangement for this evening?
b some gossip?
c a party invitation?

6 Read the messages and answer the questions.
1 Why is Natalie so happy? What do you think 'yippee' means?
2 Who is Sam and what's the news about him?
3 How do you think Natalie will feel when she hears the news? Why?
4 What arrangement does the text message show?

How communication has changed in figures

1983
The year that the first mobile phone network arrived in the US.

1990
The year that the World Wide Web became available to the public.

70–80%
The percentage of web pages that are in English.

8
The average age of a first-time mobile phone owner in the UK.

2,300,000
The number of text messages that we send around the world every day.

1,000,000
The number of new mobile phone handsets that Nokia produce every day.

60%
The percentage of young people who are addicted to mobile phones.

1,000,000,000
The approximate number of people worldwide who have joined social networking sites.

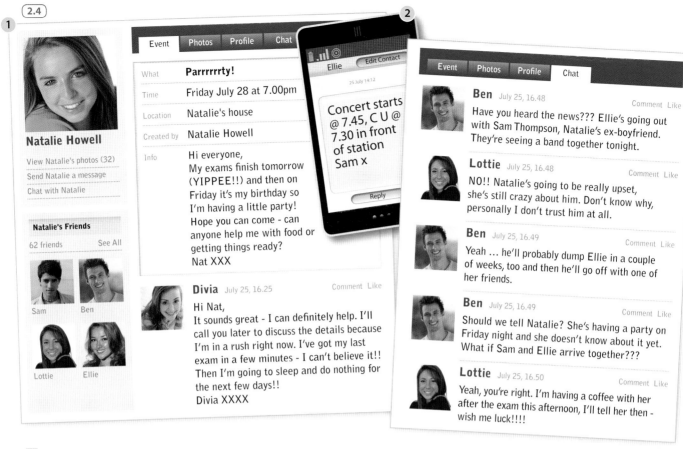

7 <u>Underline</u> the sentences in which these forms refer to the future. Read *Grammar2know* and check your answers.

• going to • *will* • present continuous • present simple

8 (2.5) Complete the dialogues with the correct form of the verb in brackets. Use the present simple, present continuous, *going to* and *will* in each dialogue. Then listen and check.

1 Al: The match ¹*starts* (start) at three tomorrow afternoon. Do you want to watch it at mine?

 Jez: I can't, I'm afraid. I ²___ (finish) my science project. I ³___ (present) it to my class on Monday.

 Al: How awful! I ⁴___ (come) and help you if you want.

2 Tom: I haven't told Liz how I feel about her yet.

 Jo: But her flight ⁵___ (leave) at six tomorrow morning.

 Tom: I know. I ⁶___ (tell) her tonight when I see her.

 Jo: ⁷___ (she come) to the party?

 Tom: I hope so but I haven't invited her yet. I think ⁸___ (call) her now.

3 Liz: It's nearly nine. We ⁹___ (be) late for the party.

 Jess: It's cool to be late for parties. Anyway, this one ¹⁰___ (not get going) until ten.

 Liz: How do you know?

 Jess: Because a lot of Tom's friends ¹¹___ (come) from Manchester and their train ¹²___ (arrive) at about half past nine.

9 Choose two topics and discuss them in pairs.

• your plans for this summer
• which celebrity couples will break up soon
• what you think will happen the rest of today
• gadgets we'll be able to buy in five years' time

MINI WORKBOOK exercises 1-3 page 110

Grammar 2 know

Future forms

Use the present simple for schedules and timetables:

*My exams **finish** tomorrow.*

*The concert **starts** at 7.45.*

Use the present continuous for fixed arrangements in the future (it's almost always possible to use *going to* instead):

*They**'re seeing** a band together tonight.*

Use *going to* for

a general intentions and plans for the future:

 *I'm **going to sleep** and **do** nothing for the next few days.*

b predictions about the future based on present evidence:

 *She**'s going to be** so upset. (there's evidence for this because she's crazy about him)*

Use *will* for

a predictions about the future based on our opinions:

 *He**'ll** probably **dump** her. (this is just the speaker's opinion)*

b decisions about the future that we make as we speak:

 *You're right … I**'ll tell** her.*

global network

25

Vocabulary & Speaking

Talking about technology

1 Discuss the questions in pairs.
- What is your favourite gadget at the moment?
- What do you like about it?

" *My favourite gadget is my portable media player.*

I like watching YouTube videos on it.

2 **Words 2 know** (2.6) Check the words in blue then do the quiz. How many questions did you get right? Do you consider yourself to be 'techie' or not?

How techie are you?

1 Which of these can you put in your bag and take to school?
a a **desktop** computer
b a **high-speed internet connection**
c a **handheld games console**

2 Which of these is probably the smallest?
a a **high-definition** TV
b a **digital** photo frame
c a **wireless** mouse

3 Which of these does not exist yet?
a a **touch-screen** phone
b a **hands-free** laptop
c a **mini projector**

4 Which of these does not require an internet connection?
a **transferring** music to your mp3 player
b **uploading** a video to the Web
c **updating** your **profile** on a **social networking site**

5 Which of these would you not want on a new laptop?
a a big **hard drive**
b a short **battery life**
c the latest **operating system**

6 Which of these statements is not true?
a You use a **search engine** to **download** music.
b You use a **web browser** to surf the net.
c You can **download apps** for some mobile phones.

Answers: 1c 2c 3b 4a 5b 6a

3 Read *Active Study* and underline three more compound nouns and three more compound adjectives in the quiz.

ACTIVE STUDY

Notice compounds
1 Compounds are combinations of two (or more) words. Together, the words make one idea.
Compound nouns: *internet connection, operating system, social networking site*
Compound adjectives: *high-speed, handheld*
2 We sometimes use two compounds together: *high-speed internet connection*

4 **a** Think of three more questions to test your partner's knowledge of technology. Use the *Words2know* and the prompts below or your own ideas.
- What do you use a … for?
- Is there such thing as a … ?
- Is this statement true or not: … ?
- What are the advantages of a … ?

Is there such thing as a touch-screen TV?

b In pairs, ask and answer your questions.

MINI WORKBOOK exercises 7–9 page 112

Grammar focus

Second conditional

5 **a** Look at the title of the article and the photos on page 27. What do you think a 'technology refusenik' is? Do you know anyone like this?

b Read the interviews with Terri and Paul. The interviewer asks them the same three questions. Match the questions 1–3 to their answers A–F.
1 Why haven't you got one?
2 What do your friends say?
3 What would you do if you had one?

6 **a** Answer the questions about this sentence from the interview with Terri.

'If your car broke down, you'd need a mobile phone.'

1 Has Terri's car really broken down?
2 Does she need a mobile phone? Why? Why not?
3 Which verb form tells you this is a hypothetical situation?

b Read *Grammar2know* to check your answers.

technology refuseniks

This week we talk to two technology refuseniks, Terri and Paul.

(2.7)

A ___ They assume I'm a technophobe but that's not true. I've got a state-of-the-art laptop, for example. Sometimes they say, 'If your car broke down, you'd need a phone.' I say, 'If I really needed one, I could borrow one from someone like you!'

B ___ I had a mobile for years but then I went travelling for six months and I didn't take it with me. When I got back last year, I just decided that I didn't really need one.

C ___ Provided that it was a touch-screen smartphone, I might use it for a while. But sooner or later, I think I'd put it in a drawer and forget about it.

Terri: 'I haven't got a mobile phone.'

Paul: 'I haven't got a social networking profile.'

D ___ When it comes to friendship, social networking sites make people value quantity over quality. I mean, who needs hundreds of online friends? What if they all got in touch at once?

E ___ Even if you created a profile for me, I wouldn't use it. I wouldn't be able to spend so much time with my real friends if I had one. You can only have about four or five proper friends!

F ___ Sometimes people say it's a hassle to get in touch with me but I think my real friends understand me. If they didn't understand me, they wouldn't be real friends, would they?

Grammar 2 know

Second conditional

Use the second conditional for hypothetical situations and things which are possible but unlikely:

What **would** you **do** if you **had** a mobile phone?

I **wouldn't be able to spend** so much time with my real friends **if** I **had** a social networking profile.

If my friends **didn't understand** me, they **wouldn't be** real friends.

We often use could or might instead of would:

If I really **needed** a phone, I **could borrow** one from someone like you!

If this phone **were** cheaper, I **might buy** it.

We sometimes use even if, provided that and supposing instead of if.

Even if you created a profile for me, I wouldn't use it. (in the extreme situation that you created a profile for me …)

Provided that it was a touch-screen smartphone, I might use it for a while. (only if it was a touch-screen smartphone)

Supposing I gave you one, would you use it? (imagine for a moment that I gave you one …)

We quite often ask questions with What if …?:

What if they all got in touch at once? (what would happen if …?)

---

7 Which gadgets below do or don't you have? Write sentences imagining life with or without these things.

- a mobile phone
- a laptop
- a TV in your room
- a games console
- an online profile
- an mp3 player
- internet access

If I didn't have a mobile phone, I wouldn't be able to text my friends.

If I had an mp3 player, I wouldn't have to listen to other people's boring conversations on the bus.

8 **a** Read the phrases 1–6. ~~Cross out~~ the ones that are likely and tick (✓) the ones that are imaginary or 'possible but unlikely'.

1 A new online friend suggests meeting up.
2 I get a job in another country.
3 I don't go to university.
4 A friend of mine is being bullied.
5 My blog becomes very popular.
6 I have a great idea for an internet business.

b Now write second conditional sentences with the phrases you have ticked. Use alternatives to if.

Supposing a new online friend suggested meeting up, I'd say no.

c In pairs, read your sentences and ask your partner about his or her sentences.

" *If I got a job in another country, I wouldn't take it. Really? Why not?*

MINI WORKBOOK exercises 4–6 page 111

Reading & Speaking

1 Discuss the questions.

- Do teenagers in your country have their own slang?
- Has teenage slang changed since your parents were young?
- Do you know any slang that English-speaking teenagers use?

2 Look at the picture. What do you think the words and phrases mean? Read the article and check your answers.

(2.8)

English is changing iNNiT?

¹ Millions of people around the world are learning English but how many of them realise that the English they are learning is constantly changing? New words are entering the language, existing words are developing new meanings and other words are falling out of use. ¹ _d_ So what drives these ⁵ changes and should we try to stop them?

New technology needs new words

Not surprisingly, technology is responsible for a lot of new words. Twenty years ago, no one knew what a 'blog' was but when people began writing web logs online, the phrase ¹⁰ was quickly shortened to 'blog' and the writer was called a 'blogger'. And nowadays, internet users are constantly warned about the dangers of 'phishing', where criminals try to get your credit card and bank details by sending fraudulent emails. ² ___ Criminals use emails to catch victims just like ¹⁵ fishermen use worms to catch fish.

New ways of communicating create new language

The arrival of texting on mobile phones created a quick and easy way to stay in touch with friends. It also created the need for a very short form of English – a text message is only 160 ²⁰ characters long. Instead of writing 'see you later', teenagers started to write 'c u l8r' and when they found something funny, they wrote 'lol', instead of 'laugh out loud'. At the moment it is still wrong to use this language in essays, job applications and so on. ³ ___ It will all change soon, I think, lol!

²⁵ ### The influence of teenagers

Teenagers use their own slang because it indicates that they belong to a group, that they are different from other people. Modern teens use 'sick' to mean 'great' and 'Wassup?' (What's up?) to mean 'Hello' but ask a typical middle- ³⁰ aged person what these phrases mean and they would

probably have no idea. ⁴ ___ A school in Manchester recently banned slang in the classroom and exam grades increased dramatically!

Human beings are lazy

³⁵ We all prefer things to be simple rather than complicated. A common phrase like 'I don't know' is often shortened to 'dunno'. In a similar way, some young people now use 'innit?' (short for 'isn't it?') to replace all question tags, for example 'He's gone home, innit?' ⁵ ___ Most adults see this as bad ⁴⁰ English and some complain loudly. But language has always evolved and although we all need to know the right language for each situation, surely it's better to enjoy the way English changes rather than complain about it?

Global culture is changing English

⁴⁵ Globalisation has been an effective way of spreading English around the world. But now many people believe that non-native speakers of English are creating their own form of the language, which has been named Globish. With its limited vocabulary and simple sentences, this form of English enables a Spanish ⁵⁰ businessman to communicate easily with a Chinese student, for example. Some people believe Globish will be the most commonly spoken language in the world one day. ⁶ ___ So if we could travel into the future, would we find people all over the world speaking a common language? Probably not but at least ⁵⁵ communication might be simpler one day … innit?

sick

cu l8tr

phishing

3 Match the sentences a–f to the gaps 1–6 in the article.

  a It's quicker and easier than using the right question tag.

  b But how long will it be before text speak is standard English?

  c The word is a variation on 'fishing'.

  d Even the grammar of English is changing slowly.

  e Perhaps it already is!

  f Some people are taking a stand against teen text speak and slang.

4 Read the article again. Tick (✓) true, cross (✗) false and write (?) if there is no information.

  1 ✓ New words enter English every year.

  2 ☐ Phishing emails are sent by fishermen.

  3 ☐ Teenagers invented the phrase 'lol'.

  4 ☐ Banning slang had a positive effect on a school's exam results.

  5 ☐ Most people know the appropriate language to use in each situation.

  6 ☐ People who speak English as a second language are creating their own form of English.

5 Circle the correct answers. Find evidence in the article to explain your answers.

  1 How would you describe the tone of the article?

    a serious   **c** informative

    b scientific   **d** negative

  2 What is the writer's attitude towards changes in English?

    a unhappy   **c** delighted

    b disapproving   **d** positive

6 **a** Read the Glossary of Informal English and Slang on the back cover.

  b (2.9) Listen to three conversations that Dan has and answer the questions.

Conversation one

1 How does Alex feel?

2 Why might Dan's mum be angry?

3 What arrangement do Dan and Alex make?

Conversation two

4 What does Greg suggest about Dan and Alex?

5 What does Greg think of Alex?

Conversation three

6 In what way is Alex's dad messing around?

7 Does Dan use any slang with Alex's dad? Why? Why not?

8 What practical joke does Dan play on Alex's dad?

7 (2.9) Listen again. Can you identify three examples of informal English in each conversation?

CAN YOU DO IT IN ENGLISH?

8 **a** In pairs, read the role card and decide:

  • what the names of the two friends are.

  • what comments and suggestions each person might make.

  • which informal expression from the back cover they could use.

  • how to make their conversation surprising or dramatic.

> Two teenage friends meet after the weekend. One of the friends went to a concert but it wasn't very good. The other friend went to a party. He met someone that he really liked but he didn't ask her out.

  b Write the conversation in pairs, then learn it off by heart. Use the phrases on the back cover to help you.

9 Take turns to perform your conversation in front of the class. Which had the most interesting ending?

MINI WORKBOOK exercise 10 page 112

Writing & Vocabulary

A 'for and against' essay

1 **a** In pairs, discuss the questions.

- How often do you get a new mobile phone?
- Do you ever wish that you had a more modern one?

b Describe what you can see in each photo. Do they show advantages or disadvantages of mobile phones? Explain why.

2 Read the 'for and against' essay and answer the questions.

1 What are the three arguments in favour of mobile phones?

2 What are the three arguments against?

3 Which point do you think the writer feels most strongly about? Why?

4 What is the writer's conclusion? Do you agree?

3 STRUCTURE Read the essay again and match the instructions a–g to the paragraphs 1–4. Some instructions fit into more than one paragraph.

a Make two or three points in favour of the statement.

b Say that there are arguments on both sides of the debate.

c Give your opinion.

d Make two or three points against the statement.

e Try to support each point with an example or a result.

f Say in the first sentence if the paragraph is for or against.

g Give a brief background to the topic.

Paragraph 1: Introduction	• b – Say that there are arguments on both sides. •
Paragraph 2: Arguments for	• f – Say in the first sentence if the paragraph is for or against. • •
Paragraph 3: Arguments against	• • •
Paragraph 4: Conclusion	•

2.10

What are the advantages and disadvantages of mobile phones to society as a whole?

1 Mobile phones have been widely used for just twenty years but already many people could not live without them. Clearly they have many benefits but they also cause a number of problems. So are mobile phones good for society in general?

2 There are several important arguments in favour of mobile phones. The first advantage is that mobile phones have huge benefits for people in developing countries where there are no landline telephones. They allow people in remote places to find work and stay in touch with relatives. **What is more**, they are useful in emergencies, for example when a car breaks down. Finally, the mobile phone industry employs large numbers of people and because of this, it helps society in general.

3 **On the other hand**, mobile phones have some serious disadvantages. Firstly, they contain coltan. Coltan mines in East Africa are dirty and dangerous and children often work in them unpaid. Not many people know that when you buy a mobile phone you are also supporting child labour. Secondly, mobile phones are bad for the environment. Although it is possible to recycle old mobile phones, they are usually thrown away and **as a result**, they produce mountains of toxic waste. **Besides this**, mobile phones are often used irresponsibly, for example when driving and this can cause accidents.

4 **To summarise**, there are strong arguments on both sides of the debate. However, I strongly believe we should all stop buying mobile phones because the disadvantages are simply too great.

4 **a** LANGUAGE Read *Language4writing*. <u>Underline</u> eight of these phrases in the essay.

Language 4 writing

1 Listing your arguments:

There are several arguments in favour/against …
The first advantage/disadvantage is …
Firstly, Secondly, Finally, **a** ___ **b** ___

2 Introducing contrasting points:

However, Although … **c** ___

3 Explaining consequences:

Because of this, For this reason, **d** ___

4 Giving your conclusion:

To sum up, In conclusion, **e** ___

b Complete the gaps a–e in *Language4writing* with the phrases in **bold** in the essay.

5 Notice the way that *however* and *although* are used in the example below. Join the other sentences using both constructions.

1 Technology is improving – it is getting cheaper.

Although technology is improving, it is getting cheaper.

Technology is improving. However, it is getting cheaper.

2 Touch-screen phones are expensive – they are extremely popular.

3 Most people have heard of computer viruses – they don't really understand the dangers.

4 Downloading movies is usually illegal – many people still do it.

5 It is the truth – it is hard to believe.

6 Circle the best linker.

> Most young and middle-aged people have access to the internet these days. ¹*Because of this,*/Firstly,/On the other hand, more and more everyday business happens online. Nearly all people in these age groups know how to use the internet, ²*however,*/what is more,/for this reason, many elderly people still cannot use it. ³*Although/As a result,/Finally,* they are unable to take advantage of many online facilities, such as email and social networking. ⁴*What is more,*/On the other hand,/Secondly, they often miss out on cheap online deals. ⁵*Although/However,*/On the other hand, many old people are poor and really need these savings, they do not have access to them.

7 **a** You are going to write a 'for and against' essay. Read the title and decide if arguments 1–3 are advantages (+) or disadvantages (–).

What are the advantages and disadvantages of social networking sites?

1 ☐ They're a way of staying in touch with people who you might otherwise lose contact with.

2 ☐ Indiscreet gossip or photos can cause a lot of trouble.

3 ☐ Shy people sometimes find it easier to chat online than they would in real life.

b In pairs, think of more advantages and disadvantages with examples or other information to support each point. Discuss the ideas with the class.

8 Write the first draft of your essay. Then read it through or swap with a partner. Work through the checklist for writing on the back cover.

9 Write the final draft of your essay.

Bright Lights radio special guest interview this week: Danny Prince, Brighton's very own rap star!

GIVING A SPEECH (1)

1 **Look at the photo, read the caption and answer the questions.**

1 Who is Danny Prince? Why is Ella interviewing him?

2 Where do you think they are?

3 Who do you think the other woman is?

2 a (2.11) **Listen to Ella interviewing Danny Prince. Choose two points below that summarise what Danny believes about rap music.**

☐ Rap music glorifies violence.

☐ Music with violent lyrics should be banned.

☐ Rap music is modern poetry.

☐ If you don't like rap music, don't listen to it.

b **In pairs, rank the statements from 1 (strongly agree) to 5 (strongly disagree). Discuss your opinions.**

❝ *In my opinion, rap music definitely glorifies violence.*

3 (2.12) **Listen to Danny's speech again. Complete the gaps 1–6 with ideas a–f.**

a Hollywood action films

b these lyrics by DJ Hi-Tone

c if you don't like it, you don't have to listen to it

d on the streets of New York

e rap should be banned

f rappers are modern poets

The start	
The topic	violent lyrics in rap
Some history	1 _____
What people say about it	2 _____
Your opinion	rap is a good thing
The main body	
Reasons for your opinion and an example or comparison	Reason: rap isn't all about violence
	Example: 3 _____
	Reason: 4 _____
	Comparison: Shakespeare or Wordsworth
	Reason: rap is entertainment
	Comparison: 5 _____
The conclusion	
Summarise	we shouldn't ban rap
A final thought	6 _____

4 Write sentences using the *Phrases2know* and the ideas in the table.

I'd like to talk about violent lyrics in rap.

5 a In pairs, read the statements below and decide if you agree (✓) or disagree (✗) with the ideas.

☐ In the future, nobody will write letters.

☐ Mobile phones are bad for society.

☐ Violent computer games should be banned.

CAN YOU DO IT IN ENGLISH?

b Choose the statement that you find most interesting and use the table in exercise 3 to make notes for a speech on this topic.

c Use the *Phrases2know* to expand your notes and prepare a speech. Then practise giving your speech in pairs.

Phrases 2 know

Giving a speech

Starting a speech

I'd like to talk about …

It all began …

Some people say/argue that …

In my opinion …

Presenting your ideas

Let me explain why.

First of all, … Secondly, … Lastly, …

Giving examples and comparisons

Take … for example.

… like …

It's exactly the same as …

Summarising and concluding

So, to sum up, …

Let me finish by saying …

ANSWERING SIMPLE QUESTIONS ABOUT YOUR SPEECH

6 a (2.13) Listen and complete the information 1–4 about Danny Prince. Is any of the information surprising? Why?

b (2.13) Listen again and complete gaps 1–3 in *Phrases2know*.

Danny Prince: rapper, ¹___ , ²___

Favourite writer: ³___

Favourite quote: A fool thinks himself to be wise but a wise man ⁴___

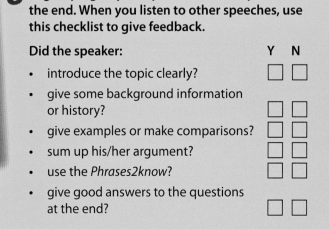

7 a Use the *Phrases2know* to write questions and answers about your speech in exercise 5.

Phrases 2 know

Asking simple questions

Why did you mention ¹_____ ?

What was your point about ²_____ ?

Why do you think that ³_____?

Answering questions

The point I'm trying to make is that ⁴_____ .

My argument is that ⁵_____ .

That's a good question. I think ⁶_____ .

b Match Danny's sentence endings a–c to the gaps 4–6 in *Phrases2know* to complete his answers.

a … a lot of people don't understand rap music.

b … rap is the same as Hollywood action films.

c … Shakespeare was writing about life, just like rappers do.

8 In groups, give your speech and take questions at the end. When you listen to other speeches, use this checklist to give feedback.

Did the speaker:	Y	N
• introduce the topic clearly?	☐	☐
• give some background information or history?	☐	☐
• give examples or make comparisons?	☐	☐
• sum up his/her argument?	☐	☐
• use the *Phrases2know*?	☐	☐
• give good answers to the questions at the end?	☐	☐

33

4 happy & successful

Grammar	Modals of obligation and advice
	Future continuous and future perfect
Vocabulary	Skills and ambitions
Phrases	Job interviews

Listening & Speaking

1 Discuss the questions in pairs.

- These 'life skills' are all part of the curriculum in British schools. Are they taught in schools in your country?

  Nutrition and healthy eating

  Alcohol and drug education

  Sex education and relationships

- Do you think schools should teach people about these things or are they a matter for parents?

- At what age do you think people should learn about these things?

> " *I think healthy eating lessons are a good idea because …*

2 **a** Look at the introduction to a news report. What new 'life skill' is being introduced at Wellington College? Whose idea is it?

b (2.14) Listen to part 1 of a news report about this story and answer the questions.

1 Where is happiness and well-being already taught?

2 How long will the course at Wellington College be?

3 Which pupils will do the course?

4 According to Dr Seldon, what do teachers and parents want for their children?

3 (2.15) Which things below do you think might happen in well-being lessons? Listen to part 2 and tick (✓) the things that are on the curriculum.

1 ☐ The teacher brings cake for the students.

2 ☐ Students learn to think positively about things that have happened to them.

3 ☐ They think about the things in their lives that they feel thankful for.

4 ☐ They think about the negative things in their lives and how they feel about them.

5 ☐ They think about what they are good at as individuals.

6 ☐ They learn that it is important to help and support other people.

Can you teach happiness?

Dr Anthony Seldon, the headmaster of Wellington College, near London, thinks so. Next year, he is introducing a new subject to the curriculum: happiness and well-being.

4 (2.16) Listen to part 3 and match the summaries 1–3 to the three speakers, Jade (J), Nikita (N) and Marcus (M).

1 ☐ If you have serious problems in your life, these lessons will not help.

2 ☐ The lessons sound like a good idea.

3 ☐ How happy you are depends on the type of personality you have. Happiness lessons will not change that.

5 Discuss the questions in pairs.

- Which ideas in the happiness course at Wellington College sound most useful?

- Which speaker(s) in exercise 4 do you most agree with and why?

> " *I think it's a good idea to think about the things in your life that you are thankful for because …*

Grammar Focus

Modals of obligation and advice

6 Which academic school subjects do you think will be most useful in your future life? Which will be least useful in your opinion? Why?

7 Read the opinions about school subjects. Which ones do you agree or disagree with?

Which school subjects are worth learning?

'I personally think people **should concentrate** on subjects they are interested in and forget the things they don't like. If you're fascinated by the past then you should do lots of History. But if you don't like computers, you shouldn't bother with ICT.'

Mia, 20

'Schools **must prepare** young people properly for work – it's essential. I'm an employer and I sometimes meet young people who don't even have basic literacy and numeracy skills so I can't give them a job.'

Simon, 34

'I'd like to give up Music because I'm tone deaf. But it's on the curriculum at my school so I'**ve got to study** it. I don't have any choice.'

Kelly, 14

'I spent hours learning the symbols for different chemicals in Chemistry and I've never used them. I **needn't have learned** them!'

Matt, 32

'I decided to do Politics this year but I **shouldn't have chosen** it. I thought it was about current affairs and the news but actually we do loads of stuff about the parliamentary system, which I find really difficult. I **should have done** something like English instead.'

Josh, 17

8 **a** Match the explanations 1–6 to the phrases in **bold** in the text.

1 The speaker says this is necessary.

2 This is necessary because someone else (not the speaker) says so.

3 The speaker thinks this is a good idea.

4 The speaker did this but regrets doing it.

5 The speaker didn't do this but regrets not doing it.

6 The speaker did this but it was unnecessary.

b Read *Grammar2know* to check your answers.

Grammar **2 know**

Modals of obligation and advice

must

Use *must* to express obligations or strong opinions that come from the speaker:

*Schools **must prepare** young people properly for work.* (the speaker thinks this is necessary)

have (got) to

Use *have (got) to* to express obligations that do not come from the speaker but from some other authority:

*Music is on the curriculum at my school so I'**ve got to study** it.* (the school rules say this is necessary)

should

Use *should* to say that you think something is a good idea or to give advice:

*People **should concentrate** on subjects they are interested in.*

should (shouldn't) + have + past participle

Use *should have* + past participle to say that it was a good idea to do something but the person didn't do it:

*I **should have done** something like English instead.*

Use *shouldn't have* + past participle to say that someone did something but it wasn't a good idea:

*I **shouldn't have chosen** politics.*

needn't + have + past participle

Use *needn't have* + past participle to say that something you did was unnecessary:

*I **needn't have learned** all the chemical symbols.*

9 Read about Molly's disastrous Maths exam. Write a response using *should, shouldn't have* or *needn't have*. More than one answer is possible.

1 She didn't do any revision before the exam.

She should have done some revision.

2 She went out the night before the exam.

3 She didn't set her alarm clock.

4 She spent half an hour putting make-up on.

5 She brought her calculator but calculators were provided in the exam.

10 Discuss the questions in pairs.

• Have you studied something that you 'needn't have bothered with'? What and why?

• Are there any subjects in which you should have worked harder? Why?

• Do you have to study anything that is a waste of time for you? Why?

• Are there any extra subjects that you think you should study at school?

" *I had dancing lessons when I was little but I needn't have bothered because I was hopeless at dancing!*

MINI WORKBOOK exercises 1–4 pages 113–114

happy & successful

35

Vocabulary & Reading

Skills and ambitions

1 **a** Rank the factors from 1 (most important) to 5 (least important) for your career. Compare your answers in pairs.

I want a job which:

☐ involves working with people.

☐ will be well-paid in the future.

☐ involves travel.

☐ will allow me to have a social life.

☐ is challenging.

☐ requires creativity or talent.

b Tell your partner about a career you are considering. Use these ideas and your own to explain why it appeals to you.

" Becoming a nurse appeals to me because it would be challenging.

2 **Words 2 know** (2.17) Check the words in blue. Read the case studies. What are Omar and Joanna doing now and what are their plans?

3 Match the explanations 1–9 to the phrases in blue in the case studies.

1 keen *enthusiastic*

2 has done courses and passed exams in this subject

3 good at using standard computer programmes

4 approaches things in a good way

5 really wants to succeed

6 is good with people

7 wants to learn

8 has experience people will recognise

9 ability to work with other people

4 WRITING Write a short description of your work-related skills using the *Words2know* and your own ideas. Give examples to explain your skills.

I have a positive attitude so I believe that I can succeed. I also have sound IT skills ...

MINI WORKBOOK exercises 8–10 page 115

the inside track

(2.18) **CASE STUDIES:** Two students have their career plan assessed by experienced professionals in their field.

Omar Kane
Age: 18
Currently studying: Journalism degree (first year)
Wants to be: a journalist

Skills
Omar says that he's **highly motivated** and when he's finished his course, he'll be **well-qualified**. He also says that he has **proven experience** of journalism from his work for the university magazine. His tutors say that he is talented but that he needs to develop **sound IT skills**.

Career plan
'I'm confident that by the time my course finishes, I'll have found a job with a national newspaper. And by the time I'm 25, I'll probably be working as a foreign correspondent, if all goes to plan. I'll be reporting on events around the world. That lifestyle appeals to me. Ultimately, I want to be the senior foreign correspondent for a big TV channel. I hope I'll have achieved that by the age of 40.'

Professional view
Amy Hirst, 30, is a journalist with a national newspaper. What does she think of Omar's career plan? Has he got the right skills? Realistically, what will he have achieved by the time he is 25? Click to listen.

Grammar Focus

Future continuous and future perfect

5 Read Omar and Joanna's career plans again. What do they think will happen in the next few years?

6 **a** According to Omar and Joanna, which activities will be

A: happening at the time in brackets

B: completed before the time in brackets

Omar

1 find a job (by the time his course finishes) *B*

2 work as a foreign correspondent (when he's twenty-five)

3 become the senior foreign correspondent for a TV channel (when he's forty)

Joanna

4 live in Spain (this time next year)

5 pass her exams (this time next year)

6 become the manager of a resort (when she's twenty-five)

b Read *Grammar2know* and check your answers.

Joanna Ball

Age: 17
Currently studying: A-levels
at school
Wants to be: a travel rep

Skills

Joanna says that she is **enthusiastic** and **willing to learn**. Her tutors say that she's got **good interpersonal skills** and a **positive attitude** but that she needs to develop her **ability to work in a team**.

Career plan

'I already have a job offer from a travel company so this time next year I'll be living in Spain and working as a travel rep, maybe in Ibiza. I'll hopefully have passed my exams by then. My boyfriend wants to work in Ibiza too but he probably won't have finished his A-levels by then so we won't be travelling there together.
By the time I'm 25, I hope I'll have become the manager of a resort but after that I don't really have any career plans.'

Professional view

Trevor Watling, 25, is a travel rep in Ibiza. What does he think of Joanna's career plan? What will she be doing in five years' time, in his view? Does she need to develop her plan further? Click to listen.

Grammar 2 know

Future continuous

Use *will* or *won't* + *be* + *-ing* to talk about events that will be in progress at a time in the future:

+ *By the time I'm 25, I'**ll be working** as a foreign correspondent.*

– *We **won't be travelling** there together.*

? *What **will she be doing** in five years' time?*

Future perfect

Use *will* or *won't* + *have* + past participle to talk about events that will be complete before a time in the future:

+ *By the time my course finishes, I'**ll have found** a job.*

– *He probably **won't have finished** his A-levels.*

? *What **will he have achieved** by the time he is 25?*

Notice the position of adverbs with these tenses:

*I'll **probably** be working as a foreign correspondent.*

*I'll **hopefully** have passed my exams by then.*

Time expressions: *by then, by the time I'm 25, this time tomorrow, in a few months' time, ten years from now*

---

7 (2.19) **Listen to the professionals' podcasts. Complete the summaries with the future continuous or future perfect form of the verbs in brackets.**

At the age of twenty, Omar [1] *will still be studying* (still study) but he [2] ___ (gain) two years' useful experience with the school newspaper. By the time he's twenty-five, he [3] ___ (probably apply) for several jobs with a national paper but it is likely that he [4] ___ (still work) with a local newspaper.

By the time Joanna is twenty, she [5] ___ (work) for two years as a travel rep and if she's good, she [6] ___ (possibly work) as a manager. However, if she's sensible, she [7] ___ (change) to another career by the time she's twenty-five!

8 **a Put the verbs in brackets in the future continuous or future perfect and complete the sentences so that they are true for you.**

1 By this time next year, I hope I (pass) …

By this time next year, I hope I'll have passed my English exam.

2 When I'm twenty, I think I (live) …

3 I think I (move) out of my parents home by the time I'm …

4 I (probably finish) studying by the age of …

5 By the time I'm thirty, I (probably work) as a …

b Compare your answers in pairs.

9 **When, if ever, do you think you will have done or will be doing these things?**

- meet the partner of your dreams
- do your ideal job
- make lots of money
- live in your dream home
- have children
- retire

" *I hope I'll have met the partner of my dreams by the time I'm twenty-five.*

I think I'll be making lots of money in the next five years.

MINI WORKBOOK exercises 5–7 pages 114–115

happy & successful

Reading & Speaking

1 Look at the cartoons and discuss the questions in pairs.

Which job do you think is:

- the most physically demanding? Why?
- the most boring? Why?
- the most unpleasant? Why?

What are the worst aspects of each job?

" *I think being a miner would be very boring.*

For me, the worst thing about being a hospital porter would be the injuries and blood.

2 Read the introduction to four extracts from books. Answer the questions.

1 When were George Orwell and Polly Toynbee writing?
2 What was Orwell's purpose in writing about the poor?
3 How did he research his books?
4 How does Toynbee's book relate to Orwell's?

These four extracts come from books by **George Orwell** and **Polly Toynbee**. George Orwell (1903–1950) is one of Britain's most famous authors, best known for his political novels *Animal Farm* and *Nineteen Eighty-Four*. In *Down and Out in Paris and London* (1933) and *The Road to Wigan Pier* (1937) he wrote about the lives of the poor and the homeless. He lived with the people he was writing about and tried to experience what they experienced so that he could show in his books what their everyday lives were like. More than fifty years after Orwell's death, Polly Toynbee, a British journalist, took a variety of low-paid jobs to find out if life for poor people had changed since Orwell's time. Her book was called *Hard Work* (2003).

3 **a** Read the extracts 1–4 from the books and match them to the cartoons A–D.

b Answer the questions.

1 Does the writer feel positive or negative about each job?
2 Can you guess which extracts come from Orwell's books and which come from Toynbee's?

(2.20)

1 At the start, to walk while bending over is rather a joke but the joke soon wears off. When the roof is four feet [120 centimetres] or less it is a tough job for anybody except a child. You not only have to bend over, you have also got to keep your head up all the time so you can see the beams and dodge them when they come. You have, therefore, a constant pain in your neck but this is nothing to the pain in your knees and thighs. After half a mile [800 metres] it becomes (I am not exaggerating) agony. You begin to wonder whether you will ever get to the end and how on earth you are going to get back. Your pace grows slower and slower.

2 I was given a script to read from. 'Good morning. My name is X and I am calling from Clean Direct. I wondered if you would like a free quotation for your office cleaning.'

I have never known the hands of a clock move so slowly. I ached with boredom as I dialled number after number and repeated the same phrases over and over again. I made 163 calls in seven hours and I got just one appointment.

4 Read the extracts again and choose the correct answer.

1 In extract 1, the most difficult aspect of the job was
  a working with children.
  b the pain in your neck.
  c the pain in your legs.
  d the hours you spend underground.

2 In extract 2, the job was:
  a boring and physically painful.
  b just boring.
  c just physically painful.
  d comfortable because it was easy.

WORK

The job is astonishingly hard. For example, you are making toast, when 'bang!' down comes an order for tea, rolls and three different kinds of jam and simultaneously 'bang!' down comes another order for scrambled eggs, coffee and grapefruit; you run to the kitchen for the eggs and to the dining-room for the fruit, going like lightning so as to be back before your toast burns and trying to remember the tea, coffee and other orders that are still pending. It needs more brains than you might think. **3**

If it wasn't for the miserable pay, however, this could have been a good and satisfying job. It meant walking all day with only a half-hour break for lunch but it was pleasing and purposeful. The porters seemed like the life-blood of the place, fetching and carrying, finding out everything that was happening, aware of the pleasant and unpleasant staff in different locations. We knew the rude nurses in some wards, the very friendly ones elsewhere. An arrogant male nurse was the worst, 'You, porter person, come here!' he snapped at me on my first day. **4**

3 In extract 3, the author found the job difficult because:
   a he was constantly hungry.
   b there was a lot to remember.
   c it was painful.
   d there was lots of physical work.

4 In extract 4, the biggest problem with the job was:
   a the low pay.
   b the constant walking.
   c the unpleasant staff.
   d the hard physical work.

5 **a** Writers help their readers to imagine situations by using vivid language. Which phrase is used to mean:
   1 you soon realise that it is not funny (extract 1) *the joke soon wears off*
   2 … is not nearly as bad as … (extract 1)
   3 the time passed very slowly (extract 2)
   4 moving very fast (extract 3)
   5 the system that makes everything work properly (extract 4)

   b Find more examples of vivid language in the extracts.

6 Discuss the questions in pairs.
   • Have you changed your mind about any of the jobs after reading the extracts?
   • Which job would you choose for two weeks' work experience? Why?
   • Which would you least like to do?

   I have changed my mind about working as a hospital porter – it sounds rewarding.

   I wouldn't like to do any of these jobs for two weeks' work experience!

   I would least like to work as a miner as the conditions sound terrible.

7 In pairs, think of three ways in which each job could be improved. Compare your answers in groups.

   CAN YOU DO IT IN ENGLISH?

   The workers should be paid more. They should also get more breaks.

8 **a** Choose one of the jobs and imagine you are the workers' representative for that job. You are meeting the managers to convince them to improve conditions for workers. Prepare a short, persuasive speech to give at the meeting. Use the phrases on the back cover to help you.

   Surely you must realise that miners need better working conditions.

   You have to remember what an important job hospital porters do.

   If we want workers to do a good job then we must give them more breaks.

   b Give your speech to the class. Listen to the other speeches. Who was the most persuasive?

A CV (CURRICULUM VITAE)

1 a Read the job advert and answer the questions.

1 Would you like this kind of job? Why? Why not?

2 Who do you think in your class would be the best candidate for the job?

b Read the advert again. What is the radio station looking for.

1 Skills: *great communication skills*

2 Knowledge:

3 Experience:

4 Ability:

2 Mary McGee has applied for the job at Bright Lights Radio. Match the section headings 1–6 to the correct place A–F in her CV.

1 EDUCATION
2 KEY SKILLS
3 PERSONAL INTERESTS
4 PERSONAL STATEMENT
5 REFERENCES
6 EMPLOYMENT AND EXPERIENCE

3 Choose phrases from Mary's CV that show she is right for the job. Use your answers to exercise 1b to help you.

4 a LANGUAGE Look at the phrases in *Language4writing* on the back cover and find them in Mary's CV.

b Rewrite the sentences 1–6 using a phrase from *Language4writing*.

1 I have just left school and I am able to learn quickly.

I am a school-leaver and I have the ability to learn quickly.

2 I know all the normal computer programmes very well.

3 I have the desire to be successful.

4 I have a lot of experience of selling to customers.

5 I know all about the latest trends in electronics.

6 I had to train new staff.

Have you got the talent to be a radio DJ?

BRIGHT LIGHTS RADIO

If you have great communication skills and knowledge of current music and culture, Bright Lights Radio has the job for you. We are Brighton's coolest radio station and we are looking for a DJ for the late night show. You must have plenty of experience of being a radio DJ and the ability to be entertaining even at three o'clock in the morning! Email your CV to daviddouglas@brightlightsradio.co.uk.

Curriculum Vitae
Mary McGee
18 New Court Road, Brighton, BN1 RG8 07932 54389
marymcgee@umail.net   DOB: 19/05/1993

(A) PERSONAL STATEMENT
A lively and popular college graduate with considerable experience of DJ-ing, extensive knowledge of the latest trends and the motivation to succeed.

(B) _____
• Excellent communication skills.
• The ability to entertain listeners.
• Up to date with the latest youth culture and music.

(C) _____
Currently: DJ for Brighton Hospital Radio
• DJ for a three-hour radio show.
• Very positive reactions from listeners.

2009–2011: Sales assistant in Ziggy's Music Store
• Served customers and helped to increase sales.
• Learned about the latest music trends.

2010–2011: DJ for school parties
• Responsible for organising all aspects of the party.

(D) _____
2003–2010: West Thorpe High School, Brighton
• 3 A-levels • 8 GCSEs

(E) _____
• Music • Films • Local Brighton issues

(F) _____
References available on request.

5 a Tick (✓) the things that Mary does in her CV.

☐ uses bullet points
☐ writes in complete sentences
☐ avoids using the word 'I'
☐ always uses a verb or article

b Rewrite your sentences from exercise 4b in the style of CV bullet points.

1 I am a school-leaver and I have the ability to learn quickly.

• *School-leaver with ability to learn quickly.*

6 You are going to write a CV. Follow the steps 1–3.

1 Look at the job advert. Underline the skills, knowledge and experience that the job requires.

Join us and see the world!

Travel rep wanted to take groups of tourists to holiday destinations around the world. The right applicant must have good English and excellent communication skills. A good understanding of other cultures is essential and some travel experience is useful.

Send your CV to sarahpark@triptravel.net

2 Write notes about yourself for each CV heading 1–6 from exercise 2. You can make up the details but make them relevant to the job.

3 Write your CV for this job.

7 In pairs, read each other's CVs. Work through the checklist for writing on the back cover. Would you give your partner an interview for the job? Why? Why not?

Mary has an interview with the Bright Lights Radio team.

A JOB INTERVIEW

8 a ⟨2.21⟩ Read the interview questions and Mary's CV. How do you think she'll answer the questions? Listen and check.

1 Why do you want to be a DJ?
2 What are your strengths and weaknesses?
3 What do you hope to be doing in five years' time?

b ⟨2.21⟩ Listen again and answer the questions.

1 In what way is Mary's CV not accurate?
2 Would you give Mary the job? Why? Why not?

9 ⟨2.21⟩ Look at the *Phrases2know*. Try to remember who said each phrase, Ella (E), Ikram (I), Mr Douglas (D) or Mary (M). Listen again and check.

Phrases 2 know

A job interview

Initial questions

☐ Why do you want to be a … ?

Asking for clarification

☐ What do you mean when you say … ?
☐ Sorry, I'm not with you.
☐ Basically, you're saying that …

Clarifying

☐ No, that wasn't what I meant. What I meant was …
☐ What I'm trying to say is …

Generalising

☐ In general …/Generally speaking …
☐ On the whole …

10 a Imagine you are going to interview someone for the job advertised in exercise 6. Make a list of questions that you would ask the candidate.

CAN YOU DO IT IN ENGLISH?

b Think about how you would answer your own interview questions. Use the CV you wrote to help you.

11 In pairs, swap questions and interview your partner for the job using his or her questions. Then decide if your partner should get the job.

41

activestudy2 (EXAMS)

Vocabulary

1 **a Match the words to form compound nouns.**

1 operating	**a**	attitude
2 search	**b**	experience
3 battery	**c**	skills
4 positive	**d**	system
5 interpersonal	**e**	browser
6 proven	**f**	engine
7 web	**g**	life

b (2.22) **Listen, check and repeat.**

2 **Complete the sentences with the verbs below.**

> browse   download ✓   transfer
> update   upload

1 I'm going to _download_ a few new apps for my phone.

2 I've moved to a different city. I'm going to ___ my Facebook profile.

3 I want everyone to see this funny video. I must ___ it.

4 I need some information for my Economics essay. I'm going to ___ the web for the next couple of hours.

5 I'm going on a long trip. I must ___ more music files from my computer to my mp3 player.

Grammar

3 **Complete the sentences with the correct form of the verb in brackets.**

1 'If you _found_ (find) a job in a very distant country, would you go?'
'I might, provided that the job ___ (be) interesting.'

2 If she spoke more languages, she ___ (can/work) as a travel rep.

3 Supposing someone ___ (offer) you one digital gadget for free, what would you choose?

4 If I lost my mobile phone, I ___ (feel) absolutely helpless.

5 Even if I had the right qualifications, I ___ (not/want) this job.

4 Underline the correct verb form.

1 Candidates for the job _must/should_ have two years' proven experience. It's essential.

2 You _should turn/should have turned_ your mp3 player down a bit or it may damage your hearing.

3 I _should/must_ have an internet connection in my hotel room or I'm not staying!

4 I _should buy/should have bought_ the other phone. The one I got has a short battery life.

5 We just _have to/should_ do what they tell us. We have no choice.

6 I _needn't have worried/shouldn't worry_ about my job interview. It turned out to be quite easy.

5 Complete the dialogue with the correct future form of the verb in brackets. Use a different form in each sentence.

Liam: Hi, Grace. Why are you looking so depressed?

Grace: Hi, Liam. Oh, I'm just so stressed out by all this school work.

Liam: Cheer up. Think about this: six months from now, the exams will be over and we [1]_will be swimming_ (swim) in the Mediterranean.

Grace: Right. And by 2018, I [2]___ (finish) my studies and I'll be making lots of money.

Liam: Exactly. In the meantime, come to a concert with me on Saturday.

Grace: I can't. I [3]___ (visit) my grandma this Saturday.

Liam: But the concert [4]___ (start) until 10.00 p.m. Look, here are the tickets. Surely you'll be free by that time, won't you?

Grace: I think so.

Liam: Then I [5]___ (pick) you up at 9.30, okay?

6 **Complete the second sentence so that it means the same as the first.**

1 I'm sorry I didn't work harder on the IT course.
I should _have worked harder_ on the IT course.

2 I can't help you because I don't live here.
If I ___ help you.

3 It wasn't necessary to download this document.
You ___ this document.

4 We've arranged to meet our old classmates on Saturday.
We're ___ our old classmates on Saturday.

5 I'm determined to pass my driving test before my nineteenth birthday.
By the time I'm nineteen, I ___ my driving test.

6 Bob can work well in a team.
Bob's got the ___ work in a team.

7 I can come with you because there's no school tomorrow.
I ___ to come with you if there was school tomorrow.

8 Imagine all technology disappeared overnight – what would we do?
Supposing ___ overnight, what would we do?

Reading skills

7 Read the article and choose the correct answer.

1 Lists of top words of the decade
   a were an idea suggested by readers.
   b reflected a decade of joy and hope.
   c show some of the problems of today's world.
   d were first published in the US.

2 The phrases 'global warming' and 'carbon footprint'
   a both appeared in the same list.
   b reflect worries about climate change and terrorism.
   c are complicated.
   d refer to the same problem.

3 The word 'Obama' appeared on the GLM list because
   a it's the US President's name.
   b the President is very popular.
   c other words have been created from it.
   d there is a mania connected with it.

4 The words related to technology
   a are the most popular of all.
   b are mostly quite recent.
   c have been with us forever.
   d are not listed in dictionaries yet.

5 The aim of the article is to
   a show how the words people use reflect their lives.
   b inform readers about new words.
   c explain which new words are correct.
   d show which words are most important.

Speaking skills

8 Express and justify your opinion on the following statement.

> 'Communication technologies such as email, texting and Facebook encourage people to hide behind their screens and stop them socialising in the real world.'

The Words of the Noughties*

(2.23)

The language we use can say a lot about our lives. What then, seen through language, was life like for the 1.5 billion speakers of English worldwide in the first decade of the third millennium?

5 As the noughties were coming to an end, various websites published lists of 'the top words of the decade'. One was produced by the BBC News magazine, with words suggested by thousands of readers. Another came from the Global Language Monitor (GLM), an American 10 online organisation that analyses trends in the English language.

'9/11' appears close to the top on both lists, reflecting the decade's greatest fear: terrorism. 'Global warming' on one list and 'carbon footprint' on the other represent worries 15 connected with climate change. 'For a decade that began with such joy and hope, the words chosen depict a far more complicated and in many ways, tragic time,' says GLM president, Paul J. J. Payack.

The BBC also included the phrase '24/7' meaning 'open 20 twenty-four hours a day, seven days a week', which says something about how hectic our lives have become in recent years. The third word on the GLM list is 'Obama'. But why is it there at all, instead of appearing among the Top Names of the Decade, also listed on the website? 25 The reason is that the US President's name has started functioning as a root word, creating around itself a whole family of words such as 'Obama-mania' and 'Obamanomics' (Obama + economics).

Predictably, many of the most popular words on both lists 30 have to do with technology. 'Google', 'dotcom', 'texting', 'blog', 'twitter', 'emoticon' – it may feel as if these have been with us forever but actually they all entered the language in the last ten years, at least in their modern meanings. The Oxford English Dictionary – the great 35 dictionary that aims to list all the words in the English language, a never-ending task – added 'blog' in 2003, 'dot-commer' in 2004 and 'Google' as a verb ('Google it!') in 2006.

Among the most recent and most famous technology 40 words is the verb 'to unfriend' – to delete someone as a friend on a social networking site such as Facebook. In 2009, the American Oxford Dictionary chose it as its Word of the Year. Its opposite, 'to friend someone', existed in English for centuries but hasn't been used since the 45 seventeenth century and has now made a return.

Looking at the most popular words of the past decade, we can see that speakers of English have worried about war and climate, that technology has been central to their lives and that President Obama has made a strong 50 impression. And what will the next ten years bring? Who knows? But one thing is almost certain: we'll continue to invent and use new technologies and with them new words, words that may soon make 'Google' sound as old-fashioned as 'floppy disk'.

* the noughties is the decade 2000–2009, formed from the word 'nought'– zero (created by analogy to the sixties, the nineties, etc.)

5 pop culture

Grammar	Passives
	More complex question forms
Vocabulary	A performance
	Pop music
	Filmmaking and publishing
	Describing a film
Phrases	Talking about statistics and trends

Vocabulary & Speaking

A performance

1 List as many artistic events as you can in a minute.
opera, concert

2 a **Words 2 know** (2.24) Check the words in blue.
Order the events 1–9 during a theatre performance.

- [ ] The audience **take their seats** in the **stalls** or the **circle**.
- [ ] The actors put on their **make-up** and **costumes** in their **dressing rooms**.
- [ ] At the end of the performance the **cast** all **bow**.
- [ ] The **curtain goes up**, the actors appear **on stage** and the **performance** begins.
- [1] The actors arrive **backstage**.
- [ ] The audience buy **refreshments** and discuss the **production**.
- [9] The audience **show** their **appreciation** of the **acting** by **clapping** and **cheering**.
- [ ] After the **first act** there's an **interval**.
- [ ] When the curtain goes up again the **set** has changed.

b (2.25) Compare answers in pairs. Listen and check.

3 a Add the words from exercises 1 and 2 to the correct section in the word map.

```
     WORK                    PLACES
     a play    PERFORMANCE   backstage
               ARTS
     ACTIONS                 PEOPLE
     to clap                 the audience
               OTHER
               the costumes
```

b Think of at least one more word to add to each section. Think of music and dance as well as drama.

4 Mark the audience's comments positive (+) or negative (−). Which comments are the most positive? Which are the least?

- [+] 'The costumes were really impressive.'
- [ ] 'I was bored out of my mind a lot of the time.'
- [ ] 'I thought the whole production was absolutely outstanding!'
- [ ] 'I thought the set was a bit weird.'
- [ ] 'The whole performance was absolutely appalling.'
- [ ] 'I found the story quite amusing.'

5 a In pairs, describe a play, concert or show that you have performed in or attended. You can make up the details if necessary. Explain what happened and what you thought of it using the *Words2know* and phrases in exercise 4.

> *Last year our school put on a play. For a school play, the costumes and set were really impressive and the acting was outstanding...*

MINI WORKBOOK exercise 7 page 117

Grammar Focus

Passives

6 a Describe what is happening in each cartoon and guess what happened next.

b Read the stories to check your answers. Guess which one is invented.

7 a Look at the underlined passive verb in the first story. Underline ten more passive verbs in the three stories.

b Read *Grammar2know* and complete with the verbs you have underlined.

Wynn Loses

Steve Wynn, the millionaire art collector, recently made one of the most expensive mistakes of his life. He put his elbow through a painting worth $139 million. *La Rêve* <u>was painted</u> by Picasso in just five hours in 1932. The painting is being restored but it is now thought to be worth only $85 million. Wynn is expected to claim on his insurance.

Passives

Use the passive if the action is more important than the person who did the action. The 'doer' is often obvious, unimportant or unknown:

*The playwright **has been arrested**.* (obviously the police arrested him)

*The man **has been asked** to stay away.* (we don't know who asked him or it doesn't matter)

We often use the passive to describe processes and procedures:

*The painting **is being restored**.* (the action is the most important thing here)

We often use the passive in reports and newspaper articles in order to say what is happening without saying who is responsible:

*The man **could be charged**.* (we don't know who wants this to happen)

We often use impersonal passive constructions with *it* in formal contexts:

It is thought *to be worth $85 million.* (people think/believe/say/expect that it's worth $85 million)

Form

The correct tense or modal form of *be* + past participle:

present simple *is expected*	past simple _____
present continuous _____	past continuous _____
present perfect _____	past perfect _____
'will' future _____	modal _____

8 <u>Underline</u> the correct tense, active or passive.

A new musical ¹*has cancelled/<u>has been cancelled</u>* before its opening night because only a few tickets ²*have bought/have been bought*. The musical, *Dubya*, ³*bases/is based* on the life of former US President George W. Bush. The producers ⁴*say/are said* that all tickets sales ⁵*will refund/will be refunded*. It ⁶*believes/is believed* that the show ⁷*may put on/may be put on* next year in a theatre in Texas, Mr Bush's home state.

9 Complete the text with the correct tense of the active or passive form of the verb in brackets.

A painting that ¹*had been thrown* (throw) into a rubbish bin in New York ²___ (sell) by the auction house Sotheby's for over a million dollars. *Tres Personajes* ³___ (paint) by the Mexican artist Rufino Tamayo in 1970 and ⁴___ (steal) from a warehouse in Texas twenty years ago. It ⁵___ (save) from the rubbish by Elizabeth Gibson, who ⁶___ (spot) it while she ⁷___ (walk) with her dog. Ms Gibson ⁸___ (keep) the painting on the wall of her apartment for several months until she ⁹___ (tell) by a friend that it might be valuable. The theft of the painting ¹⁰___ (now investigate) by the FBI. It ¹¹___ (expect) that Ms Gibson ¹²___ (reward) with a large sum of money later this month.

MINI WORKBOOK exercises 1–4 pages 116–117

A smashing visit

A museum visitor has smashed three seventeenth-century Chinese vases worth £500,000. The man from Cambridge tripped while walking down some stairs and fell into the vases which were part of a special exhibition. The 400 broken pieces are being glued together but the work won't be completed before next June. The man has been asked to stay away from the museum in future. He may be asked to pay for the repairs.

Birthday blues

A concert in honour of the conductor Augustus Caplin ended in disaster yesterday. It had been organised to celebrate Caplin's eightieth birthday but he became so excited when he was conducting the orchestra that his baton flew out of his hand and hit a woman in the audience. The performance had to be delayed while the woman was being treated.

pop culture

Listening & Vocabulary

1 **Discuss the questions in pairs.**

- What is the name of your favourite singer or band?
- What kind of music do they play?
- Do you and your partner have similar tastes?

2 **Check the *Words2know*. Which of these things have your band or singer from exercise 1 done? Which aren't you sure about?**

" *Kanye West has had several hit singles. I'm sure he's signed to a record label. I don't know if he's played gigs in small venues …*

Words 2 know (2.27)

post music on the internet
get lots of hits on the internet
get signed to a record label
release an album
have a hit single ✓
have a number one single
win a TV talent contest
play gigs in small venues
go on a world tour

3 **a** **Look at the magazine cover showing Alex and his band, Thirteen. What do you think an 'overnight sensation' is?**

b **What are the pros (+) and cons (−) for a teenager of being an overnight sensation? Make a list of ideas and compare with your partner.**

+ You earn a lot of money.

− You can't choose your own clothes.

4 (2.28) **Look at the questions and guess the answers. Listen to part 1 of an interview with Alex and check your answers.**

1 Which three things in exercise 2 did Thirteen do before they were 'discovered'?
2 Which two have they done since then?
3 Which are they going to do?

5 (2.28) **Listen to part 1 again. Tick (✓) true and cross (✗) false.**

1 ☐ A year ago Alex was still a schoolboy.
2 ☐ The band chose the name Thirteen because they are all superstitious.
3 ☐ Alex hasn't got used to being a pop star yet.
4 ☐ He likes having a stylist to choose his stage clothes for him.
5 ☐ The band were very popular on the internet before they got a recording deal.

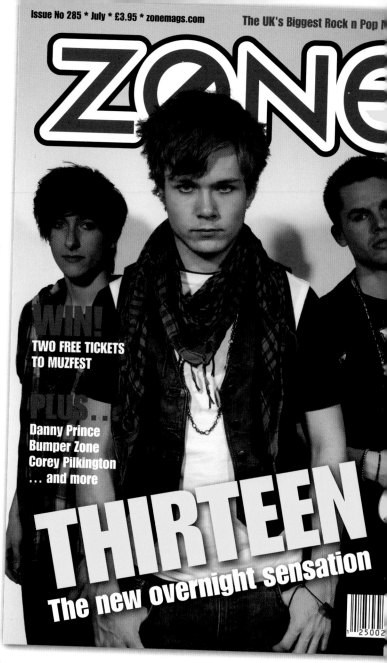

Issue No 285 * July * £3.95 * zonemags.com   The UK's Biggest Rock n Pop M

ZONE

WIN!
TWO FREE TICKETS TO MUZFEST

PLUS...

Danny Prince
Bumper Zone
Corey Pilkington
… and more

THIRTEEN
The new overnight sensation

6 (2.29) **Listen to part 2 of the interview and answer the questions.**

1 What does Alex plan to do next?
2 Where is his home?
3 Does he have a place of his own?
4 How frequently does he see his old friends?
5 What kind of music does he listen to?
6 What advice does he have for other 'pop star wannabes*'?
7 When does the world tour start?

* people who want to be pop stars

7 **SPEAKING Discuss the questions in pairs.**

- Would you like to be an overnight sensation like Alex?
- Which aspects of a pop star's life would you enjoy? Which aspects wouldn't you enjoy?

" *I wouldn't like to be an overnight pop sensation because I don't want to be famous. I like my privacy.*

MINI WORKBOOK exercise 8 page 118

Alex before he was famous

Grammar focus

More complex question forms

8 **a Compare questions 1–7 from the interview with questions 1–7 in exercise 6. Which questions have extra words in them and a different word order? Which question has changed from affirmative to negative?**

1 'Can you tell us what you plan to do next?'
2 'Tell us where your home is.'
3 'Don't you have a place of your own?'
4 'How frequently do you see your old friends?'
5 'What kind of music do you listen to?'
6 'What advice do you have for other 'pop star wannabes'?'
7 'Do you know when the world tour starts?'

b Read *Grammar2know* to check.

9 Put the words in order to make the questions from part 1 of the interview. Make negative questions into contractions.

1 have/you/'Thirteen'/did/What/for calling yourselves/reason ?
2 to be a pop star/feel/How/it/does/exactly ?
3 being/Do/you/not/rich and famous/like ?
4 not/choose/your own clothes/you/Do ?
5 hang out/you/normally/with/Who/do ?
6 how/you/Can/us/it all started/remind ?

10 Complete the questions. In pairs, choose three to ask and answer.

1 Which websites do you download music *from* ?
2 Which radio stations do you listen ___ ?
3 Do you know what the biggest music venue in this country ___ ?
4 Who do you normally go to clubs and gigs ___ ?
5 Tell me who your least favourite singer ___ .

Grammar 2 know

More complex question forms

Compound questions

a Use *What* or *Which* + noun or *How* + adverb to form compound questions:

How frequently do you see your old friends?

What advice do you have for other 'pop star wannabes'?

Negative questions

b Use negative questions to express surprise or ask the listener to confirm that something is true. Use contracted negative forms:

Don't you have a place of your own?

Notice how we answer negative questions:

No. (no, I don't have a place)

Yes. (yes, I do have a place)

Questions with prepositions

c When a verb or adjective takes a preposition, put the preposition at the end of the question. Do not omit the preposition:

What kind of music do you listen to?
NOT: ~~What kind of music do you listen?~~

Indirect questions

d Use affirmative word order in questions that follow phrases like *Could you tell me …?, Can you remind me …?, Do you know …?, Tell me …, I wonder …*

I wonder when the next train to Sheffield is.
NOT: ~~I wonder when is the next train to Sheffield.~~

Can you tell us what you plan to do next?

Do you know when the world tour starts?

Tell us where your home is.

Notice that the question auxiliary disappears in the present and past simple:

When did the tour start? ⟶ *Remind us when the tour started.*
NOT: ~~Remind us when the tour did start.~~

11 a In pairs, write the script for an interview with the singer or band you discussed in exercise 1. Use the phrases on the back cover to help you. You can invent answers.

CAN YOU DO IT IN ENGLISH?

b Learn the script and act out the interview in front of the class.

MINI WORKBOOK exercises 5–6 page 117

pop culture

Reading & Vocabulary

Melinda

Murderland
Melinda Scott

1 Look at the pictures and discuss the questions in pairs.

- What kind of novel has Melinda written?
- What kind of film has Marc made?
- Do you like these genres? If so, which books and films are your favourites?

2 **a** Read the introduction to *Making it alone!* and choose the correct answer.

The article is about young artists who:

1 have got big deals with publishers or film studios.
2 have created and publicised their work independently.
3 are very good with technology.

b Can you guess how technology has helped these young artists?

3 **Words 2 know** (2.30) Check the words in blue. Then decide who the sentences are about, a writer (W), a filmmaker (F) or both (B).

He/She:

1 ☐ has a **big budget**.
2 ☑ works out the **plot**.
3 ☐ tries to find an **original angle**.
4 ☐ does **research**.
5 ☐ **tells the story** from several characters' **point of view**.
6 ☐ **shoots scenes on location**.
7 ☐ receives **constructive feedback** from other people.
8 ☐ gets a **publishing deal**.

His/Her:

9 ☐ work is **released** in cinemas **worldwide**.

Marc

COLIN
www.COLINMOVIE.com

MAKING IT ALONE!

(2.31) If you wanted to make a film or publish a book in the past, you needed a deal with a major film studio or publisher. But thanks to modern technology, a new generation of artists are reaching an audience without the help of big corporations.

Case study 1: The filmmaker

1 Most film budgets run into millions but thirty-year-old director, Marc Price, made his horror movie *Colin* for just forty-five pounds … and took it to the Cannes Film Festival!

Marc has no training at all as a filmmaker, he picked up everything 5 he knows from watching the special features on DVDs. 'They're packed with useful information,' says Marc. He wrote the script during quiet moments in his job as a motorcycle courier. 'I didn't have a big budget so I knew I needed an original angle,' he explains. So he came up with the idea of telling the story from the zombies' 10 point of view. The film was shot with his mother's old camcorder but he claims that the same could be done with a good mobile phone. It was edited on his laptop.

The internet was vital in finding talent. He posted an advert promising free publicity to inexperienced make-up artists in return for their services and ended up with fifty brilliantly made-up zombies. 'To 15 get actors, we went on Facebook and said to friends of friends, "Who wants to be a zombie?" and lots of them were like, "Hey, I'd love to be a zombie!".'

The movie was filmed on location in suburban streets where curious local children were roped in as extras. 'We told them to 20 walk around really quickly and in the film it looks like a big crowd!' says Marc.

The film was initially shown at a small local festival but an enthusiastic fan talked Marc into taking it to Cannes, where it got fantastic reviews. It is now being released in cinemas worldwide by a 25 Japanese company. 'Technology has given filmmakers much more freedom,' says Marc. 'Potentially, anyone can make a movie.'

Colin will be released in cinemas on 23 October.

4 a In pairs, Student A read the case study about Marc on page 48 and Student B read about Melinda on page 143. Make notes about the questions below. Write (?) if there is no information.

1 What exactly is his or her story or film about?

2 How has he or she tried to make it interesting and original?

3 What role did the internet and technology play in his or her work?

4 In what ways did other people help him or her?

5 Are big companies now involved with his or her work?

6 What successes has he or she had?

b Ask and answer the questions in exercise 4a to find out about your partner's case study.

" How has Marc tried to make his film interesting and original?

He told the story from the zombies' point of view.

5 Read the case study you haven't read. Which ideas in exercise 3 are mentioned in each case study? What is said about them?

Marc says that he didn't have a big budget.

6 Discuss the questions.

• Who do you admire most, Marc or Melissa? Why?

• Do you know any other artists, for example musicians, who have used the internet to achieve success? How did they do this?

7 Match the phrasal verbs 1–6 from case study 1 to the correct definition a–f. Use the context to help you.

1 ☐ to pick (something) up (line 4)

2 ☐ to come up with something (line 9)

3 ☐ to end up (with) (line 15)

4 ☐ to rope (somebody) in (line 20)

5 ☐a to walk around (line 21)

6 ☐ to talk (somebody) into (line 24)

a to walk in different directions

b to think of an idea

c to learn informally

d to persuade (somebody) to do something

e to arrive at a final situation or place

f to involve or get help from somebody (informal)

8 Read *Active Study*.

Notice phrasal verbs (2)

Some phrasal verbs have several meanings:

*He **picked up** everything he knows from DVDs.*
(learn informally)

*Can you **pick** your rubbish **up**, please?*
(take from the floor)

*My dad **picked** me **up** from the party.*
(give someone a lift in a car)

A good dictionary will give you all the different meanings of a phrasal verb. Read all of them to find the meaning you are looking for.

---

pick up

1 pick sb/sth ↔ up to lift someone or something: *Pick me up, Daddy! | I picked up the phone just as it stopped ringing.* → see picture on page A11

THESAURUS LIFT

2 pick sth ↔ up to buy something while you are going somewhere or doing something: *Do you want me to pick up some milk while I'm out?* **THESAURUS** BUY

3 pick sb/sth ↔ up to collect someone or something from a place, especially in the car: *What time should we pick you up at the airport?*

---

9 Write the two different meanings of the common phrasal verbs in **bold**. Use a dictionary to help you if necessary.

1 a We thought about the problem for a while and eventually we **worked out** the best solution. *solve logically*

b Anna **works out** at the gym for an hour every day.

2 a Can you **wind up** the old clock in the hall?

b I can't stand waiting in traffic jams – it really **winds** me **up**.

3 a Her husband has died so she is **bringing up** their children alone.

b You **brought up** some interesting issues during the discussion.

4 a I must **send off** this application form today.

b The referee **sent** the player **off** because he had kicked one of the other players.

5 a The artists **made** him **up** so that he looked like a zombie.

b The story isn't true – Melinda **made** it **up**.

MINI WORKBOOK exercises 9–10 page 118

pop culture

49

Writing & Vocabulary

A review

1 **a** Look at the film review website and think of an example for each film genre shown.

b Look at photos from the series *Twilight*. Have you seen the film or read the book? What did you think of it?

2 **a** Words **2** know (2.32) Check the words in blue. What other factors are important in a good film?

b Choose the three most important factors and compare answers in pairs.

❝ *For me, a good film needs a satisfying ending and ...*

3 **a** Read three reviews of the film. Are they positive, negative or mixed?

b Which review did most people find useful? Give three reasons why this review is better than the others.

4 STRUCTURE Read Filip's review again and match the ideas a–g to the paragraphs 1–4.

a He says what he thinks the good and bad things about the film are.

b First, he gives his opinion of the film.

c He says who would enjoy the film.

d He introduces the characters and setting.

e He says whether or not he recommends the film.

f He mentions the writer or director.

g He briefly explains the story but doesn't give away the ending.

Paragraph 1: Introduction	• • •
Paragraph 2: Description of the plot	•
Paragraph 3: Evaluation and opinion	• *a – He says what he thinks the good and bad things about the film are.*
Paragraph 4: Conclusion and recommendation	• •

TV	Music	Games	**Film genre**	Downloads

adventure
animation
comedy
crime
fantasy
historical
horror
romance
sci-fi
thriller
war

Twilight (2008)

twilight

STEPHENIE MEYER

Your Reviews (32)

12 out of 36 people found this review useful

It rocks!!!!

This movie rocks! I loved it. **Great acting, wonderful soundtrack** and Robert Pattison is sooooooo cool as Edward Cullen. Go see it!

Jenny Wetz, the US

20 out of 40 people found this review useful

If you loved the book, you'll be disappointed.

The books capture the excitement and danger of young love. The film, unfortunately, doesn't. It lacks **drama** and the **special effects** are poor. Overall it's disappointing.

Didem Yilmaz, Turkey

(2.33)

48 out of 50 people found this review useful

Exciting and annoying at the same time.

1 *Twilight* is an exciting and sometimes annoying film which is still enjoyable. It is based on the hugely popular *Twilight* books by Stephenie Meyer and is set in a rainy town in the US called Forks. The story centres on the relationship between Bella Swan, a shy, emotional teenager and Edward Cullen, a young man who is not what he seems.

2 The film begins as Bella starts a new school and meets the mysterious Edward Cullen. Edward saves Bella's life twice and in saving her, he shows superhuman strength and speed. The film reaches a turning point when Bella realises that Edward is a vampire. The **twist** is that Edward and his family are 'vegetarian' vampires who kill wild animals rather than humans. As the story progresses, Edward and Bella fall in love but is it safe for Bella to be with Edward and can he protect her from other vampires who want to harm her?

3 For many people, the best thing about *Twilight* is the relationship between Bella and Edward. The lead characters are played by Kristen Stewart and Robert Pattinson, who give **great performances**. For me, however, the film succeeded because of the **strong storyline**. The **original theme** of a 'vegetarian' vampire is interesting and creates a lot of **suspense**. Unfortunately, *Twilight* has its faults. The special effects are disappointing and the **characters** are not very **well-rounded**.

4 Overall, however, I would recommend going to see *Twilight*. If you like romances with a twist, then this is for you.

Filip Nowak, Poland

5 LANGUAGE Read *Language4writing*.
<u>Underline</u> the phrases used in the review on page 50.

Language 4 writing

The introduction

The film <u>*centres on*</u> …/*is about* …/*tells the story of* …

The film *is set* …/*takes place* …

It *is based on* …/*was directed by* …

The main characters are played by …/*The film stars* …

The plot

The film *opens* …/*begins with* …

The film reaches *a turning point/a climax* when …

As the story progresses, …/In the end…

The film has an interesting *twist/message*.

Your opinion

The *best/worst* thing about 'Twilight' is …

The film *succeeded/failed* because …

'Twilight' also has its *faults/good points*.

The conclusion

Overall, I *would recommend/wouldn't recommend* going to see …

If you *like/love* … then this is for you.

6 Complete this short film review using the phrases in *Language4writing*. There may be more than one possibility.

7 Think of a film that you would like to write a review about. In pairs, tell your partner about the film and what you thought of it.

8 **a** Make notes about your film using the questions below.

1 Do you know the names of the director and main actors?

2 Think of two adjectives to describe the film. Is it worth seeing?

3 What is the film about? Try to explain in one sentence.

4 How does the film begin? What is the turning point?

5 What happens as the film progresses? What is the climax?

6 What is the best or worst thing about the film?

7 Does the film fail or succeed? Why?

8 If it succeeds, what are its faults? If it fails, what are its good points?

b Look again at the table in exercise 4. Match the information in exercise 8a to the correct paragraph. Do you need to add any more details?

9 **a** Write the first draft of your review. Then read it through or swap with a partner. Work through the checklist for writing on the back cover.

b Write the final draft of your review.

10 Circulate your reviews among the class for other students to read. Which of the films would you most like to see?

MINI WORKBOOK exercise 11 page 118

32 out of 41 people found this review useful (2.34)

A fantastic experience!

The blockbuster film *Avatar* [1]<u>*was directed by*</u> James Cameron and [2]____ on a distant planet called Pandora. It [3]____ an ex-soldier who travels to the planet and discovers a magical world. [4]____ Sam Worthington and Sigourney Weaver.

[5]____ the main character, Jake, who finds himself on a spaceship heading towards the planet. He agrees to work with a team of scientists who are looking for minerals on Pandora. [6]____ , he gets to know the beautiful planet and falls in love with an alien woman. The film reaches [7]____ when he decides to side with the alien people against the American corporation who want to exploit their world.

For most people, [8]____ *Avatar* is the stunning 3D special effects. For me, however, the film [9]____ because it has an important environmental [10]____ . However, the film has its [11]____ . The characters are not very well-rounded and the storyline is quite weak. Overall, however, I [12]____ *Avatar* – it is a fantastic experience, [13]____ fantasy films.

REAL TIME

The Brighton Doughnut – a gift from the Mayor of Naples.

The Wave by a local sculptor

Graff Jam Wall – graffiti created by Brighton's youth.

TALKING ABOUT STATISTICS

1 Look at the photos. Which work of art do you prefer and why?

Personally, I prefer The Doughnut. I love the shape and colour.

2 a (2.35) Listen to Ikram and Ella's show about public art and answer the questions.

Which work of art did:

1 listeners like the most and the least?

2 artists like the most and the least?

b (2.35) Read *Phrases2know*. <u>Underline</u> the numbers and phrases Ikram and Ella used. Listen again and check.

3 Use the *Phrases2know* to talk about the information.

The pie chart shows that two-thirds of teenagers prefer pop concerts. The majority of …
What the statistics prove is …

Do you prefer films, plays or concerts?

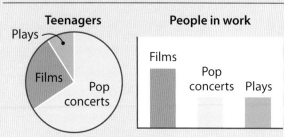

Teenagers

Plays
Films
Pop concerts

People in work

Films
Pop concerts Plays

Senior citizens	
Films	75%
Plays	24%
Pop concerts	1%

Phrases 2 know

Talking about statistics

Fractions
a half/a third/two-thirds/three-quarters of listeners voted for …

Percentages
five/fifty/seventy-five percent of people chose …

Other phrases
a tiny minority/the vast majority chose …
one in three/four/five listeners think that …

Drawing conclusions
The statistics prove/show that …
What the statistics prove/show is that …

4 a In pairs, predict the answers to the questions below for your class. Use *Phrases2know*.

1 Which artist do you prefer, Leonardo da Vinci, Vincent Van Gogh or Pablo Picasso?

I'd imagine that the vast majority of the class prefers Van Gogh.

2 What is the most popular public work of art in your town? What is the least popular?

3 Do you think that graffiti is art or a crime?

b Choose a question from exercise 4a. Do a class survey and make a chart. Explain your results.

We thought that most people would like Van Gogh. In fact, we were … , two-thirds of the class prefer …

TALKING ABOUT TRENDS

5 a (2.36) **Listen to Jake's idea for the radio show and answer the questions.**

1 What does Jake want Ikram and Ella to include on the radio show?

2 Does he succeed?

b (2.36) **Listen again and complete Jake's presentation with *Phrases2know*.**

> The graph shows how many students have been to the theatre recently. As you can see, numbers have ¹*risen* steadily over the last four years. In fact, they've ² _____ . This year, about a third of students say that they have been to the theatre recently. ³ _____ the theatre is popular with students.
>
> What about art galleries and museums? The bar chart shows that ⁴ _____ teens are going. In contrast, there has been ⁵ _____ in the number of adults going to galleries and museums. In fact, it has ⁶ _____ while the number of senior citizens has ⁷ _____ .
>
> So ⁸ _____ more and more teens are interested in the arts and it's a trend that's likely to continue.

Phrases 2 know

	more than doubled.	
	risen slightly/steadily/dramatically.	
Numbers have	stayed pretty much the same.	
The number of people who … has	fluctuated a little/a lot.	
	fallen slightly/steadily/dramatically.	
	roughly halved.	
There has been a	slight/ steady/ dramatic	rise fall	in numbers. in the number of people who …

More and more people are …

Fewer and fewer people are …

6 Use *Phrases2know* and the prompts to talk about the trends.

1 slight rise/number of students going to the theatre

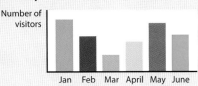

> *There has been a slight rise in the number of students going to the theatre.*

2 popularity of exhibitions/fluctuated

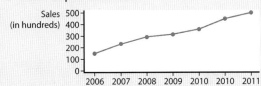

3 numbers/tourists/fallen

Year	2009	2010	2011
Number of tourists	70%	60%	50%

4 sales of posters/risen

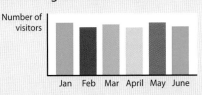

5 visits to art galleries/the same

7 In pairs, tell your partner what you think the trends are for your town. Give reasons for the changes.

1 the number of tourists in your town

> *I think that the number of tourists in our town has risen slightly. This is probably because of the new airport.*

2 the number of things for teenagers to do

3 the number of fast food restaurants

4 the number of cars on the road

5 the amount of litter

8 a You are going to talk about some statistics on music and teenagers. Study the information and think about how to present it.

CAN YOU DO IT IN ENGLISH?

b In pairs, present the information to your partner. When you listen to your partner, note the *Phrases2know* that he or she uses.

	2001	2011
buy on CD	65%	35%
download from the internet	15%	45%
borrow from friends	20%	20%

6 something different

Grammar	Quantifiers
	Relative clauses
Vocabulary	Food
	Describing dishes
	Travel
Phrases	Dealing with unexpected problems
	A description of an event

Listening & Vocabulary

1 WORD RACE In pairs, how many items of food can you write down for each category in one minute? Try to think of words that other students might not know.

1 Fruit: *kiwi*

2 Vegetables:

3 Meat:

4 Fish and seafood:

5 Herbs and flavouring:

6 Sweet things:

7 Other:

2 **a** Check the *Words2know* and put them into the categories in exercise 1. Which ones can you see in the photo?

Words **2** know (3.1)

aubergines   beans   chicken drumsticks
chilli   curry powder   garlic   liver
mangoes   muffins   nuts   prawns
tuna   turnips   watermelon

b In pairs, test each other like this:

❝ *What's a turnip?*
It's a kind of vegetable.
Name two types of fruit.
Watermelon …

3 Read the preview of a TV programme and answer the questions.

- What was last week's challenge? What is this week's?

- Why do you think this challenge is difficult?

- Are there any similar programmes in your country? What happens?

- Would you be able to cook a three-course meal? If not, where would you get advice?

- Would you be able to plan a nutritious, well-balanced menu for a week?

Pick of the Day

Student Cookery Challenge Channel 5, 7.30

Each week, two students face a different challenge in the kitchen. Last week's challenge was to cook a three-course meal for their friends. This week, contestants have to feed themselves for a week. And they can't just live on ready meals and processed food – their menus have to be nutritious and well balanced … all on a budget of only twenty-five pounds.

4 **a** (3.2) Listen to part 1 of the TV programme and answer the questions.

1 What is Claudia's strategy?

2 What is Ed's strategy?

3 Which strategy do you think will work best? Why?

b (3.3) Listen to part 2. Tick (✓) true and cross (✗) false. Correct the false answers.

1 ☐ Ed is getting a lot of recipes from his mum.

2 ☐ He isn't getting much protein because he can't afford to buy meat.

3 ☐ He has made a mistake with today's recipe.

4 ☐ Claudia is planning her meals carefully.

5 ☐ She hasn't been eating fruit and vegetables.

6 ☐ She is managing well with the twenty-five pound budget.

5 **a** (3.4) Who do you think won the challenge? Why? Listen to part 3 and check.

b If you did this challenge, would you be more like Ed or Claudia?

MINI WORKBOOK exercise 9 page 121

Grammar focus

Quantifiers

6 **a** Read the sentences from the TV programme. If you think the words in bold describe large quantities, write (L) and if they describe small quantities, write (S).

1 You just need ☑ **a couple of** tins of tuna and ☐ **a bit of** curry powder.

2 ☑ **A large number of** special offers are on ready meals.

3 I bought ☐ **plenty of** vegetables and ☐ **quite a lot of** fruit but ☐ **very little** meat.

4 I bought ☐ **a few** packs of muffins.

5 Yesterday I had ☐ **loads of** prawns.

6 There are ☐ **very few** special offers on fruit and vegetables.

7 He ate ☐ **plenty of** fresh food and spent ☐ **hardly any** money on packaged food.

8 ☐ **A little** salt is okay but there's ☐ **loads of** added salt in processed food.

9 She ate ☐ **a great deal of** processed food.

10 There were ☐ **hardly any** fresh vegetables in her diet.

11 She ate ☐ **quite a lot of** cakes.

b Read *Grammar2know* and check your answers. Is each quantifier followed by a countable noun, uncountable noun or could be both?

Grammar 2 know

Expressing large and small quantities

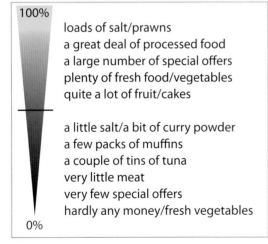

100%
loads of salt/prawns
a great deal of processed food
a large number of special offers
plenty of fresh food/vegetables
quite a lot of fruit/cakes

a little salt/a bit of curry powder
a few packs of muffins
a couple of tins of tuna
very little meat
very few special offers
hardly any money/fresh vegetables
0%

Notice that *a couple of, a bit of* and *loads of* are informal but they are very common. Use *plenty of* in positive contexts:

*She ate **plenty of fresh food**.*
NOT: ~~She ate plenty of sugar.~~

7 Look at the picture and <u>underline</u> the correct quantifier.

1 He ate *quite a lot of/loads of/very little* pizza.

2 He drank *very little/plenty of/hardly any* orange juice.

3 He ate *loads of/a bit of/quite a lot of* fruit.

4 He ate *very few/hardly any/plenty of* vegetables.

5 He ate *quite a lot of/a large number of/a couple of* bananas.

6 He ate *very few/quite a lot of/loads of* muffins.

7 He had *hardly any/quite a lot of/loads of* protein.

8 He probably spent *a great deal of/plenty of/very little of* his money on pizza.

Harry's parents went away for a week and left him thirty pounds to feed himself. On the table you can see what he ate.

8 **a** In pairs, talk about what you eat using quantifiers and the prompts below. Give examples.

bread   fish   fizzy drinks   fruit
meat   pizza   processed food   salad
sweet things   vegetables

❝ *I eat hardly any salad, just a bit of cucumber sometimes.*

I eat a couple of pieces of fruit every day, especially kiwis and oranges.

b Tell the class whether or not your partner has a healthy diet, explaining why.

❝ *Marta has a fairly healthy diet because she eats loads of fruit ...*

MINI WORKBOOK exercises 1–3 page 119

Vocabulary & Listening

Describing dishes

1 **a** Which dishes from the restaurant menu would or wouldn't you try? Compare your answers in pairs.

" I might try exotic fruit salad but I'd never try roast pigeon.

Starters
Today's specials

Spicy fish soup
Raw tuna in a hot chilli sauce

Main courses

Grilled liver in a garlic sauce with mashed potatoes
Roast pigeon with pickled red cabbage

Desserts

Exotic fruit salad of mango, kiwi and watermelon

b Discuss the questions in groups.

- Are you adventurous with food?
- Is there any food that you refuse to eat?

" I'm quite adventurous with food but I refuse to eat rabbit.

2 Look at the website tastesomethingdifferent.com and answer the questions.

- What is the purpose of the website?
- Which foods can you see on the 'top recommendations' page?
- What do you imagine they taste like?

3 **a** Check the *Words2know*.

Words 2 know (3.5)

☑ lean	☐ soft and runny	☐ high in protein
☐ delicious	☐ rich	☐ tender
☐ boiled	☐ a strong flavour	☐ a strong smell
☐ fried	☐ disgusting	

b (3.6) Listen to three people talking about the dishes in the photos.

- Have they eaten the food they are describing? If so, do they like it?
- Would you try any of these foods?

c (3.6) Listen again. Match the descriptions in *Words2know* to the dishes 1–3 on the website. Some words might be used to describe more than one dish.

tastesomethingdifferent.com

HOME CULTURE SPECIALITY MORE

Do you like to try exotic new dishes when you travel? Specialities that only the locals eat?

Welcome to **tastesomethingdifferent**, the guide to the most interesting local dishes wherever you travel. Share local traditions, then share your experiences with other travellers.

🍴 TOP RECOMMENDATIONS

1 Haggis

2 Kangaroo

3 Maggot cheese

4 **a** Put the *Words2know* into the correct group.

1 Ways of cooking or serving food: *fried*
2 Words to describe taste: *delicious*
3 Other words to describe food: *a strong smell*

b Look again at the menu in exercise 1. Underline eight adjectives to describe food then add them to the correct group in exercise 4a.

5 Think of another food that can be described using the *Words2know*.

Curry has a really strong smell.

6 **a** Write a description of the most exotic, disgusting or delicious dish you have ever eaten but do not say which of these it is. Use the *Words2know* to help you.

… is a kind of grilled lamb mixed with vegetables. It's served with boiled rice. It's very … and it tastes really …

b Read your description to the class. Can they guess whether or not you enjoyed the dish?

MINI WORKBOOK exercise 10 page 121

Grammar Focus

Relative clauses

7 Read information from the website about the three dishes and answer the questions.

1 In what forms is kangaroo meat served today?

2 What ingredients go into haggis?

3 How do the maggots get into 'maggot cheese'?

8 **a** Look at the sentences in **bold** in text A. Then read each sentence without the relative clause.

- Which relative clause defines the thing or person described?

- Which just adds extra information?

b Underline the relative clauses with *where* and *who* in the texts. Are they defining or non-defining clauses? Read *Grammar2know* to check.

Grammar 2 know

Defining and non-defining relative clauses

Use defining relative clauses to say which thing or person we are talking about:

*Australians eat sausages **that are made from kangaroo meat.*** (this tells us what kind of sausages)

Use non-defining relative clauses to add extra information to the sentence. They are not necessary to define what we are talking about:

*In Australia, some friends offered me kangaroo meat, **which was traditionally eaten by Aboriginal people.***

*The ingredients, **which are mixed with spices,** are boiled in the sheep's intestines.*

Relative pronouns

Use the relative pronouns *which, who, where* and *when* in both types of relative clause:

*The maggots must be alive at the time **when the cheese is eaten**.*

*The dish is served on 25 January, **when Scots celebrate the birthday of their national poet**.*

Use *that* instead of *which* or *who* in defining relative clauses but not in non-defining clauses:

*Haggis is a sausage **which/that** is made from the sheep's heart, liver and lungs.*

Notice that we cannot use *what* in these sentences.

3.7 🍴 TOP RECOMMENDATIONS

A **In Australia, some friends offered me kangaroo meat, which was traditionally eaten by Aboriginal bush people.** However, it is becoming increasingly popular with modern Australians, who often barbeque the meat in the form of steaks. **Australians also eat sausages that are made from kangaroo meat.**

B In Edinburgh, I went to a restaurant where haggis is served. Haggis is a kind of sausage that's made from sheep's heart, liver and lungs. The ingredients, which are mixed with oatmeal and spices, are boiled inside the sheep's intestine for three hours. The dish is traditionally served on Burns Night, when Scots celebrate the birthday of their national poet.

C In Sardinia, I came across casu marzu or 'maggot cheese', which has been produced on the island for thousands of years. Special 'cheese flies' lay their eggs in the cheese, where they hatch into maggots. The maggots must still be alive at the time when the cheese is eaten. If the maggots are dead, the cheese is considered toxic. Sometimes the maggots jump out of the cheese into the eyes of the person who is eating it!

9 Underline the correct relative pronoun and add a comma if necessary.

Burns Night

Burns Night is a celebration ^{1}◯ *that/when* takes place on 25 January. It is the night ^{2}◯ *which/when* Scots celebrate the birth of poet Robert Burns. Burns ^{3}⊘ *who/that* was born in 1759, wrote many famous poems and songs. His most famous song is *Auld Lang Syne* ^{4}◯ *which/that* is sung on New Year's Eve. For 'Burns Supper', Scots eat haggis ^{5}◯ *which/what* is a traditional dish. At the beginning of the meal ^{6}◯ *which/when* the haggis is brought in on a large plate, it is toasted with whisky. The music ^{7}◯ *that/what* traditionally accompanies Burns Supper is played on the bagpipes.

10 **a** Join the sentences using either defining or non-defining relative clauses. Add commas and make any other changes if necessary.

Australia day

1 Australia Day commemorates a day. The British first landed in Australia on this day.

Australia Day commemorates the day when the British first landed in Australia.

2 They landed at Sydney Cove. The modern city of Sydney is situated there.

3 Australia Day is on 26 January. It is a public holiday in Australia.

4 Australians often celebrate Australia Day with a barbeque. This usually takes place on a beach or near a swimming pool.

5 A lot of people also go to big cities like Sydney. There are fantastic firework displays there.

b **3.8** Listen and check.

11 Think of a national celebration in your country which is similar to those in exercises 9 and 10. Write sentences about it using relative clauses.

In my country we celebrate ...

MINI WORKBOOK exercises 4–8 page 120

57

Reading & Speaking

1 Discuss the questions in groups.

- What holidays have you been on in the last few years? Which one was the best and why?
- Would you like to travel more in the future? Where to?
- What are the cheapest ways of travelling or having a holiday?

" *In the last few years I've been on a beach holiday to … and I've been ….*
Camping is a cheap way of having a holiday.

2 **a** Look at the picture. Can you guess what 'couch surfing' is?

b Read the article and check. Then answer the questions.

1 What does the CouchSurfing website do?

2 What does a traveller gain from couch surfing?

3 What does a host gain?

4 How did Alex and Zsolt find people to help them?

3 Put the sentences a–d in the correct gaps 1–4 in the article. In pairs, explain how you made your decision.

a They relied entirely on social networking websites like Facebook and Twitter.

b But the best bit isn't the free accommodation, it's the people you meet.

c Very few people managed to really meet the locals, experience local culture or taste genuine local food.

d So why do people agree to let a stranger sleep on their sofa?

4 Read the article again and choose the correct answer.

1 Couch surfing is a way for

a people to make money from their sofa.

b travellers to meet other travellers.

c people to be kind to strangers.

d travellers to get advice from locals.

2 According to Jamie Redstone, when you couch surf you

a learn how to cook.

b always get a great meal.

c often have to rough it.

d learn about a different culture.

Couch Surfing (3.9)

How to travel the world … for free!

Simon Wheater reports

1 Going abroad used to mean a package holiday in a beach resort, a guided tour to see the local area and meals in an over-priced tourist restaurant. [1]___ But websites like CouchSurfing.org are changing that.

5 CouchSurfing.org connects travellers with people around the world who are happy to let them stay on their sofa. The traveller might bring a gift for the host but no money changes hands. The spirit of couch surfing is all about strangers helping strangers in order to make the world
10 a better place. CouchSurfing.org now has millions of members in 238 different countries and it has changed the face of travel forever. Jamie Redstone, 21, from Australia, has couch surfed all over the world, including some places off the beaten track. 'Before I discovered couch surfing, I
15 used to really rough it to save money,' says Jamie. 'Now I stay in really nice houses and apartments. [2]___ A couch surfing host will usually cook you a meal – that really helps to break the ice. Then they'll often introduce you to their friends and take you to the places they enjoy. Basically,
20 you become part of their life. Couch surfing allows you to experience a country and its culture as if you were a local. For people like me, who don't have much money, it's easily the best way to see the world.'

3 Delphine is a couch surfing host because

a she enjoys cooking for people.

b she wants to meet vegetarians.

c she wants to help people go round the world.

d she is a professional chef.

4 Alex Boylan discovered that all over the world

a people drink fine wine.

b food brings people together.

c it is important to bring your own food.

d it's not easy to travel without money.

5 Discuss the questions in pairs.

- Would you ever use CouchSurfing.org to travel? Why? Why not?
- Would you like to be a couch surfing host? Why? Why not?

³___ Delphine Lambert, who is an experienced host
25 from Paris, has an answer: 'They say that money
makes the world go round but I try to help people
go round the world without much money!' she says
with a smile. To date she has hosted more than
one hundred travellers. 'I enjoy meeting people
30 from different cultures and I've made friends from
all over the world,' says Delphine, who is also a
professional chef. 'And of course, I like sharing a
bit of French cuisine with them. Usually, my guests
love trying French food but I have had the occasional
35 problem. Once I cooked roast lamb for a guest but
unfortunately, when she got here, she told me she
was vegetarian!'

The concept of travelling the world for free has even
been made into a TV series. Alex Boylan and Zsolt
40 Luka from the US set out with no money at all. ⁴___
'We would go online and write "Hey, I'm in Lima, Peru
tonight and I'm heading to Santiago in Chile. Do you
know anyone who can help out?",' explains Alex. 'And
it was amazing - wherever we went we were always
45 provided for, whether it meant sharing a bowl of rice
with monks or having a luxurious dinner with fine
wine. All over the world, food is a common bond.'
They travelled 45,000 miles through sixteen different
countries and the results were turned into the TV
50 show *Around the World for Free.*

Vocabulary & Speaking

Travel

6 **a** Words **2** know (3.10) Check the phrases in blue in the quiz.

b What kind of traveller are you? Do the quiz in pairs and find out. Do you agree with the conclusions in the key?

7 **a** Work in groups of three. Student A, look at page 134, Student B at 142 and Student C look at page 143.

CAN YOU DO IT IN ENGLISH?

b You are going to persuade your group to go on this holiday with you. Decide what the advantages of the holiday are and what objections your partners might have. Use the phrases on the back cover to help you.

8 **a** Take turns to present your holiday option to your group and persuade them of the advantages. Answer their objections.

"*Don't you think we should go to ...? There are loads of things to do.*

Yes, but on the other hand we can only stay a few days.

b Take a vote on the holiday you prefer. Explain to the class which holiday your group has chosen and why.

MINI WORKBOOK exercise 11 page 121

What kind of traveller are you?

1 Which holiday would you rather have?
a a **package holiday** at a **beach resort**
b a **hiking holiday**
c a five-star city break

2 What do you enjoy most on holiday?
a **sunbathing**, swimming and **chilling out**
b exploring places that are **off the beaten track**
c shopping, **eating out** and **nightlife**

3 How do you prefer to eat when you're on holiday?
a choose a hotel with **full board** or a **self-catering apartment**
b look for small restaurants where **the locals** eat
c choose an international hotel with a top restaurant and twenty-four-hour **room service**

4 How do you go sightseeing when you're on holiday?
a **take a guided tour**
b put on a **backpack** and set off, taking a map to help you
c **hire** your own personal **tour guide**

5 You want to visit a famous local landmark but you can't find any buses that go there. What do you do?
a ask your **travel rep** for advice   b **hitch-hike**   c order a taxi

Key

Mostly answered . . .
a You enjoy going on holiday but you are not an adventurous traveller! You prefer to stick with things that you know.
b You want to experience new cultures and you don't mind roughing it.
c You enjoy travelling and experiencing new things but you travel in luxury or not at all.

something different

59

REAL TIME

DEALING WITH UNEXPECTED PROBLEMS

1 a In pairs, say what you would do in these situations.

1 You are on a train and you realise that you have lost your ticket.

❞ *I'd tell the ticket inspector.*

2 You arrive at a hotel but it is full and they have no record of your reservation.

b (3.11) Listen. What did Ikram do? What was the outcome?

Ikram arrives at his hotel but there's a problem …

2 a Read *Phrases2know*. Complete the extracts from Ikram's conversations with the correct phrases.

1 On the train

Inspector:	You must have a valid ticket when you board the train, sir.
Ikram:	¹_____ I had a valid ticket.
Inspector:	I'm sorry, sir but there's nothing I can do.
Ikram:	²_____ show you the receipt? That proves I bought a ticket at Brighton station, doesn't it?
Inspector:	I'm afraid not, sir. The rules are the rules.
Ikram:	³_____ to resolve this?

2 In the hotel

Receptionist:	We don't seem to have a record of your reservation.
Ikram:	⁴_____ you don't have a room for me. ⁵_____?
Receptionist:	That's right, sir.
Ikram:	So ⁶_____?
Receptionist:	Well, why don't you try another hotel?
Ikram:	I'm sorry but ⁷_____.
Receptionist:	I'm very sorry, sir.
Ikram:	Can I ⁸_____? ⁹_____ offer me the luxury room for the standard room price?

b (3.12) Listen and check.

Phrases 2know

Dealing with unexpected problems

Clarifying the problem
So the problem is that …
Is that right?

Asking for solutions
What do you suggest?
Is there anything I can do to resolve this?

Suggesting solutions
Can I make a suggestion? Why don't you …? What if I …?

Standing your ground
I understand that but …
I'm sorry but I don't think that's fair.

3 In pairs, act out the conversations in exercise 2. Add any details that you can remember.

❞ *Can I see your ticket please, sir?*
I've got a ticket somewhere.
You must have a valid ticket when you board the train, sir.

4 a In pairs, read the situation below and write a conversation. Use the *Phrases2know*.

CAN YOU DO IT IN ENGLISH?

Vanessa bought two tickets for a concert to see her favourite band. She bought the tickets online from the official band website. When she got to the concert the man on the door said that she could not come in because the tickets were fake.

b Act out your conversation for the class.

A DESCRIPTION OF AN EVENT

5 Read Ikram's blog and answer the questions.

  1 Why did Ikram go to the event?

  2 How was it organised?

  3 What inspired Ikram at the exhibition?

  4 What decision did he make while he was there?

6 STRUCTURE Match the questions a–e to the paragraphs 1–5 in Ikram's description.

  a How did you spend your time?

  b What was the best part?

  c Would you recommend it?

  d How was it organised?

  e Why did you go?

  1 Introduction _Why did you go?_

  2 Description (place) _____

  3 Description (time) _____

  4 Highlights _____

  5 Conclusion _Would you recommend it?_

7 a LANGUAGE <u>Underline</u> phrases Ikram uses to:

  1 introduce an event and explain why he attended (paragraph 1)

  2 describe the place (paragraph 2)

  3 describe his time at the event (paragraph 3)

  4 describe the highlight of the event (paragraph 4)

  5 conclude his description and make a recommendation (paragraph 5)

  b Read *Language4Writing* on the back cover and check.

8 a You are going to write a description of an event. Think of an organised event that you have experienced recently. It might be:

a sporting event, an exhibition or show, a big family meal or celebration, a guided tour, a concert

  b Make some notes about the event. Use the structure in exercise 6 to help you.

9 a Write the first draft of your description then read it through or swap with a partner. Work through the checklist for writing on the back cover.

  b Write the final draft of your description.

Blog

The Student Travel Exhibition

Ikram Kahn
Wednesday, 21.30
Article History

1 The Student Travel Exhibition in London is an annual event aimed at students in their late teens and early twenties. It brings together organisations involved in student travel and students who want to travel. I had been looking forward to this event because I needed an answer to my burning question: what should I do with my gap year?

2 The exhibition is divided into three areas. In the 'theatre area' you can watch talks and presentations from experienced travellers. In the 'vacation area' you can find information about recreational holidays. And in the 'volunteer area' students who want to do charity work can find out about their options.

3 I arrived early on the first day, in order to listen to a very eloquent speaker who had done voluntary work in Sierra Leone, a country in West Africa. This talk encouraged me to find out more about volunteering and I spent most of my time in this fascinating area. Although the vacation area was also interesting, it simply wasn't as stimulating.

4 The highlight of the exhibition for me, personally, was talking to a very informative representative from VSO, an organisation that sends volunteers to fight poverty around the world. I learned about the work that VSO is doing in places like Cambodia, India and South Africa and I finally made up my mind that voluntary work is what I want to do.

5 All in all, then, I found the Student Travel Exhibition an inspiring and enjoyable event and I would definitely recommend it to any student who is thinking of travelling. It might change your life!

activestudy3 EXAMS

Vocabulary

ACTIVE STUDY Learn words in groups

1 Put the words below into the categories in the table. Some words belong to more than one category.

> acting ✓ backstage curtain
> gig plot shoot

Theatre	Music	Film
acting		acting

2 Match words with similar meanings.

1 gig   **a** place
2 venue   **b** uncooked
3 plot   **c** money available
4 budget   **d** concert
5 raw   **e** story

3 Complete the text with the words below.

> aubergines disgusting muffins runny
> spicy tender ✓ watermelon

We went to the new restaurant in our neighbourhood, The Chilli Grill, last Saturday. I had some grilled meat – it was excellent, very ¹*tender*. Tess ordered a vegetarian dish with ²___ and peppers but it was so hot and ³___ that she couldn't finish it! Then we decided to have some French cheese. It was soft and ⁴___ and it had a strong smell. I found it delicious but Tess thought it was ⁵___ . She ordered some fresh fruit for dessert and she got some lovely pink ⁶___ . (It certainly looked nicer than the cheese.) To finish the meal off, they gave us mini chocolate ⁷___ with our coffee.

Grammar

4 Underline the correct verb form.

1 When we arrived at the theatre, all the seats *had/have* been taken.

2 The stolen painting has *damaged/been damaged* and is *restored/being restored*.

3 The singer *is said/says* to have problems with her voice.

4 The sculpture was discovered in a farmhouse where it *has/had* been hidden for one hundred years.

5 The concert had to *cancel/be cancelled* because of bad weather.

5 Complete the questions with one word in each gap.

1 What *kind* of films do you like?

2 How ___ is it from here to the concert venue?

3 Who did you stay ___ in Barcelona?

4 Can you tell me what vegetables these ___ ?

5 I wonder how old this singer ___ .

6 ___ you notice anything? It happened outside your window!

6 Underline the correct relative pronoun and add commas if necessary.

THE PILGRIMS

'The Pilgrims' is the name given to the group of settlers ○ ¹*that/which* founded the town of Plymouth, Massachusetts in North America. The Pilgrims ⊘ ²*who/that* had escaped England because of religious intolerance ○ came to North America on the ship *Mayflower* in 1620. The day ○ ³*when/which* the *Mayflower* landed in North America ○ is celebrated in Plymouth as Forefathers' Day. Plymouth Rock ○ ⁴*where/that* it landed ○ is a popular tourist destination. The festival of Thanksgiving was also started by the Pilgrims. They celebrated the first Thanksgiving in the autumn of 1621 ○ ⁵*when/that* they had their first harvest in North America.

7 Complete the text with one word in each gap.

Last Thursday's charity summer concert was a great success, with a rich programme of music-making by students, staff and parents and a great ¹*deal* of additional attractions. The patio, ² ___ the event took place, had been decorated with lanterns. The whole school cheered as the evening's youngest musician, Nick, appeared ³ ___ stage to play his drum set. Another highlight was *California Dreamin'* performed by the whole Irvine family, ⁴ ___ had been practising since Christmas. During the interval, refreshments were served in a tent. There was plenty ⁵ ___ excellent home-made food and drink. Two hundred raffle tickets ⁶ ___ sold.

Halfway through the second part of the concert it started to rain but hardly ⁷ ___ of those in the audience seemed to notice. Amy Chang's brilliant performance of *Black or White* inspired even ⁸ ___ few of our grandparents to start dancing!

The total proceeds from this month's charity events are still ⁹ ___ calculated. They ¹⁰ ___ expected to reach £1,500.

Listening skills

8 (3.13) Listen to an interview with a couch surfer and choose the best answer.

1 Chris has stayed with couch surfers:
   a in France and northern Europe.
   b in Europe and Iran.
   c in Europe and India.
   d in Europe, Iran and India.

2 For Chris, the best thing about couch surfing is:
   a going to Paris, Berlin and Helsinki.
   b the free accommodation.
   c meeting interesting people.
   d discovering someone is a couch surfer.

3 When Chris met his friend Jacques for the first time:
   a they didn't spend much time together.
   b they talked a lot about films.
   c Chris was very busy.
   d they went hitchhiking together.

4 What's a major problem with couch surfing?
   a Some people don't treat others with respect.
   b Some hosts and guests are uninteresting.
   c You have to go to big meetings.
   d There aren't any major problems.

5 One problem with Chris's host in Iran was that:
   a he wouldn't let him meet his sister.
   b there was too much food.
   c he wouldn't let his guest pay for anything.
   d he wanted Chris to read poetry.

Speaking skills

9 Look at the photos below and discuss the following in pairs.

A local cultural centre is going to organise creative activities for people in your neighbourhood. The ideas in the photos below have been suggested. Talk about how useful and interesting these activities would be. You can suggest other ideas, too. Agree on the two most interesting and useful activities.

a pottery course

an art class

a filmmaking course

a dance class

a cookery course

63

7 body & mind

Grammar	Articles
	Modals of ability
Vocabulary	Qualities of mind
	Health
	Describing people
Phrases	Giving a speech (2)
	Answering challenging questions

Vocabulary & Listening

Qualities of mind

1 Discuss the questions in pairs.
- What does the photo show?
- What kind of information can scientists get from brain scans?

2 **a** Read the text about the human brain. Which statements do you think are facts and which are myths? Compare answers in pairs.

b (3.14) Listen to a radio programme and check. Which statements do scientists disagree on?

3 **a** Words 2 know (3.15) Check the words in blue. Try to remember who the statements are associated with, men (M), women (W), 'left-brained' people (L), 'right-brained' people (R), video game-players (V) or teenagers (T).

1 ☑ They are quick-thinking and good at multi-tasking.
2 ☐ They tend to be empathetic and have good verbal skills.
3 ☐ They are good at processing information and learning languages.
4 ☐ They tend to be imaginative and artistic.
5 ☐ They can be badly organised and impulsive.
6 ☐ They are practical and analytical.
7 ☐ They are more independent have good spatial skills.

b (3.14) Listen again and check.

4 Write one sentence about five of the people in the box below, using *Words2know*. Explain your ideas.

> teenagers   middle-aged people
> elderly people   men   women   my friend
> my father   my sister   artists   architects
> scientists   business people   politicians

My sister is very artistic – she's always drawing.

Architects need good spatial skills because they have to design buildings.

The human brain: facts and myths

Thanks to modern science, we know more about the human brain than ever before. So are these common ideas facts or myths?

- Men have bigger brains than women.
- Some people are 'left-brained' and some are 'right-brained'.
- Video games are bad for the brain.
- The brain is fully developed by the time we enter our teens.
- Eating fish makes you brainy.

5 **a** Write four sentences about yourself using the *Words2know*. One sentence should be false but the others should be true.

b In pairs, read your sentences to each other. Guess which sentence is false.

" *I'm very imaginative and artistic, I write a lot of poetry.*

False – I don't believe that!

MINI WORKBOOK exercises 6–7 page 124

Grammar Focus

Articles

6 **a** (3.16) Listen to some sentences about the ideas in the programme. Complete the sentences with the articles you hear or write (ø) if there is no article.

1 Men and women have different brains. ᵃ _ø_ Women have better verbal skills but men have better spatial skills.

2 We use both sides of ᵇ___ brain but in some people the left side is dominant. In others, the right is dominant.

3 This is an interesting subject. Many people worry that video games are bad for ᶜ___ young but ᵈ___ latest research into the subject suggests that the opposite is true. The brains of video gamers are actually very sharp. They process information faster than the average person.

4 ᵉ___ teenage brain is highly effective in many ways. But the front of the brain develops last and this is the part that is responsible for organisation.

5 Some scientists claim that ᶠ___ vitamins that are found in oily fish are good for the elderly because they help stop memory loss.

b Underline eleven more nouns with articles and circle eleven nouns with no article.

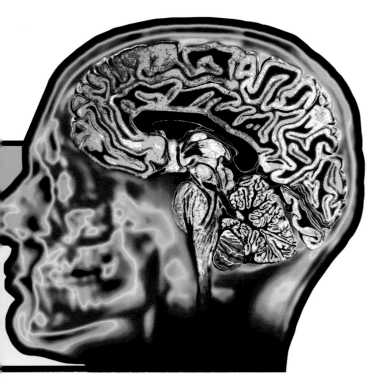

7 Read *Grammar2know*. Then match articles a–f in exercise 6a to rules 1–6 below.

Grammar 2 know

Articles

We use *a* or *an* if we don't know which noun we are talking about because it is one of many and we haven't mentioned it before:

*This is **an** interesting subject.* (this is the first mention, there are many subjects)

We use *the* if we have referred to a noun before so we have defined which one we mean:

*… research into **the** subject suggests …* (this is the second mention, we know which subject)

We use *the* if it is clear from the context exactly which thing we are talking about. This might be because:

1 The noun is defined by the clause or phrase that follows it:

   *This is **the** part **that is responsible for organisation.*** (we know which part)

   *… **the** brains **of video gamers** …* (we know which brains)

2 The noun is unique or unique in that context:

   ***The front** of the brain.* (each brain has only one front)

3 The adjective before the noun makes the noun unique:

   ***The left side** is dominant.* (there is only one left side)

   Also: *right, only, next, last, latest, first.*

Making generalisations

4 To generalise, we usually use plural or uncountable nouns with no article (ø):

   *ø **Men** and ø **women** have ø **different brains.***

5 We can also use *the* + singular noun :

   *They process information faster than **the average person**.*

6 Use *the* with certain adjectives to generalise about groups of people:

   *Oily fish is good for **the elderly**.* (elderly people)

8 **a** ⟨Circle⟩ the correct article in paragraph 1.

   b (3.17) Complete paragraph 2 with the correct article where necessary. Then listen and check.

9 In pairs, discuss whether you agree with the generalisations made in these articles.

" *I disagree with the claim that …*

Why teens are grumpy...

1 According to ¹*a/the* new piece of research, there is ²*a/the* good reason why ³*the/ø* adolescents (aged twelve to fourteen) often have ⁴*the/ø* conflicts with ⁵*the/ø* older people. ⁶*A/The* research claims that ⁷*a/the* brains of ⁸*the/ø* young people are physically changed by ⁹*a/the* hormones that are associated with ¹⁰*the/ø* adolescence. Apparently, because there are so many hormones in their brains, ¹¹*the/ø* young teenagers often do not recognise ¹²*the/ø* sadness and ¹³*the/ø* anger in ¹⁴*the/ø* faces of ¹⁵*the/ø* other people.

... and grandparents are embarrassing!

2 We all know that ¹___ old people often ask ²___ personal questions and say what they think. But according to Australian psychologist, Dr Bill von Hippel, there is ³___ good reason for this. It seems that ⁴___ part of ⁵___ brain that controls ⁶___ rude thoughts gets weaker as we get older! ⁷___ doctor's research has shown that ⁸___ young people aged eighteen to twenty-five are better at keeping their opinions to themselves than ⁹___ people over sixty-five. '¹⁰___ Old people often know that what they are about to say will cause ¹¹___ embarrassment but they just can't stop themselves from asking ¹²___ personal questions,' says ¹³___ doctor.

MINI WORKBOOK exercises 1–3 pages 122–123

body & mind

Listening & Speaking

1 In groups, look at the photos and discuss the questions.

- Did you have a favourite superhero when you were a child? Who was it and why was he or she your favourite?
- What superhuman ability would you like to have? What would you do with it?

I'd like to be able to turn invisible or read minds. If I could do that I'd ...

2 a Which people in the photos do you think these words and phrases relate to?

> memorise   climb without a rope
> bend and twist   a gift for numbers
> turn his head 180 degrees   be autistic

b Can you guess what superhuman abilities these people have?

3 (3.18) Listen to a TV programme about people with superhuman abilities and check your answers to exercise 2. Write one amazing thing that each person has done.

4 (3.18) Listen again and complete the sentences.

1 The Petronas Twin Towers are ___ metres high.
2 Alain Robert had unsuccessfully tried to climb the towers ___ times before.
3 As a child, he climbed ___ storeys of his apartment block because he didn't have ___ .
4 As a teenager, he fell ___ metres.
5 Daniel Browning Smith can turn his ___ 180°.
6 Daniel Tammet once memorised a sequence of ___ numbers.
7 He speaks ___ languages.
8 He learned to speak Icelandic in ___ .

5 a Rank Alain Robert, Daniel Browning Smith and Daniel Tammet from 1 (most extraordinary) to 3 (least extraordinary). Explain your order to the class.

b Discuss the questions in pairs.

- Do you think people should be free to do what Alain does or are the police right to try and stop him?
- Would you like to watch Alain climbing a building or Daniel folding himself into a box? Why? Why not?
- Do you know of anyone else with amazing abilities like this?

I would like to see Daniel folding himself into a box because ...

Grammar focus

Modals of ability

6 Match the sentences 1–6 to the people A–C in the photos.

1 He can bend and twist his body in incredible ways. *B*
2 At the age of four, his parents discovered that he could do extraordinary things.
3 He was able to climb eight floors and get in through a window.
4 He was unable to complete the climb.
5 He managed to climb through a tennis racket.
6 He succeeded in answering all the questions in Icelandic.

SUPERHUMAN ABILITIES

Alain Robert

A

B

Daniel Browning Smith

C

Daniel Tammet

7 **a** <u>Underline</u> the ways of expressing ability in the sentences in exercise 6. Read *Grammar2know* to check.

b Write alternatives for the <u>underlined</u> words in exercise 6.

He is able to bend and twist his body ...

Grammar 2 know

Modals of ability

can, *could* and *be able to*

Use *can* or *is able to* to talk about present abilities:
*Daniel **is able to** speak twelve languages.*

For a general ability in the past, use *could* or *was able to*:
*As a child Alain **was able to** climb very well.* (this was possible for him if he wanted to do it)

For a specific action in the past, use *was able to*:
*Alain **was able** to get to the top in just two hours.* (he actually did this)

Notice that in the negative both are possible and *be unable to* is also common:
*I **couldn't** see him at first.*
*The police **were unable** to catch him.*

managed to + verb and *succeed in* + verb + *-ing*

When a specific action was hard to achieve, we often express ability using *managed to* or *succeeded in* + gerund:
*Daniel **managed to** memorise 22,500 numbers.*
NOT: ~~Daniel could memorise 22,500 numbers.~~

*He **succeeded in** answering all the questions in Icelandic.*
NOT: ~~He could answer all the questions in Icelandic.~~

Forms and tenses of *be able to*

In other tenses and forms we use *be able to* instead of *can* or *could*:
*Not many twelve-year-olds **would be able to** climb eight storeys.*
*He claims **to be able to** speak twelve languages.*

8 Complete the sentences with the correct modal verbs. There may be more than one answer. Explain why the others are incorrect.

1 Mozart __ write music even at the age of six.
a could ✓   c succeeded in
b was able to ✓   d can

2 Ben Underwood __ to see since he was born but he doesn't use sight. He uses sounds like a dolphin.
a couldn't   c has been able
b could   d has been unable

3 Tanya Streeter used to be a free diver. On one occasion she __ dive 160 metres below the waves without oxygen.
a managed to   c be able to
b succeed in   d could

9 Complete the text about Sonya Thomas with a modal verb from *Grammar2know* and the correct form of the verb in brackets. There may be more than one answer.

10 Complete the sentences to make them true for you. Compare answers in pairs.

1 I'd love to be able to play *the saxophone* .
2 When I was young I could ___ quite well but not any more.
3 I hope that I'll be able to ___ by the time I'm thirty.
4 Last year I managed to ___ which I was pleased about.
5 Recently I wasn't able to ___ because my parents didn't let me.

MINI WORKBOOK exercises 4–5 page 123

Sonya Thomas

1   Sonya Thomas is one of the superstars of the strange world of competitive eating. She [1]___ (consume) more food in a shorter time than almost anyone else on the planet. In July 2009, for example, she [2]___ (eat) forty-
5   one hot dogs in their buns in just ten minutes!

Sonya always knew she [3]___ (eat) a lot but she had never thought about competing until she saw a contest. In her first competition, in 2003, Sonya [4]___ (not set) a world record but she did [5]___ (eat) eighteen
10   hot dogs in one go. She knew that she [6]___ (do) much better. She started training and the same year she [7]___ (eat) sixty-five hard-boiled eggs in just six minutes and forty seconds. In June 2004, she [8]___ (consume) thirty-two hot dogs in one go – a huge improvement! Since
15   then she has [9]___ (win) many contests in a variety of foods, including chicken wings (173 in twelve minutes) and lobster (forty-four in twelve minutes). In a good year she [10]___ (earn) over $60,000 from competitions.

body & mind

Reading & Speaking

1 Read the statement and discuss the questions in pairs.
- Do you agree with the statement?
- Can you think of any circumstances where this is not true?
- Can you think of any real life examples of ethical dilemmas that doctors face?

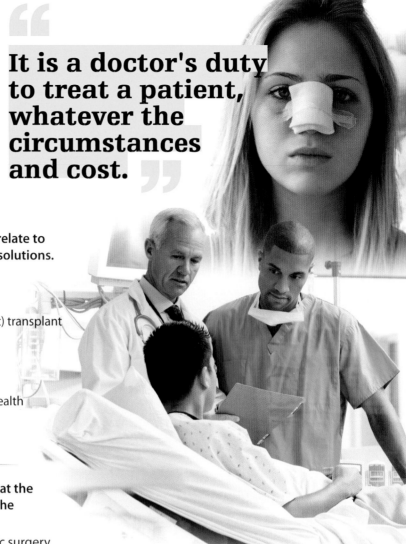

" **It is a doctor's duty to treat a patient, whatever the circumstances and cost.** "

2 Check the *Words2know*. Write (P) if they relate to health problems and (S) if they relate to solutions.

Words 2 know (3.19)

- [ ] have surgery
- [S] treatment
- [ ] suffer from an illness
- [ ] (kidney or liver) failure
- [ ] keep someone alive
- [ ] be obese
- [ ] (state funded) healthcare
- [ ] (kidney or heart) transplant
- [ ] chemotherapy
- [ ] (lung) cancer
- [ ] cure someone
- [ ] damage your health
- [ ] organ donor

3 Look at the prompts and try to guess what the three case studies are about. Then read the website and check.

Case study A fifteen-year-old/nose/plastic surgery

Case study B smoker/lung cancer/expensive treatment

Case study C kidney failure/no donors/buy on the internet

MedicalEthics.com   home | case studies | your comments

(3.20)

Case study A

1 Fifteen-year-old J wants her parents to pay for her to have plastic surgery to reduce the size of her nose. She claims that other pupils at school tease her and call her 'Pinocchio', which is affecting her
5 confidence. Her parents think her nose is okay but are worried about her being depressed. They could afford to pay for the operation. Should her parents pay for plastic surgery?

Case study B

Forty-five-year-old K smoked forty cigarettes a
10 day until he gave up two years ago and is now suffering from the early stages of lung cancer. He is married and the father of three children, aged sixte, thirteen and five. He could be given a new form of chemotherapy, which would cost
15 approximately $250,000. This would keep him alive for between one and three more years, although it might not cure him. K lives in a country where healthcare is funded by the state. Should the ex-smoker be given this treatment?

Case study C

20 Several years ago, seventeen-year-old R suffered from complete kidney failure and now needs dialysis* to keep him alive. Each dialysis session takes four hours, three times a week, making it difficult for him to lead a normal life. R has
25 been waiting for a kidney transplant for five years in his own country but there simply aren't enough donors. In desperation, R's parents have been looking at websites where people sell their 'spare' kidney for around $200,000. These
30 people generally come from poor countries and need money. The transplant would take place in a well-equipped modern hospital and should be perfectly safe for R but there is no way of knowing what healthcare the donor would
35 receive after the operation. Should his parents buy him a kidney on the internet?

*dialysis is a treatment in which waste is removed from the body through the blood

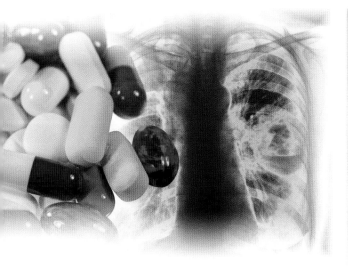

4 Read the three case studies again and answer the questions.

1 What does J want and why?

2 How do her parents feel about it?

3 In what way is K responsible for his own illness?

4 What are his family circumstances?

5 What three things do you learn about the treatment that he might receive?

6 What is R's problem and why is his treatment difficult for him?

7 Why are his parents looking on the internet for a solution?

8 What kind of people sell their kidneys on the internet and what are the risks for them?

5
a Match the comments 1–6 from the same website to case studies A–C. Are they answering *yes* or *no* to the questions at the end of each case study?

b Which comment on each case was posted first? Explain your answers.

6
a What arguments does each comment make and which opinions do you agree with? Think of more arguments to support your ideas.

b Think about how to express your ideas. Use the phrases on the back cover to help you. Underline a phrase in each comment for expressing agreement or disagreement.

7
a Compare opinions about each case study in pairs, giving all the reasons you have thought of. Do you agree or not?

b Discuss the three case studies with the class. Then have a class vote about the questions at the end of each case study.

---

1 The way I see it, if people do something they know will damage their health, they shouldn't expect us, the taxpayers, to pay for their treatment. There are other sick people who deserve expensive treatment more than this guy.
Alison, Southport

2 I disagree. Why not have the operation if it makes her life better and they can afford it? You only have one life, you should be able to enjoy it.
Ben, Cardiff

3 I think you're completely wrong! Following the logic of your argument, anyone who doesn't take care of their body shouldn't get healthcare. Would you also include people who are obese? And what about people who do dangerous sports like skiing or people who sunbathe? Almost everyone does something that is not good for them. And anyway, smokers pay taxes, too so they should get the same treatment as everyone else.
Mariella, Boston

4 In my opinion, if someone wants to sell a part of their body like this, it's their own choice. They should be able to do what they want.
Jeff, London

5 My view is that she should wait until she is older and see how she feels then. All teenagers lack self-confidence sometimes. Her parents should not encourage her to become obsessed with her looks.
Sandra, York

6 I don't agree at all. Organs are often sold online by money-making agencies. The donor himself may only receive a fraction of the $200,000 and will risk his health.
Rohan, Bristol

---

8 Which *Words2know* in exercise 2 are the same or similar in your language? Can you find any other words in the comments that are similar?

9 Read *Active Study*.

ACTIVE STUDY

Notice cognates

a Cognates are words that are the same or very similar in your own language. Which medical words below are cognates in your language?

therapy   infection   medicine   bacteria antibiotics   virus

b 3.22 Cognates are easy to understand when you read them but the pronunciation is often different. Listen and practise saying the words.

10
a Look at these adjectives from the unit. Which are cognates in your language?

a ethical   d medical   g analytical

b practical   e autistic   h superhuman

c empathetic   f physical

b 3.23 In pairs, say each cognate. Listen and check.

MINI WORKBOOK exercise 8 page 124

body & mind

Writing & Vocabulary

A description of a person

1 Answer one of the questions below. You can name someone famous or someone you know personally. Compare answers in groups.

1 Who do you really admire?

2 Who made a strong impression on you when you were a child?

3 Who is a good role model for teenagers?

4 Who has inspired you to take action?

2 Skim read the two description essays. Which two questions from exercise 1 are they answering?

3 Read the descriptions again and answer the questions.

- What are the most memorable things about the people being described, in your opinion? Why?

- Why do you think Betsy and Harry chose these people to write about?

- Which description do you think is better? Give two reasons why.

4 **a** STRUCTURE Read Betsy's description again and match the questions a–j to the paragraphs 1–4.

a Does he or she look like anyone famous? Who?

b How does he or she make you feel?

c What is the first thing you notice about him or her?

d What has he or she taught you?

e What is his or her body type?

f How does this person relate to the title of the description?

g Does he or she look older or younger than his or her age?

h How does he or she behave at a party or on holiday?

i What was his or her greatest achievement?

j What aspects of his or her character are most obvious?

Paragraph 1: Introduction	• *f – How does this person relate to the title of the description?* •
Paragraph 2: Appearance	• • • •
Paragraph 3: Character/ Achievements	• • •
Paragraph 4: Conclusion	•

b Find examples of things that Aunt Ollie does which illustrate her character.

(3.24)

Q. Who _____?

by Betsy Lane

1 Last year I was inspired to run a half-marathon by my Auntie Ollie. Auntie Ollie is receiving treatment for cancer but she is also raising money for cancer charities by taking on physical challenges. She has taught me that with the right attitude, you can achieve anything.

2 The first thing you notice about Auntie Ollie is that she is a **petite**, very **slender** woman. She's in her early fifties but most people think she looks ten years younger. She has a mass of curly brown hair that makes her look rather wild and she tends to wear **very colourful**, **rather unusual** clothes. Some people say she looks a bit like Catherine Zeta-Jones.

3 Although Auntie Ollie is small, as soon as you meet her, you realise that she has a huge personality. She's very quick-thinking and practical but at the same time she can be very **impulsive and unpredictable**. I will never forget the time when I called round to her house and found her dancing to a seventies disco classic with her dog! She's **incredibly energetic** despite her recent illness. At parties she always dances until the end. One of her greatest achievements is climbing Ben Nevis, the highest mountain in the UK, to raise money for cancer charities.

4 Auntie Ollie makes me feel that anything is possible. Her attitude to life is an inspiration to everyone who meets her and I am sure that the half-marathon is not the only thing she will inspire me to do.

Q. Who _____?

by Harry Dein

I admire Stephen Hawking. Hawking is a **famous** scientist and author. He is paralysed and he is unable to speak due to motor-neuron disease. Although he is very ill, he has achieved many **good** things.

Hawking is in a wheelchair and he uses a computer to communicate. He's quite small and he's in his seventies now but he looks younger.

However, his mind is very interesting. Hawking is **very clever**. He was a Professor of Mathematics at the University of Cambridge. He is famous for his work on cosmology* and in particular, black holes. He met the US President in the White House in 2009. The President seemed **happy** to meet him. Hawking has written a **good** science book for ordinary people called *A Brief History of Time*. It was on the bestseller list for almost five years. Because of Stephen Hawking, I think that anything is possible. He has achieved so much despite being ill. I really admire him.

*cosmology is the study of the Universe

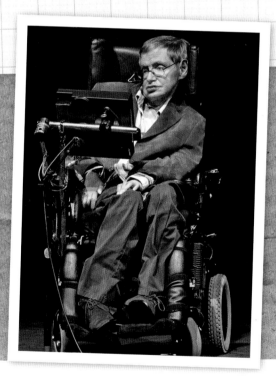

5 **a** LANGUAGE Match the phrases in **bold** in Betsy's description with the words below.

> surprising   big   small
> lively   interesting   thin

b Replace the words in **bold** in Harry's description with more interesting alternatives.

famous → world-famous, celebrated

6 **a** Underline seven phrases from *Language4writing* in Betsy's description.

b Add four phrases from *Language4writing* to improve Harry's description. Look at the examples below to help you. You can change the sentences to make the phrases fit.

A person who I really admire is Stephen Hawking.

The first thing you notice about Stephen Hawking is that he is in a wheelchair.

Language **4** writing

Introduction or conclusion

A person who really inspires me is …
A person who I really admire is …
… and for that reason I really admire him.
He or she has taught me that …
He or she makes me feel …

Description of appearance

The first thing you notice about him or her is …
Most people think he or she looks …
Some people say he or she looks like …

Description of character/achievements

As soon as you meet him or her, you realise that …
What is most interesting about him or her is …
I will never forget the time when …
He or she has … which is one of his or her greatest achievements.

7 Choose a question from exercise 1 and decide who to write about. Before you start, answer these questions:

- Which questions in exercise 4a are relevant to your description?
- What are the answers to these questions?
- Can you complete the sentences in *Language4Writing* about him or her?
- What interesting things has he or she done?
- Which ones can you use as examples in your description?

8 **a** Write the first draft of your description then read it through or swap with a partner. Work through the checklist for writing on the back cover.

b Write the final draft of your description.

REAL TIME

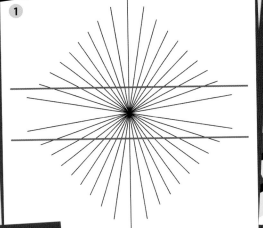

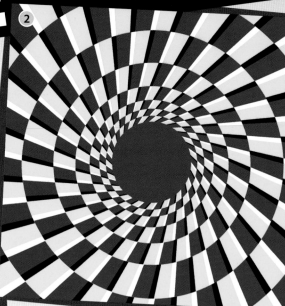

Ikram and Ella's special guest this week is psychologist and author, Barbara Peters, author of *How Your Brain Lies to You*. Here are some pictures from Barbara's book.

GIVING A SPEECH (2)

1 Look at the pictures, read the caption and answer the questions.

1 Are the red lines in image 1 curved or straight? Use a ruler to check.

2 Does image 2 seem to move? Is it really moving?

3 What do you think Barbara's book is about?

2 a (3.25) Listen to Ikram and Ella interviewing Barbara and answer the questions.

1 Is Barbara's book fact or fiction?

2 What examples does she give of ways that our brains lie to us?

b (3.25) Listen again and tell your partner anything you find surprising or unbelievable.

3 (3.26) Listen and put the notes from the speech in order. Then say if they are in the introduction (1), the main body (2) or the conclusion (3).

☐	*look at optical illusions*
☐	*we can't trust everything we see and feel*
☐	*interesting = scientists have studied it for centuries*
1	*begin by saying the brain is very complex*
☐	*we know our brains lie to us all the time*
☐	*brain lies about what it sees and what it doesn't see*
☐	*final thought: need our brain to lie to us*
☐	*look at chemicals in the brain*

4 a Match the phrases in **bold** in a–d from Barbara's speech to the gaps 1–4 in *Phrases2know*.

a **What's really interesting is that** you can't actually see that.

b **Let me** leave you with this final thought.

c What does dopamine do to us?

d **It makes us feel** great. **It makes us feel** excited. **It makes us feel** in love.

b Why do you think good speakers use the techniques in *Phrases2know*?

Phrases **2** know

Giving a better speech

Rhetorical questions (no answer is expected)

Why do we think it's moving**?**

1 _____

Repetition

Only the centre of your vision is in focus.
Only it can see colour.

2 _____

Phrases with *What* … or *The thing* …

The important thing is we assume that our brain tells the truth.

3 _____

Phrases with *Let me* … or *Let's* …

Let me give you an example.

4 _____

5 a Use the *Phrases2know* to make the notes from exercise 3 into sentences.

Let me begin by saying that the brain is very complex.

b (3.26) Listen to Barbara's speech again and check your answers.

6 **a** You are going to prepare and give a speech. Choose a question below to answer.

1. 'Men and women have very little in common.' To what extent do you agree with this statement? Justify your opinions.
2. Are teenagers 'difficult' or do they simply have different brains to adults? Provide examples supporting your point of view.

b Use the table from Unit 3, page 32 to prepare your speech. When you are ready, practise giving your speech to your partner.

ANSWERING CHALLENGING QUESTIONS

7 **a** (3.27) Listen to some callers ask Barbara questions about the brain. Say what each caller finds hard to believe.

1 William finds it hard to believe that _____.
2 Tanya finds it hard to believe that _____.
3 Georgina finds it hard to believe that

_____.

b (3.27) Listen again and complete the conversations from the interview with the correct *Phrases2know*.

William: Okay, Barbara, ¹*surely you don't believe that* love is just chemicals in the brain?

Barbara: ² _____, William. I don't think love is just chemicals. ³ _____ the feeling of being in love is the result of chemicals.

Tanya: Barbara, ⁴ _____ our brains lie to us all the time?

Barbara: ⁵ _____ that yes, our brains lie to us all the time but ...

Georgina: Barbara, ⁶ _____ our brains paint a picture for us? I mean, that's so weird!

Barbara: ⁷ _____ . Look, do a simple experiment.

After her speech, Barbara answers some listeners' questions.

Phrases 2know

Asking and answering challenging questions about your speech

Questions

What do you mean when you say ... ?
Surely you don't believe that ... ?
Do you really think that ... ?

Answers

I understand why you're asking that.
I know it sounds odd but I believe it's true.
That's not exactly what I mean. What I mean is ...
All I'm saying is that ...

8 Use the *Phrases2know* to write challenging questions and answers about the speech you made in exercise 6b.

9 Work in groups. Give your speech from exercise 6b again. Take questions at the end. When you listen to other speeches, ask challenging questions and use this checklist to give feedback.

Did the speaker:	Y	N
• follow a logical structure?	☐	☐
• have an interesting introduction?	☐	☐
• have an effective conclusion?	☐	☐
• use the *Phrases2know* in exercise 4?	☐	☐
• give good answers to the questions at the end?	☐	☐

8
consumer society

Grammar	Reported speech Reporting verbs
Vocabulary	Advertising Shopping Money
Phrases	Agreeing and disagreeing

Vocabulary & Speaking

Advertising

1 Discuss the questions in pairs.

- Are you influenced by advertising? Which adverts have made you want to buy something? Why?

- Do you have any favourite adverts? Are there any adverts that really annoy you? Which aspects of them do you like or dislike?

- Do you think advertising will change in the future? In what way?

" *I love the advert for … . It's really funny and I love the jingle.*

2 **Words 2 know** (4.1) Check the words in blue. Think of a different company, brand or product to match each statement. Compare answers in pairs.

- It has a very famous logo.
  McDonald's
- It's a famous international brand.
- It's got a memorable slogan.
- They're doing a big advertising campaign at the moment.
- It's got a very annoying jingle.
- It uses celebrities to promote its products.
- It's aimed at young children.
- The target audience is young women.

3 **a** Think of two well-known adverts and write a short description for each one using at least four of the *Words2know*.

b In pairs, describe the adverts to other students, without saying what they advertise.

" *It's an online pop-up advert aimed at teenagers. There's a monkey in it and it's got a very annoying slogan …*

MINI WORKBOOK exercise 7 page 127

Grammar Focus

Reported speech

4 **a** Read the first paragraph of the article on page 75. What is 'stealth marketing' and why is it becoming more common?

b Read about Michael and Anna and answer the questions.

1 Why do they do stealth marketing?

2 What kind of people do they talk to?

3 Do you think what they are doing is morally acceptable?

4 Would you do this kind of advertising? Why? Why not?

5 **a** Look at the words actually used by the speakers then underline the reported version in the text.

1 'You're the best.'

2 'It's the best book I've ever read.'

3 'Who's the author?'

4 'I'll promote them.'

5 'Do you stock Danny's Delicious Ready Meals?'

6 'No, we don't.'

b Write down the difference between the verbs in the two versions. Read *Grammar2know* to check your answers.

WARNING! These people are not what they seem!

1 Do you pay attention to every advert you encounter? No? It's not surprising. Every day we hear or see over a thousand billboards, pop-ups,
5 fly posters or TV adverts. There are simply too many – we stop taking notice of them. So now advertising agencies are returning to the oldest method of all: word-of-mouth. The
10 agencies recruit ordinary people to 'recommend' products to people they meet. So what exactly does stealth marketing involve and can we still trust our friends?

15 **Michael:** 'I'm a student and I do stealth marketing because I get free CDs and DVDs as payment. Actually I'm good at it. The guy at the agency said I'm the best. At the moment I'm
20 promoting a book. I haven't read it but I've told all my friends to buy it. Yesterday I was pretending to read it on a bus and I saw someone looking at the cover. I told her that it was the
25 best book I'd ever read. She asked me who the author was so I told her. I really think she'll buy the book!'

Anna: 'I'm a housewife with three children but I also do stealth
30 marketing sometimes. For example, last month the agency sent me some ready-meals. They were okay so I said I would promote them. I went to my local supermarket
35 and asked a shop assistant if they stocked them. He said that they didn't so I told him that they should get them. I also told some of the other shoppers about them. It's
40 easy! I don't do it for the prizes, I do it because I like to know what's new and I like meeting people.

Grammar 2 know

Reported Speech

Report what people said using *tell someone (that)* or *say (to someone that)*.

The tense shift

In reported speech, move verbs one tense into the past:

'It *is* the best book I *have* ever *read*.' –> I told her it *was* the best book I *had* ever *read*.

'I *will* promote it.' –> I said I *would* promote it.

However, do not change the tense if the speaker's words are still relevant:

'You're the best.' (this is generally true) –> My boss said I'm the best.

Reporting questions

Report *wh-* questions with *ask + wh-* word. Report *yes* or *no* questions with *ask + if* or *whether*. Notice the change in word order:

'*Who is* the author?' –> She asked *who* the author *was*.

'*Do you stock* these meals?' –> I asked *if they stocked* the meals.

Shortening reported speech

We do not always report everything that the speaker said. Use constructions like this to shorten or summarise what the speaker said:

I *told* some of the other shoppers *about* the meals.

She asked who the author was so I *told her*. (who the author was)

---

6 Report some more things that Michael and Anna said when they were stealth marketing.

Michael

1 'Did you read his last book?'

Michael asked if she had read his last book.

2 'Everyone's talking about his books.'

3 'You'll really like the story.'

4 'It's one of the most exciting books I've ever read.'

Anna

5 'The meals are really good value for money.'

6 'They taste fantastic.'

7 'My kids absolutely love them.'

8 'Have you tried any of their other meals?'

7 **a** Imagine you have agreed to do stealth marketing to promote 'Sweet and Dry' deodorant for men and women. Decide what to say in these situations.

1 You are in a supermarket. You see a man take a different deodorant from the shelf.

Have you ever tried Sweet and Dry?

2 You play basketball and after the game you discuss with some friends which deodorant you use.

3 Your best friend asks you what he should buy for his girlfriend for her birthday.

b In pairs, roleplay the situations. Take turns to do the stealth marketing.

c Tell the class or write a description of what you said, using reported speech.

I asked the man if he had ever tried Sweet and Dry. He said that …

MINI WORKBOOK exercises 1–2 page 125

consumer society

Listening & Vocabulary

Shopping

1 Discuss the questions in pairs.

- What kind of things do you enjoy or not enjoy buying?
- Which of the following shops do you use most and what do you buy in each one?
  - department stores and chain stores
  - small independent shops
  - markets and second-hand shops
  - online stores

" *I enjoy buying clothes and jewellery. I mostly shop in small independent shops.*

2 **Words 2 know** (4.3) Check the words in blue in situations A and B. Cross (X) the sentences that are wrong in that situation. Compare answers in pairs.

A You are buying a designer bag from a market stall.

- ☐ You find a fantastic **bargain**.
- ☒ The item you want isn't **in stock** so you **order** it.
- ☐ The stallholder **wraps** the bag **up** and gives it to you.
- ☐ You receive a **receipt** by email.
- ☐ You find out later that the bag is **fake**.

B You are buying a new camera online.

- ☐ You use a **secure website**.
- ☐ You find that the camera you want is **on special offer**.
- ☐ You type in your **credit card details** and your card is **charged**.
- ☐ You pay **in cash** and get your **change**.
- ☐ The charge appears later on your **credit card statement**.
- ☐ The camera arrives in a lot of **packaging**.
- ☐ When you try the camera, it's **faulty** so you send it back and **get a refund**.

3 Answer the questions using the *Words2know*.

- What was the last important purchase that you or your family made? Describe the purchase step by step.

I wanted to buy a new laptop from a department store. It wasn't in stock so I ordered it ...

- Which shops in exercise 1 are safest? What can go wrong in the other situations?

4 **a** Look at the picture and read the story about Izzie. Make three predictions about what happened next.

Izzie wanted a special type of designer boots and found them online at a price that was 'too good to be true'. Izzie's friend **warned** her not to trust the website and her mother **refused** to let her use her credit card to make the purchase but Izzie **insisted**. She tried to **persuade** her mum to let her use her credit card but her mum refused. However, Izzie was determined ...

b (4.4) Listen to Izzie and Greg's story and check if your predictions were true.

5 (4.4) Listen again. Tick (✓) true, cross (X) false or write (?) if there is no information. Explain why your answers are true or false.

1. ☐ Izzie looked on the internet because she knew the boots were cheaper abroad.
2. ☐ Izzie realised that the boots were fake when she opened them.
3. ☐ She wore the boots several times.
4. ☐ Greg was angry because Izzie had used his credit card again.
5. ☐ Nobody would help Izzie and Greg.
6. ☐ Greg had to pay the credit card bill.
7. ☐ Izzie's dad didn't let her wear the boots.

6 Discuss the questions in groups.

- Do you feel sorry for Izzie or Greg?
- Has anything like this happened to anyone you know?

" *I don't feel sorry for Izzie because ...*

MINI WORKBOOK exercise 8 page 127

Grammar Focus

Reporting verbs

7 Look at the verbs in **bold** in the story on page 76 and match to the speakers' words below.

1 'I've got to have those boots.' *insist*

2 'Don't trust that website; it looks fake.'

3 'Mum, please will you let me use your credit card? Oh, please, Mum!'

4 'No, Izzie.'

8 **a** Match the sentences 1–5 to the reporting verbs a–e. Use a dictionary if necessary.

1 'You've used my credit card again to do more shopping.' *b*

2 'No, I haven't used it.'

3 'Actually Mum, I bought those new boots online, even though I told you I bought them in town.'

4 'It's actually illegal to own fake designer goods, you know.'

5 'I'll never buy anything online again, I promise.'

a deny   b accuse   c promise   d explain   e admit

b Read *Grammar2know* to check how these verbs are used.

Grammar 2 know

Reporting verbs

Use these verbs to report the speaker's main point. Do not repeat every word:

'It's actually illegal to own fake designer goods, you know.' —> *He* **explained** *that it's* ~~actually~~ *illegal to own fake designer goods* ~~you know~~.

Change the tense in the same way as with *say* and *tell*:

'I **bought** *the boots online.'* —> *I admitted that I* **had bought** *the boots online.*

Structures with reporting verbs

We use different structures with different verbs:

a Verb (+ object) (+ *not*) + infinitive:

Her mum **refused to lend** *Izzie her credit card.*

Rose **warned Izzie not to buy** *the boots online.*

(also: *agree, offer, promise, threaten, advise, remind*)

b Verb (+ object) (+ preposition) + gerund:

Izzie **denied using** *Greg's credit card to do more shopping.*

Izzie **insisted on buying** *the boots.*

Greg **accused** *Izzie* **of using** *his credit card without asking him.*

(also: *admit, apologise for, criticise someone for, congratulate someone on*)

c Verb (+ person) + *that* + clause:

Her father **explained that** *it was illegal to own fake designer goods.*

Izzie **promised her mum that** *she would not buy anything online again.*

(also: *add, accept, admit, suggest, point out, remind, persuade, warn*)

9 Write reported speech sentences using the people and reporting verbs in brackets. Make any other changes necessary.

1 'Okay, I'll lend it to you.'
(Greg/agree/Izzie)

Greg agreed to lend Izzie his credit card.

2 'I'm really sorry for asking to use your card.'
(Izzie/apologise/Greg)

3 'You should phone the bank straight away.'
(Izzie's mum/advise/Greg)

4 'Don't use that kind of website again or you'll have more problems.'
(bank clerk/warn/Greg)

5 'You've got to throw those boots away.'
(Izzie's dad/insist/Izzie)

6 'I was really stupid, I know.'
(Izzie/admit/Rose)

10 Put each line of the dialogue into reported speech using the verbs in *Grammar2know* where possible.

Mum: Emma, you've taken some money from the kitchen, haven't you?

Emma's mum accused her of taking some money from the kitchen.

Emma: Yeah, I took five pounds on Tuesday. I needed it to pay for a schoolbook and you were at work. Sorry I didn't tell you.

Mum: Well, don't take money again without asking or there'll be trouble.

Emma: But I absolutely needed to pay for the book and you weren't here! I wasn't stealing the money!

Mum: Okay, I know you weren't stealing. But perhaps in future you should remember things like that before I go to work.

Emma: Okay, I'll do that next time, I promise.

MINI WORKBOOK exercises 3–6 pages 125–126

consumer society

Reading & Speaking

1 Look at the photos and the facts and figures and discuss the questions.
- How is the young man feeling and why?
- Which facts and figures do you find most shocking? Why?

2 **Words 2 know** (4.5) Check the words in blue then discuss the questions in pairs.
- Do you ever borrow money to buy things that you **can't afford**?
- Are you often **in debt** or is it something you avoid?
- Do you have a **bank account**? If so, do you always stay **in credit** or have you ever been **overdrawn**?
- Would you ever get a **bank loan** or do you prefer to **save up** to buy things?
- If you **owed** money, would you **ignore** the problem and still go out and spend money or would you **repay** the **debt** first?

3 Read the text quickly then match the summaries a–d to the paragraphs 1–4.
- **a** Young people face constant temptation to borrow and spend.
- **b** University fees cause a lot of debt among young people.
- **c** Ignoring debt is the worst thing you can do.
- **d** More and more young people around the world are getting into debt.

4 Choose the correct answer. Find ideas in the text to support your answers.
- **1** What age do you think the author is?
  - **a** a young person or a teenager
  - **b** an older person
- **2** Where do you think the writer is from?
  - **a** the UK
  - **b** the US
  - **c** a non-English speaking country
- **3** What is the writer's attitude towards young adults in debt?
  - **a** critical
  - **b** sympathetic
  - **c** angry
- **4** What is the writer's purpose in writing this article?
  - **a** to show how stupid some young people are
  - **b** to persuade banks not to lend to young people
  - **c** to show how easy it is to get into debt and help young people avoid it

Generation DEBT

(4.6)

1 ¹ Have you heard the joke about the young woman whose credit card was stolen? She didn't report it to the police because the thief was spending less than her! Debt is ⁵ increasingly common for young people all over the world but it certainly isn't funny. Nine out of ten people in the UK are in debt by the time they reach twenty-one. The average eighteen-year-old Australian ¹⁰ has debts of around $3,000 while in the US the average college graduate has debts of $20,000. So why are young people today so much more likely to be in debt than previous generations?

2 ¹⁵ Older people often accuse young people of getting into debt too easily. But the truth is a little more complicated. Of course, there are a lot more things for us to buy now than there were in the past and advertisers are ²⁰ continually telling us to spend, spend, spend. At the same time, it is much easier to borrow money – it often seems as if anyone can get a loan or credit card these days. So is it surprising that some young people go too ²⁵ far? Emilio West is a typical example. Despite having a job, Emilio ended up owing his bank £8,000. He admits that he was stupid. 'My friends were earning more than me and I couldn't afford to live the high life like them ³⁰ but I did anyway.' It took Emilio four years to repay his debts.

90%
The proportion of young British people who are in debt by the time they reach the age of twenty-one.

£25,000
The debts of the average British person graduating from university.

22%
The proportion of young Americans who take a job they don't like, in order to pay off debt.

The proportion of people who ignore the first signs of debt. **45%**

3 And it's not just consumer goods that are to blame. Higher education used to be free in the UK but we now have to cough up thousands of pounds. Here,
35 the average debt at the end of a degree course is £25,000, while medical students in the US often leave college with debts of $150,000 or more. Rebecca Cartwright graduated with a BA in Furniture Design and a fairly typical debt of £28,000. After finishing her
40 degree, Rebecca fell ill. She claims that the reason was stress. 'I was worried sick about my debt,' she says. 'I just didn't know if I would ever be able to pay it back.' Debt can have an impact in other ways, too. In the US, 11% of college graduates say that they
45 have delayed marriage plans in order to repay debt.

4 If you find yourself in debt, remember that the worst thing you can do is to bury your head in the sand. Martin Avery, twenty-two, took out £10 from his bank account one day when he was only nine pounds in
50 credit. His bank fined him for going overdrawn and then he was charged every day that he stayed in the red. Martin admits that he didn't take any notice of the letters from his bank and his overdraft grew to £600! Fortunately, he eventually sought advice.
55 Martin has now made a video and posted it on YouTube to warn other young people of the dangers of ignoring even a very small debt.

5 Discuss the questions.
- Is debt among young people a problem in your country?
- If not, why is the situation different from the countries mentioned in the article?
- Look at the tips for avoiding debt. Which advice do you think is the best?
- Can you think of any more tips?

6 You are going to write a dialogue between A (who has money problems) and B (a friend). In pairs, read the prompt card on page 134.

CAN YOU DO IT IN ENGLISH?

7 In pairs, write the dialogue. Use the phrases on the back cover to help you.

Have you tried paying for things in cash?

Perhaps you should destroy your credit card?

I think you should tell your parents because ...

8 **a** Practise the dialogue with your partner then act it out in front of the class.

b Listen to each other's dialogues. Write down the main problem in each case and the advice that the friend gave.

MINI WORKBOOK exercise 9 page 127

DON'T GET INTO DEBT!

Enjoy a debt-free future by following these simple tips!

1 Work out a weekly budget and stick to it.
2 Don't get a credit card or overdraft unless you're sure you can use it sensibly.
3 Pay for things in cash rather than with a card. You will be more aware of what you are spending.
4 Never ignore letters from your bank or credit card company.

REAL TIME

VOX POP INTERVIEWS

1 a In pairs, discuss how much pocket money you need a month to be happy.

b (4.7) Listen to part 1 and answer the questions.

1 What did the report in the news suggest?

2 How much does the average seventeen-year-old spend on haircuts and trainers a year?

3 What did Ikram do last Saturday?

2 a (4.8) Listen to part two. Tick (✓) the people who agree with the report and cross (✗) the people who disagree.

Interview 1 ☐ Andy ☐ Kim

Interview 2 ☐ Helen ☐ Callum

Interview 3 ☐ Derek ☐ Jody

b (4.8) Read *Phrases2know* and complete the interviews. Then listen and check.

Andy:	In my opinion, it's all hype.
Ikram:	¹_____
Andy:	Yeah, the media love this kind of thing.
Kim:	Yes, but just a ²_____ . I don't think that's ³_____ ! When I was a teenager …

Ikram:	Sorry to ⁴_____ don't you think there's some truth in the report?
Helen:	Well, no, not really.
Callum:	Oh I don't ⁵_____ that. I think it's quite shocking actually.
Ikram:	Why do you ⁶_____ that?

Ikram:	Did you find that report into teen spending shocking?
Derek:	⁷_____ ! Some parents have lost control of their children.
Ikram:	And what do you think, Jody?
Jody:	Well, I think that's ⁸_____ , actually.

Ikram went out last Saturday to ask Brighton's teens and their parents what they thought about a report into teen spending.

Phrases 2 know

Agreeing and disagreeing

Agreeing
Absolutely!   I totally agree.   I think that's true.

Disagreeing
I don't think that's true.   I don't know about that.

Encouraging someone to speak
Why do you say that?   Hype? [Repeat the last word or phrase]

Politely interrupting
Sorry to interrupt you but …
Yes, but just a minute.

3 (4.9) Listen and respond by agreeing or disagreeing using *Phrases2know*.

I don't think this is true …

CAN YOU DO IT IN ENGLISH?

4 a Work in groups of three. Student A chooses a question and interviews Student B. Student B answers Student A's question. Student C agrees or disagrees with Student B.

• Is debt becoming a problem for teenagers?

• Is it really wrong to buy fake designer goods?

• Should advertising be targeted at children?

b Change roles so that everyone has a chance to be the interviewer.

Last Saturday, Ella went to buy a mobile phone and got more than she bargained for …

AN ANECDOTE

5 Look at the photo and caption and answer the questions.

1 Have you ever bought something that you didn't really want? Why did you buy it?

2 How did you feel after you'd bought it?

6 a Read Ella's anecdote on the Bright Lights Radio blog and answer the questions.

1 What did Ella want at first?

a ☐ a cheap, basic phone

b ☐ a mid-range phone

c ☐ a top-of-the-range phone

2 What did she buy?

3 Why did she buy it?

b Choose the best definition of an anecdote.

a a short and funny account of something that happened to you

b a short and serious account of something that happened to you

7 STRUCTURE Read the anecdote again and answer the questions.

Paragraph 1: Introduction

- When and where did this event happen?
  in a mobile phone shop in town
- Who are the main characters?

Paragraph 2: Main event

- What happened before the main event?
- What was the main event?

Paragraph 3: Consequences

- How did other people react?
- What were the consequences?

8 a You are going to write a personal anecdote. Choose one of the topics below (or use the topic in exercise 5) and make some notes. Use the questions in exercise 7 and the techniques in *Language4writing* on the back cover to help you.

- Have you ever wanted something because of an advert and then been disappointed when you got it?
- Have you ever been persuaded to do something that you didn't want to do? How did you feel after you'd done it?

b Write the first draft of your anecdote then read it through or swap with a partner. Work through the checklist for writing on the back cover.

c Write the final draft of your anecdote.

BRIGHT LIGHTS RADIO Blog

Tell us your stories and anecdotes about money and we'll read out the best ones on air!

Here is my personal anecdote on the topic of money.

Ella Campbell
Friday, 17.55
Article History

1 Last Saturday I went into town to buy a cheap, basic mobile phone. You might think that's an easy task but it's not when you meet someone like Kevin, the greatest salesperson in the world! I had no idea that Kevin was going to sell me a phone that I didn't need and couldn't afford. Why didn't anyone warn me?

2 My story begins a few days ago when, all of a sudden, my mobile phone died. I wasn't desperately sad because I knew that I could afford a cheap replacement. So I went into a shop and asked Kevin for his advice. Huge mistake! He said if I bought a more expensive one, I'd save money because it would last longer. That sounded sensible. He showed me a mid-range phone. 'It can play mp3s,' said Kevin, 'so you'll never be bored on long journeys again.' I don't make long journeys but still, I was hooked! I nearly bought it. Then Kevin showed me a top-of-the-range phone. 'All the smart people are buying this,' he said. I desperately wanted to be smart. Kevin showed me its amazing features. Within no time at all I'd bought it.

3 When I told my mum, she freaked out. I quickly realised that I couldn't afford it and I shouldn't have bought such an expensive phone. A few hours later, when I had the courage, I went back into the shop and asked for a refund. 'We don't do refunds,' said Kevin, 'but I can offer you an even better phone!'.

activestudy4 (EXAMS)

Vocabulary

1 **a Match the words to form compound words.**

1	verbal	a	account/loan
2	advertising	b	organised
3	target	c	thinking
4	badly	d	audience
5	quick	e	skills
6	bank	f	campaign

b (4.10) Listen, check and repeat.

2 Complete the sentences with one preposition in each gap.

1 The shop wouldn't accept my credit card so I had to pay _in_ cash.

2 These T-shirts were ___ special offer – that's why I bought four.

3 The advertising campaign is aimed ___ independent young women.

4 We are ___ debt because we got a bank loan to buy our flat.

5 My grandfather suffers ___ heart disease.

6 Mike apologised to James ___ borrowing his book without asking.

7 The shopkeeper accused the man ___ stealing.

8 I'm saving ___ for a trip to Egypt after I finish school.

Grammar

3 Complete the sentences with the correct form of the verbs below.

> afford   charge   get ✓
> process   promote   repay

1 I finally _got_ a refund for those faulty jeans.

2 I can't ___ this new camera right now. I owe some money to a friend and I mustn't spend any more until I've ___ the debt.

3 One possible definition of intelligence is that it is the ability to ___ information.

4 I find your methods of ___ your products unacceptable.

5 Your credit card will be ___ after the products are sent to you.

4 Complete the text with the correct article. Write (ø) for no article.

I've just seen [1] _a_ new TV commercial for [2]___ well-known make of car. It shows [3]___ woman and [4]___ man in [5]___ car. What's interesting about it is that [6]___ woman is driving [7]___ car. I think it is [8]___ only commercial I've seen which shows a man in [9]___ passenger seat. This is a pleasant change after all the adverts which repeat the same old stereotypes: [10]___ women look after [11]___ children and smile in [12]___ delight at [13]___ new washing powder, while [14]___ men drive [15]___ cars, have fun and watch sports on television!

5 Complete the second sentence so that it means the same as the first.

1 My brother could swim at the age of five.
My brother was _able to swim_ at the age of five.

2 We managed to reach the top of the mountain in four hours.
We succeeded ___ the top of the mountain in four hours.

3 He says he can memorise a sequence of fifty numbers.
He claims to ___ a sequence of fifty numbers.

4 'Have you seen my credit card?' Laura asked Tom.
Laura asked Tom ___ credit card.

5 'No, I won't buy you this computer game,' said Sammy's dad.
Sammy's dad ___ the computer game

6 'No, I didn't steal anything from the shop!' the man said.
The man ___ anything from the shop.

7 'We won't be able to use credit cards there,' John said.
John explained ___ use credit cards there.

EXAM PRACTICE   Word formation

6 (4.11) Complete the text with the correct form of the word in brackets. Then listen and check.

Asperger's syndrome

Asperger's syndrome is a disorder similar to autism. People with Asperger's have problems with social [1] _interaction_ (interact) as they lack empathy and find it difficult to understand other people's [2]___ (feel) and to interpret non-verbal signals. If you're not used to such people, their behaviour may seem [3]___ (predict): you never know how they might react.

At the same time, some 'aspies' have extraordinary mental abilities. They can often [4]___ (memory) numbers and words much more effectively than other people. They have good [5]___ (analyse) skills and can be excellent at Maths. On the other hand, they are seldom [6]___ (imagine) as they tend to understand the world literally.

In educating children with Asperger's, the main aim is to help them develop enough social skills to live [7]___ (depend) lives as adults.

Reading skills

ACTIVE STUDY | Read for specific information

7 **Read the article. Match the phrases a–g to gaps 1–6. There is one extra phrase.**

a As the two groups mix

b While the person is replying

c Because you often have to react quickly to emergencies and opportunities

d but quickly forgets them

e because our visual memory isn't very good

f because we imagine that we remember more details than we really can

g who carries on the conversation as if nothing had happened

Listening skills

8 **(4.13) Listen to a radio programme about safe online shopping. Tick (✓) true, cross (X) false or write (?) if there is no information.**

1 ☐ You should buy only from websites recommended by your friends.

2 ☐ Read other customers' online comments about their experiences.

3 ☐ You should check if the company is registered in your country.

4 ☐ Find out how much the delivery will cost before you order.

5 ☐ Your browser will probably show if the connection is secure.

6 ☐ Don't put credit card data in an email unless your bank asks you to.

Speaking skills

9 **Express and justify your opinion on the following statement.**

> 'Advertising should be controlled by the government and some advertising practices should not be allowed.'

(4.12)

Can you trust your brain?

From *Welcome to your Brain*
by Sandra Aamodt and Sam Wang

1 Your brain lies to you a lot. We're sorry to have to tell you this but it's true. Even when your brain is doing important and difficult stuff, you're not aware of most of what's going on.

Your brain doesn't intend to lie to you, of course. For the
5 most part, it's doing a great job, working hard to help you survive and achieve your goals in a complicated world. ¹ _c_ , your brain usually tries to get a simple answer in a hurry rather than a perfect answer that takes time to work out. But as the world is not simple, this means that your brain has to
10 take shortcuts and make a lot of assumptions. Your brain's lies are in your best interests – most of the time – but they also lead to predictable mistakes.

The problems start when the brain takes in information from the world through the senses. Even if you are sitting quietly
15 in a room, your brain receives far more information than it can hold on to or than you need to decide how to act. You may be aware of the detailed pattern of colours in the rug, the photographs on the wall and the sounds of birds outside. Your brain perceives many other aspects of the scene initially
20 ² ____ . Usually these things aren't important so we don't often notice how much information we lose.

When people look at complicated pictures, they can identify differences if the images remain still. But if the image flickers, then they have a lot more trouble. This happens ³ ____ .
25 Experiments of this sort led psychologists to try more outrageous ways of getting people to fail to notice things. In one of our favourites, a researcher approaches someone on the street and asks for directions. ⁴ ____ , workmen carry a large door between the two people, blocking their view of
30 each other. Behind the cover of the door, the person who asked for directions is replaced by another researcher, ⁵ ____ . Even when the second person looks very different from the first, the person giving the directions has only about a fifty per cent chance of noticing the change.

35 In another experiment, people watch a video in which three students in white shirts pass a basketball around, while another three students in black shirts pass a second basketball. The viewers are asked to count the number of passes made by the white-shirted team. ⁶ ____ , a person in
40 a gorilla suit walks into the game from one side, stops to face the camera and beats his chest and walks out the other side. About half of the viewers fail to notice this event. These experiments illustrate that you perceive only a little bit of what's going on in the world.

Grammar	Gerunds and infinitives
	Modals of deduction
Vocabulary	Crime and justice
	Truth and lies
	Punishment
Phrases	Interpreting headlines and articles
	Talking about photos, statistics and headlines

Vocabulary & Reading

Crime and justice

1 Look at the cartoons on page 134. Close your book and say what you can remember using words you already know.

❝ *Three criminals were arrested ...*

2 **a** **Words 2 know** (4.14) Check the words in blue then fill the gaps with sentences 1–3.

1 The two sides presented **evidence** and questioned **witnesses**.

2 The gang **were sentenced to** ten years in prison by the **judge**.

3 They were **charged with** armed robbery.

a A gang of robbers **committed a crime** and **were arrested**.

b _____

c One of the gang **confessed** but the others decided to **plead not guilty**.

d There was a **court case** and the men **went on trial**.

e The **prosecution lawyer** tried to prove that **the accused** were guilty and the **defence lawyer** tried to show that they were **innocent**.

f _____

g The **jury** found all the members of the gang guilty.

h _____

b Memorise the sentences from *Words2know* in order then look again at page 134 and describe the cartoons using the sentences.

3 **a** Look at the photos and read the introduction to the newspaper article. What was the crime and how did it become famous?

b Read the rest of the newspaper article and answer the questions.

1 What did the gang steal and how did they commit the crime?

2 What violence was used?

3 Did the whole gang go on trial?

4 How did the gang plead, guilty or not guilty? What did the jury decide?

5 What sentences did the train robbers receive?

6 What is the importance of these numbers in the story?
   a 240   b 600   c 51   d £80,000

(4.15)

THE GREAT TRAIN ROBBERY

1 One of the most famous crimes in British history, it inspired songs, films and books and it made two of the robbers, Ronnie Biggs and Buster Edwards, into celebrities. So what exactly happened?

5 On 8 August 1963, a train travelling from Scotland to London, carrying £2.6 million* was stopped by a gang of fifteen men. **They forced the driver to take the train to a bridge** where a van was waiting to take the money. The gang attacked and seriously injured
10 the train driver. He was unable to work again for the rest of his life. After the robbery the gang hid in a farmhouse and celebrated their success by playing Monopoly** with real money!

Committing the crime, however, was the easy part.
15 The gang found it more difficult to avoid being arrested and only Buster Edwards managed not to get caught. In 1964, thirteen members of the gang went on trial, including Ronnie Biggs. Just one of the accused, Roger Cordrey, pleaded guilty. **He regretted**
20 **taking part in the robbery** and returned his share of the money – £80,000. **The rest refused to confess.**

When the case came to court, the trial lasted fifty-one days, the prosecution questioned 240 witnesses and the jury were shown over 600 pieces of evidence,
25 including the game of Monopoly that the gang had used! Eventually, the men were found guilty and were sentenced to between ten and thirty years in prison. But that wasn't the end of the story: Ronnie Biggs had been sentenced to thirty years in prison but he was
30 determined not to spend the rest of his life in jail. And Buster Edwards was still free ...

*the equivalent of about £40 million today

**a board game involving large amounts of money

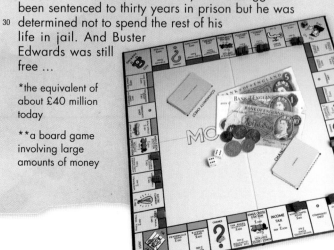

4　**a**　(4.16) Predict what happened to Buster Edwards and Ronnie Biggs and why they became celebrities. Listen and check.

　b　Do you know any criminals who have become celebrities? Do you think this should happen?

MINI WORKBOOK exercise 7 page 130

Grammar focus

Gerunds and infinitives

5　**a**　Look at the sentences in **bold** in the first article. <u>Underline</u> the ones that have a gerund and ⃝circle the ones that have an infinitive.

　b　<u>Underline</u> three more gerunds and five more infinitives in the article.

　c　Read *Grammar2know* and put the sentences in **bold** from the article into the gaps 1–4.

Grammar 2 know

Gerunds

Use a gerund after

- prepositions: *The gang celebrated by playing Monopoly.*
- some verbs: ¹_____

(also: *admit, avoid, spend time, suggest, enjoy*)

We can also use gerunds as the subject of a sentence: ²_____

Infinitives

Use an infinitive after

- adjectives: *He was unable to work.*
- some verbs: ³_____

(also: *choose, expect, attempt, offer, wait*)

Note that some verbs take an object before the infinitive: ⁴_____

(also: *inspire, allow, encourage*)

Infinitives also give the reason for doing something: *A van was waiting to take the money.*

Other forms

passive: *They avoided being arrested.*

negative: *He was determined not to spend his life in jail.*

6　**a**　Complete the sentences in *What happened next?* with the gerund or infinitive form of the verbs in brackets.

　b　(4.16) Listen again and check.

MINI WORKBOOK exercises 1–2 page 128

What happened next?

1　Even while Biggs was waiting ¹___ (be sentence) he was planning ²___ (escape). In 1965, he climbed over a prison wall and got away in a van. He had plastic
5　surgery ³___ (change) his appearance then fled to Brazil to avoid ⁴___ (be caught). There he became a minor celebrity. For many years, the British government were desperate ⁵___ (bring) him back – they
10　even attempted ⁶___ (kidnap) him! In 2001, however, Biggs chose ⁷___ (return) to the UK voluntarily because, he said, he wanted ⁸___ (walk) into a pub and buy a pint of English beer. He was immediately
15　sent back to jail. In 2009, he became very ill and the government finally decided ⁹___ (release) him.

Edwards, meanwhile, spent three years ¹⁰___ (hide) in Mexico with his wife and
20　daughter. But ¹¹___ (live) in Mexico did not suit the family – they got fed up of ¹²___ (be) away from home. In 1966, Edwards returned to Britain ¹³___ (give) himself up. He was sentenced to fifteen years in
25　prison. He was fortunate ¹⁴___ (not get) more, as he later admitted ¹⁵___ (attack) the train driver. After ¹⁶___ (be release) he became a flower seller outside Waterloo Station in London but Edwards missed the
30　old times and enjoyed ¹⁷___ (be ask) about his life on the run. 'I know I'm lucky ¹⁸___ (have) this flower stall but it's so boring compared with the time I spent on the run,' he would say. His story inspired the
35　singer Phil Collins ¹⁹___ (make) a film about his life. The film was a big success but Edwards suffered from depression and in 1994, he committed suicide.

right & wrong

85

Listening & Vocabulary

1 Read the introductions to three famous hoaxes and answer the questions.
- Where and when did the hoaxes take place?
- Who was involved?
- What deception took place?

2 (4.17) In pairs, predict the answers to the questions then listen and check.

1 What was the motive for each hoax?
2 Were many people taken in?
3 Did Anne and John Darwin carry out the third hoax together?
4 How was the Darwin hoax discovered?

3 Words **2** know (4.18) Check the words in blue. Listen to each story separately and decide which statement is wrong. Correct the mistakes.

Story 1

a Parker used **forged** documents to 'prove' to his **victims** that he owned the bridge.

b He **claimed** that he had sold the bridge twenty or thirty times.

c He got a long prison sentence for **cheating** people **out of** so much money.

Story 2

a Most viewers were familiar with food from other countries and **were not taken in** by the joke.

b When the documentary makers **admitted the truth**, many viewers were angry that they had been **fooled**.

Story 3

a At first, John Darwin **pretended** that he had lost his memory.

b Anne Darwin **conned** everyone into believing that her husband was dead, although he was living right next door.

c She even **lied to** their sons – they thought her grief at their father's death was **genuine**.

d John was sentenced to prison for **fraud** and **deception** but Anne was found not guilty.

4 **a** In groups of three, each choose one story to retell. Plan what to say, using the *Words2know*.

b Take turns to retell the stories.

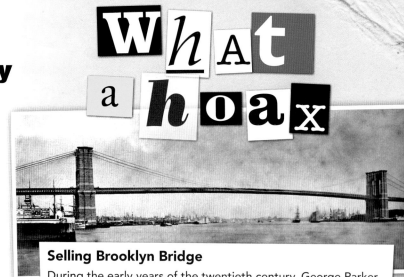

What a hoax

Selling Brooklyn Bridge

During the early years of the twentieth century, George Parker repeatedly managed to 'sell' Brooklyn Bridge in New York. He persuaded his victims that they could make a fortune by setting up toll booths and charging the public to cross the bridge.

The Spaghetti Harvest

On 1 April 1957, the BBC broadcast an apparently serious documentary about growing spaghetti on trees in Switzerland.

'Canoe Man'

After her husband John had apparently died in a canoeing accident in 2002, Anne Darwin received over £250,000 from his life insurance policies. John Darwin turned up five years later, alive and well.

5 Discuss the questions in groups.
- Do you find any of these hoaxes amusing?
- Which victims do you feel sorry for? Which don't you feel sorry for?
- Which hoax do you think is the most immoral? Why?
- Have you ever been taken in by a hoax or practical joke?

" *I think story … is quite funny because …*
I feel sorry for … because …

MINI WORKBOOK exercise 8 page 130

Grammar Focus

Modals of deduction

6 Read an online news article written the day that John and Anne Darwin were sentenced. Answer the questions.

   1 Which information about the case did you already know from exercise 3?

   2 Which information is new?

   3 Which comments do you agree with?

7 **a** Read and tick (✓) the best description of the comments.

   ☐ The writers know what the Darwins' motives were and how they felt.

   ☐ The writers are speculating about the Darwins' motives and how they felt.

   b Which modal verbs tell you this? <u>Underline</u> eight examples then read *Grammar2know* and check.

OnlineNews Wednesday 23 July 2008

Canoe couple sentenced (4.19)

Back-from-the-dead canoeist John Darwin and his wife Anne have today been jailed for more than six years after wrongly claiming £250,000 in life insurance. The couple conned sons Mark and Anthony, friends, police and insurance companies into believing that Mr Darwin had drowned in 2002. John Darwin pleaded guilty to the charges but Mrs Darwin pleaded not guilty, claming that her husband had forced her to help him. She has written to her sons from prison to express her regret.

Conned sons, Mark and Anthony

Read more →

(Have your say) Join the online debate

I feel so sorry for Mark and Anthony Darwin. First, they suffered the grief of their father's 'death' when they were young, then they discovered that their parents had deceived them for all those years. They must feel devastated.
AK, London

To me, Anne Darwin is worse than her husband. Imagine your own mother lying to you like that – she must be evil. She can't care about her children at all.
Robbin

Don't be so judgemental! She might have been frightened of her husband. Or she may have wanted to prevent her sons from getting into trouble, too. She may feel genuinely sorry now.
Suzie, France

Personally, I don't believe that the sons knew *nothing*. They must have suspected something, surely?
LM, Los Angeles

I disagree, the police have investigated them thoroughly and they haven't been charged with anything so they can't have known anything.
AK, London

Grammar 2know

Modals of deduction

Use the modal verbs *must, might, may, could* and *can't* to speculate or make deductions. We do not know this information for a fact.

Present form

*She **must be** evil.* (I'm sure she is)

*She **might/may/could feel** genuinely sorry.* (perhaps she is)

*She **can't care** about her children.* (I'm sure she doesn't)

Past form

***must/might/may/could/can't** + have + past participle:*

*They **must have suspected** something.*

*She **might/may/could have been** frightened of her husband.*

*They **can't have known** anything.*

---

8 Rewrite the comments about the other hoaxes in exercise 1 using past modals of deduction.

   1 I'm sure Parker was very convincing.

   He must have been very convincing.

   2 Perhaps Parker's victims were greedy.

   3 Surely lots of people reported him to the police.

   4 I'm sure he didn't persuade everyone that he approached.

   5 I'm sure the documentary makers had a lot of fun making the film.

   6 Perhaps the viewers didn't know what spaghetti was like.

   7 I'm sure there have been other April Fool's Day jokes on TV.

9 **a** Look at the pictures and read the story on page 142.

   b Discuss the questions on page 142 using a modal of deduction from *Grammar2know* in each answer. Give a reason for your answers.

10 (4.20) Listen to two students discussing the case and check if they make any of the same points as you.

MINI WORKBOOK exercises 3–6 pages 128–129

right & wrong

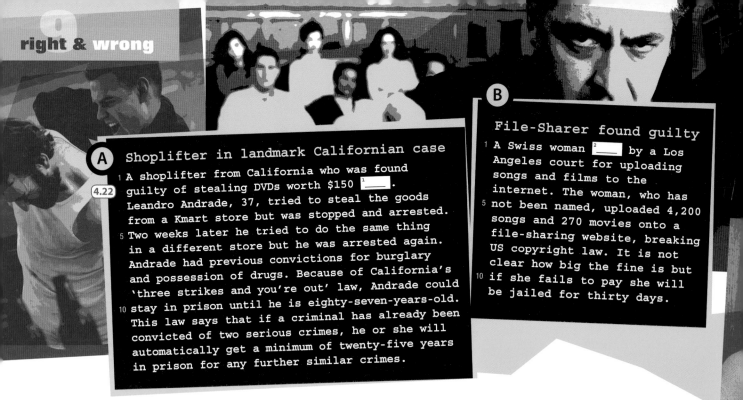

A Shoplifter in landmark Californian case

1 A shoplifter from California who was found guilty of stealing DVDs worth $150 ___[1]___. Leandro Andrade, 37, tried to steal the goods from a Kmart store but was stopped and arrested.
5 Two weeks later he tried to do the same thing in a different store but he was arrested again. Andrade had previous convictions for burglary and possession of drugs. Because of California's 'three strikes and you're out' law, Andrade could
10 stay in prison until he is eighty-seven-years-old. This law says that if a criminal has already been convicted of two serious crimes, he or she will automatically get a minimum of twenty-five years in prison for any further similar crimes.

B File-Sharer found guilty

1 A Swiss woman ___[2]___ by a Los Angeles court for uploading songs and films to the internet. The woman, who has
5 not been named, uploaded 4,200 songs and 270 movies onto a file-sharing website, breaking US copyright law. It is not clear how big the fine is but
10 if she fails to pay she will be jailed for thirty days.

Reading & Vocabulary

1 Which statements do you agree with? Compare answers with a partner.

1 'Prison doesn't work. It's better to re-educate criminals, and help them to find jobs and so on.'

2 'Courts should give criminals long, harsh sentences because they act as a deterrent to others. If punishments are too lenient they encourage criminals to commit more crimes.'

3 'The feelings of victims and their families should be the most important factor in deciding the sentence for a crime.'

2 **Words 2 know** (4.21) Check the words in blue then put the sentences for criminals in order from most lenient (1) to harshest (6).

a ☐ (He or she) has been **fined** and given a two-year **suspended sentence**.

b ☐ (He or she) was given 300 hours **community service**.

c ☐ (He or she) was sentenced to three years **imprisonment**.

d ☐ (He or she) was sentenced to **life imprisonment**.

e ☐ (He or she) was **sentenced to death**.

f ☐ (He or she) has been sentenced to fifty years' imprisonment. (He or she) cannot get **parole** for at least twenty-five years.

3 Read the news articles A–D to find out what crimes these people committed.

- Leandro Andrade
- Tony Martin
- Douglas Ramsay
- Brendon Fearon
- An unnamed Swiss woman

4 **a** Complete the gaps 1–5 in the articles with the sentences a–f in exercise 2 that you think each criminal received. There is one extra answer.

b Compare answers in pairs then check on page 142.

5 Choose the best answer according to the articles. Explain your answer.

1 What does California's 'three strikes and you're out' law mean?
   a If you are found guilty of three or more crimes you go to prison for a minimum of twenty-five years.
   b Shoplifting is a very serious crime.
   c All thieves get harsh sentences.
   d Criminals in Andrade's position have to spend at least fifty years in prison.

2 Why was the Swiss file-sharer found guilty?
   a She had made a lot of money by selling songs and films illegally on the internet.
   b She had broken US law.
   c She refused to give her name in court.
   d She refused to pay a fine.

3 What did farmer Tony Martin do?
   a He shot two burglars because they had attacked him.
   b He phoned the police because he heard burglars.
   c He got angry with the police because they didn't help him.
   d He used a gun that he shouldn't have owned.

4 What did Douglas Ramsay's representative tell the court?
   a That Ramsay was angry at his sentence.
   b That he thought his sentence was too lenient.
   c That he was very upset about what had happened.
   d That he wanted to apologise to the girls' families.

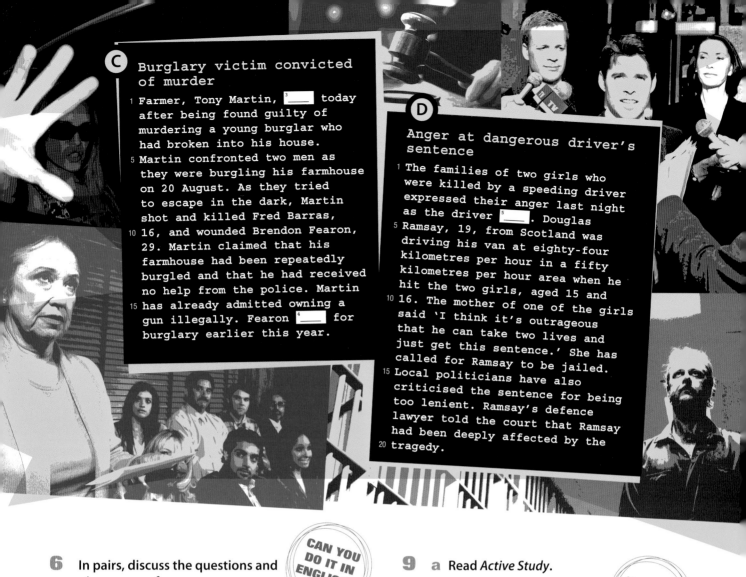

C Burglary victim convicted of murder

1 Farmer, Tony Martin, ³☐☐☐ today after being found guilty of murdering a young burglar who had broken into his house.
5 Martin confronted two men as they were burgling his farmhouse on 20 August. As they tried to escape in the dark, Martin shot and killed Fred Barras,
10 16, and wounded Brendon Fearon, 29. Martin claimed that his farmhouse had been repeatedly burgled and that he had received no help from the police. Martin
15 has already admitted owning a gun illegally. Fearon ⁴☐☐☐ for burglary earlier this year.

D Anger at dangerous driver's sentence

1 The families of two girls who were killed by a speeding driver expressed their anger last night as the driver ⁵☐☐☐. Douglas
5 Ramsay, 19, from Scotland was driving his van at eighty-four kilometres per hour in a fifty kilometres per hour area when he hit the two girls, aged 15 and
10 16. The mother of one of the girls said 'I think it's outrageous that he can take two lives and just get this sentence.' She has called for Ramsay to be jailed.
15 Local politicians have also criticised the sentence for being too lenient. Ramsay's defence lawyer told the court that Ramsay had been deeply affected by the
20 tragedy.

6 In pairs, discuss the questions and give reasons for your answers.

CAN YOU DO IT IN ENGLISH?

- Do you think the sentences given in these cases were fair, too lenient or too harsh?
- Why do you think these sentences were given?
- What sentences do you think they should have got?
- Do you know of any other crimes where the sentence was either too harsh or too lenient?

I think this was far too lenient. He should have got ten years' imprisonment.

7 Prepare a short talk about one of the crimes in exercise 3 or another crime you know. Use the phrases on the back cover to help you.

- Say briefly what the crime and sentence were.
- Explain why you think this sentence was given.
- Give your opinion about the sentence explaining your reasons.

Personally, I think this sentence is far too harsh because .... Some people might say that it's a deterrent to other people but in my view ...

8 Take it in turns to give your talk to the class. Listen to each other and say whether you agree or disagree with the points of view.

I completely agree with Marta ...
You're right about that but on the other hand ...

9 a Read *Active Study*.

ACTIVE STUDY

Notice word families and their exceptions

Many crime words have a number of different forms, which you can find in a good dictionary:

noun	personal noun	verb
a robbery	a robber	to rob
a burglary	a burglar	to burgle

However there are exceptions:

| theft | a thief | to steal |
| a crime | a criminal | to commit a crime |

b Complete the word families using a dictionary to help you. Circle the exceptions.

noun	personal noun	verb
kidnap	1 ___	2 ___
murder	3 ___	4 ___
5 ___	shoplifter	6 ___
fraud	7 ___	8 ___
9 ___	judge	10 ___
11 ___	prosecutor	12 ___
defence	13 ___	14 ___
15 ___	16 ___	to convict

MINI WORKBOOK exercises 9–10 page 130

right & wrong

Writing & Vocabulary

An opinion essay

1 Read the opinions and check the phrases in **bold**. Then answer the questions.

---

piers15 03/06 5:45 pm
I think **the death penalty** is an **effective deterrent** – it makes people think before committing a serious crime like murder or terrorism.

angelcakes 03/06 6.01 pm
I'm **against** it. I think it's murder by the state and it's **barbaric**. Most countries have **abolished** it. That's a good thing.

olivia_is_cool 03/06 6.34 pm
I'm not **in favour of** this idea. Some people are convicted because they can't afford a good lawyer. After the **execution** you can't correct the mistake.

stan the_man 03/06 6.40 pm
It costs a lot of money to keep a serious criminal in jail. **It makes more economic sense** to execute them.

- What topic is being discussed?
- Which people support the death penalty and which are against it?
- Which arguments do you agree with?

2 a Read opinion essay 1 below. Work out if the writer is in favour of capital punishment or against it. <u>Underline</u> the first sentence that tells you this directly.

b Read the essay again and note which opinions from the online forum are mentioned. Mark the paragraphs you can find them in.

3 a STRUCTURE Read the essay again and match the instructions a–h to the paragraphs 1–5.

a Give an initial opinion about the question.

b Make the most important points to support your opinion.

c Describe the arguments on the opposite side.

d Introduce some of the important issues.

e Give other arguments to support your opinion.

f Counter the arguments on the other side and restate your opinion.

g Say that the issue is controversial.

h Don't introduce any new arguments at this stage.

b Look at the instructions for paragraph 1 again. In what order do these things appear in the model essay?

Paragraph 1: Introduction	• *d – Introduce some of the important issues.* • •
Paragraph 2: Explaining your opinion	•
Paragraph 3: Explaining your opinion further	•
Paragraph 4: Presenting the other point of view	• •
Paragraph 5: Conclusion	•

Q1. The death penalty is an appropriate punishment for serious crimes. Do you agree or disagree? Why?

(4.23)

1 The death penalty is one of the most controversial issues in modern society. Some people argue that certain crimes are so serious that the death penalty is the only suitable punishment. **Despite this**, I strongly believe that it is barbaric and is never appropriate.

2 Firstly, **it is important to remember that** innocent people may be executed. Sometimes people are convicted of crimes that they didn't commit. If they are sentenced to life imprisonment, it is possible to correct the mistake. If they are sentenced to death, it is not. **Furthermore**, the verdict in a trial can depend on the quality of the lawyers. Poorer people cannot afford the best lawyers so they have more chance of being found guilty.

3 What is more, the death penalty seriously affects others. **Even though** they have not committed a crime, the criminal's family may suffer a lot. They often have to wait many years between the sentence and the execution, which is unfair.

4 **Having said that**, there are some important arguments in favour of the death penalty. Supporters argue that it is a very strong deterrent, which may stop criminals from committing crimes and so save lives. They also point out that it is very expensive to keep criminals in prison for life so the death penalty makes better economic sense.

5 **Nevertheless**, the possibility that an innocent person could be executed outweighs any advantages, **in my view**. I am convinced, **therefore**, that no modern state should consider returning to the death penalty.

90

4 LANGUAGE Complete *Language4writing* with the phrases in **bold** in the essay.

> ## Language 4 writing
>
> **Giving an opinion**
> *I strongly believe that …* ¹_____
>
> **Emphasising a point**
> *We mustn't forget that …* ²_____
>
> **Giving more points to support the argument**
> *What is more, …* ³_____
>
> **Explaining consequences**
> *For this reason … Because of this …* ⁴_____
>
> **Making a contrasting point**
> *However, …* ⁵_____ ⁶_____ ⁷_____
> *Although …* ⁸_____

5 ~~Cross out~~ the phrase that is wrong or does not make sense in these contexts.

1 *In my view,/Furthermore,/I strongly believe* downloading music illegally is theft. *Having said that,/Nevertheless,/Although* many people don't believe they are doing anything wrong.

2 *Although/Despite this,/Even though* capital punishment has been abolished in most countries, some people want to bring it back.

3 *In my view,/Even though/I strongly believe* prison sentences these days are too short. *Furthermore,/Despite this/What is more*, life in prison is too comfortable.

6 a DEVELOPING AN ARGUMENT
Look at how the writer supports his statements throughout the essay. Find another supporting argument in the essay.

- *The death penalty seriously affects others …* **the criminal's family may suffer a lot.**
- *It is very expensive to keep criminals in prison for life* **so the death penalty makes better economic sense.**

b Read essay question 2 and the notes below then match the statements 1–5 to the supporting arguments a–e.

7 a You are going to write an opinion essay to answer essay question 2. Think of more arguments for or against and decide on your opinion.

b Make notes using the paragraph headings in exercise 3 to help.

8 a Write the first draft of your essay. Then read it through or swap with a partner. Work through the checklist for writing on the back cover.

b Write the final draft of your essay.

Q2. Sending people to prison doesn't stop crime. Do you agree or disagree? Why?

Agree
1 Criminals often learn more about crime in prison.
2 There are other more effective punishments than prison.
3 Long prison sentences don't encourage people to reform.

Disagree
4 Prison is a more effective deterrent than other punishments.
5 Prison is the only safe place for certain criminals.

Supporting arguments
a Many murderers and other criminals are a constant danger to society.
b Punishments like community service mean that criminals give something back to society.
c Young criminals often meet more experienced criminals or become involved in criminal gangs.
d Most people are very frightened of losing their freedom.
e They know they will not get out for many years.

REAL TIME

Ella, Ikram and Jake are searching for interesting stories for their radio show in the newspapers.

INTERPRETING HEADLINES AND ARTICLES

1 Tell the class the most interesting newspaper headline that you've seen recently. Explain what the story is about and why you think it's interesting.

2 a Look at the newspaper headlines and say what the topic of each headline is.

1 **BRIGHTON IN BID TO BAN LIGHTING UP IN PUBLIC**

❝ smoking

2 **Mayor Pledges to Tackle Graffiti**

3 Jeans Spark Anti-Social Behaviour Arrest

4 **ROW AS MURDER SUSPECT RELEASED**

5 **Fans expect new €50m Chelsea striker to shine**

b Match the underlined words in the headlines to the meanings a–i.

a try to *in bid to*
b promise
c to take action against
d a disagreement
e someone who might have committed a crime
f make illegal
g cause
h to do very well
i offensive or unpleasant behaviour

3 a Say which headline from exercise 2a you think Ella, Ikram and Jake will choose for their radio show.

b (4.24) Listen and check. Which headline from exercise 2a <u>don't</u> they discuss?

c (4.24) Listen again and complete the *Phrases2know* 1–7 with the phrases a–g.

a … police officers will have to arrest smokers …
b … anti-social behaviour.
c … Chelsea have paid €50 million for a new striker.
d … the teenager was wearing low-slung jeans.
e … there's a lot of graffiti in Brighton.
f … a teenager in Brighton who was arrested for wearing jeans.
g … the town of Brighton is trying to pass a new law to …

Phrases **2**know

Interpreting headlines and articles

1 According to this article … *c*
2 It suggests that …
3 It's related to the topic of …
4 It means that …
5 It implies that …
6 The article talks about …
7 The article explains that …

4 In pairs, talk about the headlines and articles using *Phrases2know*.

❝ *This headline means that … It suggests that …*

1 *Schools to ban mobile phones*

2 **Government pledges to tackle online fraud**

3 'Crime in London has fallen dramatically for the third year in a row. The Mayor of London thanked the police for their "amazing work" in reducing crime and arresting criminals. He also thanked the public for their help.'

CAN YOU DO IT IN ENGLISH?

5 (4.25) Listen to the interview and look at the pieces of information 1–3. Write who mentions the information, Ikram (I) or Sergeant Watson (SW).

1 ☐ Teenagers frequently complained that they were seen as trouble-makers simply because they wore a hoodie or low-slung jeans. 'Adults just don't understand teen culture,' said one seventeen-year-old boy. 'Everyone at my school wears a hooded top, even the really good kids.'

2 ☐

3 ☐

The biggest anti-social behaviour problems		
	Five years ago	Now
Vandalism	35%	30%
Litter	30%	45%
Noise	15%	25%

6 a (4.25) Listen again and complete the revision of *Phrases2know* from previous lessons.

Phrases 2 know

Interpreting headlines and articles
It's related to the [1]_____ of anti-social behaviour
It [2]_____ that teenagers feel misunderstood.
According to this [3]_____, teenagers feel that …

Talking about photographs
It looks as [4]_____ they're falling down.
It [5]_____ you think of gangs and violence.

Talking about statistics and trends
Around a [6]_____ of residents think that vandalism …
That has fallen [7]_____ over the last five years.
Around a [8]_____ of residents think that litter …
That's risen [9]_____ over the last five years.

Expressing and justifying your opinions
You have to bear in mind the fear of …
In my opinion, it's often because …

b What other phrases can you remember for talking about photographs, statistics and trends and for expressing your opinion?

7 In groups, discuss the question. Use *Phrases2know* on page 13 for expressing and justifying your opinion.
• Should the police arrest people for wearing certain types of clothing?

❝ *To my mind, it's necessary to arrest people if they wear certain types of clothing. You have to bear in mind that …*

8 a You are going to present the information below (4–6). In pairs, look at the material for a few minutes. Think about the topic and how each piece of material relates to it.

4

5

Government pledges to ban all cigarettes

6

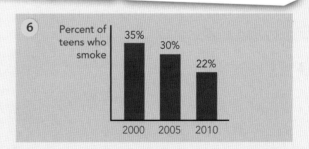

b Present the visual material to your partner. When you listen to your partner, use this checklist to give feedback.

Did the speaker: Y   N
• say what the topic was?   ☐   ☐
• relate the material to the topic?   ☐   ☐
• use appropriate phrases for the photos?   ☐   ☐
• use appropriate phrases for the graphs, charts and tables?   ☐   ☐
• use appropriate phrases for the headline?   ☐   ☐

10
life changes

Grammar	*wish* and *if only*
	Third and mixed conditionals
Vocabulary	Home and environment
	Buying and selling houses
Phrases	Inviting and persuading

Listening & Vocabulary

1 **a** Match the places to live 1–3 to the photos A–C.

1 An apartment in the city centre.

2 A house in the suburbs.

3 A cottage in the countryside.

b In pairs, describe the places in the photos. Which is most like the place where you live? What are the similarities and differences?

" *I live in an apartment in the city centre. My building is modern ...*

2 Words **2 know** (4.26) Check the words in blue. Which places in exercise 1a do you think the sentences describe? Compare answers in pairs.

1 There's a really **lively atmosphere**. C

2 It's really friendly and there's a **strong sense of community**.

3 There's lots of **entertainment** and **nightlife**.

4 There's **nothing to do** in the evenings.

5 It is surrounded by **green spaces**.

6 It's very **culturally diverse**.

7 It's very **family-friendly**.

8 It's got **good local facilities** like a sports centre and a shopping mall.

9 There's a lot of **traffic**, **pollution** and **litter**.

10 The **transport links** are very poor.

11 It's a little **cramped**.

3 Look at the photos again and put them in order from 1 (favourite place to live) to 3 (worst place to live). Explain your order in pairs, using the *Words2know*.

" *My first choice would be the cottage in the countryside because I love green spaces.*

But there'd be nothing to do!

4 (4.27) Listen to Alice and Ollie who have moved to a new place recently. Answer the questions for each person.

1 Where did they use to live and why did they move?

2 Which aspects of their new homes do they like? Which don't they like?

5 **a** (4.27) Listen again. Tick true (✓) and cross (✗) false. Explain your answers.

1 ☐ Alice's parents are fulfilling their dreams by moving.

2 ☐ Alice has found people of her own age very welcoming and doesn't miss her friends.

3 ☐ Not being able to drive is a problem for her.

4 ☐ There was more to do where Ollie lived before than there is in Madrid.

5 ☐ Overall, Ollie likes going to an international school.

6 ☐ Ollie likes everything about the apartment in Madrid.

b Would you like to move to these places? Are Alice and Ollie happy in their new places? Why? Why not?

MINI WORKBOOK exercises 7–8 page 133

Grammar Focus

wish and *if only*

6 (4.28) Listen and complete the comments that Alice (A) and Ollie (O) made.

1 ☐A̸ I wish _____ hadn't lost his job!

2 ☐ If only there was more to do in the _____ !

3 ☐ I really wish I could _____ !

4 ☐ If only I could speak _____ properly!

5 ☐ If only I could see my old _____ a bit more often.

6 ☐ I wish we'd moved to a _____ place.

7 ☐ I really wish we had a _____ in our new place.

8 ☐ If only _____ had waited until I was older!

9 ☐ I really wish we didn't live _____ .

7 Answer the questions.

• Would Alice and Ollie like the situations they mention to be different?

• Can they change these situations at the moment?

8 **a** Look at sentences 1–3 in exercise 6. Underline the verb form used after *wish* and *if only* in each sentence. Is Alice making wishes about the present (PR) or the past (PA)? Read *Grammar2know* to check.

b Match Ollie's wishes in exercise 6 to rules a–c in *Grammar2know*.

Wishes about the present

a Use *wish* or *if only* + past simple to describe present situations that you would like to be different but which you can't change:

*I **wish** we **didn't live** here.* (but we do)

*If only there **was** more to do in the evening.* (but there isn't)

b Use *wish* or *if only* + *could* to describe something you want to do that is not possible or which you are not able to do at the moment:

*I **wish** I **could drive**.* (but I can't – I'm not eighteen)

*I **wish** I **could see** my old friends more often.* (but I can't – they're too far away.)

Wishes about the past

c Use *wish* or *if only* + past perfect to describe something that happened in the past which you would like to have been different:

*I **wish** my dad **hadn't lost** his job.* (but he did)

*If only my parents **had waited** until I was older!* (but they didn't)

9 Jed has moved to London. There are some things he isn't happy about. Write sentences using *I wish* or *if only*.

1 The student house he lives in isn't very nice.

I wish I lived in a nicer house.

2 He chose accommodation a long way from the city centre.

3 His rent is very expensive.

4 He can't afford to go out in central London.

5 He brought his car with him but there's nowhere to park.

6 He spends a long time travelling to university every day.

7 He can't see his girlfriend from home very often.

10 Make three wishes about each of the topics below. Compare wishes in pairs, giving reasons for them.

1 Abilities that you don't have but would like.

If only I could play the guitar really well! I'd love to be in a band!

2 Events (large or small) in your life that you regret.

3 Changes you would like in your local area/ home, which you don't think will happen.

MINI WORKBOOK exercises 1–3 pages 131–132

Vocabulary & Reading
Buying and selling houses

1 Do you think you will ever buy a house? Why? Why not?

2 a **Words 2 know** (4.29) Check the words in blue. Put the activities in the correct order 1–8.

- ☐ A **buyer** sees an advert in an estate agent's window and he arranges to **look round** the house.
- ☐ The buyer and seller **negotiate** until they **agree a price**.
- ☐ [1] A **homeowner puts** her house **up for sale** with an **estate agent**.
- ☐ The seller **rejects the offer** because she thinks it's too low.
- ☐ After several weeks the sale **goes through**.
- ☐ The buyer likes the house and **makes an offer**.
- ☐ The buyer gets a **mortgage** with the bank.
- ☐ The old owner **moves out** and the new owner **moves in**.

b (4.30) In pairs, compare answers then listen and check.

3 In pairs, study the *Words2know*. Close your book and describe how a house is bought and sold from start to finish.

❝ *Firstly, a homeowner puts ...*

4 Look at the adverts below. In what way are these house sales unusual?

5 a Answer the questions about each story.
1 What was for sale in each case?
2 What reasons did each person have for buying or selling?
3 Did the sale go through in each case? What exactly happened?
4 How does Kimberley describe herself? Do you agree?

b In pairs, discuss the questions.
- Do you think Kimberley and Ian made good decisions? Why? Why not?
- Would you like to make a dramatic change to your life like this? If so, what would you do?

MINI WORKBOOK exercise 9 page 133

More than just a house for sale

(4.31) Two unusual adverts selling houses … and the life-changing stories behind them.

FOR SALE: SIX ROOM CAVE WITH OLIVE GROVE
Village location near Granada, Spain. £50,000

1 In 2010, Kimberley Duff, 34, saw this advert in a magazine and
5 promptly flew to Spain to look round the cave. She instantly fell in love with it, made an
10 offer and managed to negotiate a good price. She then flew home, put her own flat up for sale and quit her job as a high-flying lawyer. It was only then that she told her boyfriend what she had
15 done. 'I'm a little bit impulsive,' admits Kimberley.

Fortunately, her boyfriend was also keen to quit the rat race and within six weeks the couple had moved out of their London flat and into the cave. They are now growing olives and lemons and plan to keep
20 goats and chickens. Kimberley says she just wanted to live a simpler, greener life. 'I've always been concerned about the environment and the kind of world we are leaving to our children but I had never really done anything about it,' she says. 'If I hadn't
25 seen that advert, I would still be in London, living the same stressful life.'

A life for sale

Item condition: Used
Time left: 6 days

Current bid: **$95**
Enter maximum bid:

Description

I am putting my entire life up for sale. That includes my house, my car, my job, my hobbies and ...

In 2008, Australian Ian Usher put his entire life up for sale on the internet! He included not just his house but his car, his motorcycle, his jet ski, a two-week trial in
30 his former job and an introduction to his friends. Ian's marriage had recently broken up and his possessions reminded him of his ex-wife. He had hoped to get an offer of around £500,000 but eventually he agreed a price of £192,000. Ian wasn't disappointed, however –
35 the money would be enough to travel the world and that was his dream.

Unfortunately, in the end, the sale didn't go through and the buyer never moved in. Perhaps he was unable to get a mortgage or perhaps he simply changed
40 his mind – we'll never know. However, Ian's life did change as a result of the advert; he became a minor celebrity in Australia and even received offers of marriage. If he hadn't placed the advert, none of that would have happened!

Grammar **focus**

Third and mixed conditionals

6 Look at the sentences about Kimberley and Ian. ~~Cross out~~ one sentence about each person that doesn't fit in with the story.

Kimberley

1 If she hadn't been so passionate about the environment she might not have bought the cave.

2 If she hadn't seen the advert, she might still be a lawyer.

3 She would have bought the cave if she had been more impulsive.

Ian

4 If his wife hadn't left him, he wouldn't have put his life up for sale.

5 If the sale had gone through, he wouldn't have gone travelling.

6 If he hadn't placed the advert, he wouldn't be famous now.

7 a <u>Underline</u> the main verb in each clause of sentences 4 and 6 in exercise 6. Does each clause refer to the past or the present? Read *Grammar2know* to check.

Grammar **2 know**

The third conditional

Use the third conditional to imagine a different past (in the *if* clause) and the effects of that in the past (the main clause):

If + past perfect, *would* + *have* + past participle:

If his wife **hadn't left** him, he **wouldn't have put** his life up for sale.

       PAST   PAST

Mixed conditional

If + past perfect, *would* + verb

Use a mixed conditional to imagine a different past and the effects of that in the present:

If he **hadn't placed** the advert, he **wouldn't be** famous now.

       PAST   PRESENT

Use *might* in the main clause if the effect is not certain:

If she **hadn't been** so passionate about the environment, she **might not have bought** the cave.

If she **hadn't seen** the advert, she **might** still **be** a lawyer.

b Look back at the two stories. Find one mixed conditional sentence and one third conditional sentence.

8 Complete the third and mixed conditional sentences with the correct form of the verb in brackets. Use *might* if you think it is appropriate.

1 If Kimberley ___ (not buy) the cave house, her boyfriend ___ (not give up) his job.

2 If they ___ (not leave) their jobs, they ___ (have) more money now.

3 If Ian's sale ___ (go through), he ___ (travel) round the world.

4 If his wife ___ (not leave) him, he ___ (still be) happily married.

9 a Use ideas in columns A and B to create at least six third or mixed conditional sentences. There are many possibilities.

A	B
I split up with my girlfriend/boyfriend.	I am depressed.
I failed all my exams.	I didn't go on holiday.
I spent all my money on a motorbike.	I haven't gone out this week.
I've lost my phone.	My parents are annoyed with me.

If I hadn't spent all my money on a motorbike, I might have gone on holiday.

If I hadn't lost my phone, my parents wouldn't be annoyed with me.

b Compare answers in groups.

10 a Think of three important chains of events in your life. Imagine if things had been different, using third and mixed conditionals.

I went to my cousin's party. I met Alex there. Now we're together.

If I hadn't gone to my cousin's party, I wouldn't have met Alex and we wouldn't be together.

I moved house when I was thirteen. I joined this school.

If I hadn't moved house when I was thirteen, I wouldn't be at this school.

b Compare answers with a partner.

MINI WORKBOOK exercises 4–6 page 132

Reading & Speaking

1 Read the newspaper headlines and the title of the article. What problems do the headlines suggest about housing in the future?

> World population could reach 9 billion by 2050, warn experts

> **GLOBAL WARMING 'MAY MAKE PARTS OF THE EARTH UNINHABITABLE'**

2 Skim the article quickly. Tick (✓) the sentence that describes it best.

1 ☐ It presents a debate between experts about where we will live in the future.

2 ☐ It provides detailed facts and figures for environmental studies students.

3 ☐ It answers questions from the general public in a friendly accessible way.

3 Look at the photos and the readers' questions. Think about which housing solutions are being discussed and the advantages to each solution.

4 **a** Read the article and make notes under the headings according to what the experts think about each case. Write (?) if there is no information.

- features of the housing
- potential benefits
- practical problems *expensive, ugly*
- likely to happen?

b Compare answers in pairs.

5 Find words in the article to match the definitions 1–9. Use the context to help you.

1 energy that replaces itself naturally, for example solar power (text A) *renewable*

2 to clean (text A)

3 to take control of an area or country and go and live there (text B)

4 something such as land, oil and minerals that is useful to humans (text B)

5 to consist of (text C)

6 to pull down or destroy (text C)

7 ordinary or traditional (text D)

8 to dig from under the ground (text E)

9 plants such as wheat that are grown for food (text E)

Q&A
Our experts answer your questions

(4.32)

This week's topic:
Where will we live in the future?

1 **A** With sea levels predicted to rise and places like London, New York and Tokyo at risk, are floating cities the answer?
Agata Cabrera, Buenos Aires

5 I wish there were one simple answer, Agata! The risk of rising sea levels, caused by melting ice caps, has persuaded some people that our future lies on floating cities like Vincent Callebaut's The Lilypad. The Lilypad would house 50,000 people. Renewable energy would provide the power and the
10 central lake would collect and purify rainwater. However, no one has even estimated the cost yet and some countries that are at risk from rising sea levels, for example Bangladesh and the Republic of Maldives, simply couldn't afford it. For now The Lilypad remains a dream but if sea levels started to rise, then
15 that might change very quickly.

Dr Alberto Mancini

B Will we ever live in human colonies in space?
Ili Nemes, Budapest

If you had asked me this question
20 twenty years ago, my answer would have been 'yes'. Now, I'm not so sure. The obvious place to colonise would be Mars. It is believed that Mars almost certainly has the natural resources to
25 support life, agriculture and industry. The really big problem, though, is money. Experts estimate that sending the first man to Mars would cost between $20 billion and $400 billion!
30 And would we want to live in the colonies once they were built? They would almost certainly be cramped and limited at first and there would be very little in the way of facilities,
35 entertainment and so on. Personally, I'd rather stay on Earth!

Dr Alberto Mancini

The experts:

Professor Miriam Field is Professor of Architecture at Liverpool Technical University

Doctor Alberto Mancini teaches Ecology and Design at Milan Academic University

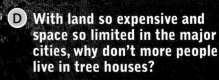

C Are 'skyscraper cities' a realistic possibility?

Lukasz Duda, Warsaw

40 Not at the moment, Lukasz. Back in 1989, a company in Japan designed 'Sky City 1000' – a 1,000 metre-high skyscraper that could provide houses for 35,000 people and workspace for 100,000 more. It comprises green spaces, apartments, offices, schools, theatres and much 45 more all in one building. But experts estimate that it will be 2030 or later before we have the technical know-how to build such structures. And do we really want them? Huge buildings like this can destroy the beauty of a city. In the 1920s, Le Corbusier, a famous 50 French architect and designer, proposed demolishing large parts of Paris to make room for rows of sky-scrapers. If he had succeeded, we wouldn't have the beautiful city that we know and love today.

Prof. Miriam Field

55 D With land so expensive and space so limited in the major cities, why don't more people live in tree houses?

Adam Sidorov, Moscow

60 The idea is not as extreme as you might think. Some architects, such as Andreas Wenning from Germany, have created a business out of building homes in trees. They are held in place by steel cables and come equipped with a kitchen, 65 bathroom and flat-screen TV. But with prices as high as €140,000, they're not exactly a cheap alternative to conventional housing. I certainly wish I could afford one though!

Prof. Miriam Field

70 E If global warming is really happening, then will places like Northern Siberia and Greenland become more habitable in the future?

Julie Rye, London

Good question, Julie. Glaciers are already melting in Greenland, 75 opening up the possibility of mining its rich natural resources, such as oil and minerals. And as summers become longer it may be possible to grow crops, raise animals and build more towns and villages there. Greenland is the largest island in the world so there should be plenty of space and the scenery is certainly spectacular. The trouble is that 80 no one really knows how exactly the climate will change and how fast that change will be. Right now, very few people are planning to move to Northern Greenland – there just aren't enough facilities, roads and so on up there.

Dr Alberto Mancini

---

6 Rank the places to live in the article from most appealing (1) to least appealing (5). Compare and explain your answers in pairs.

7 **a** In groups, you are going to design a 'home of the future'. Decide which idea in the text to develop or think of an alternative possibility.

CAN YOU DO IT IN ENGLISH?

b Read the brief below and think of a few ideas individually.

---

1 **You do not need to worry about technical and financial issues; however, your design must be:**
- healthy and attractive to live in
- practical and convenient for the inhabitants
- environmentally-friendly
- family-friendly

2 **You have to decide:**
- what features and facilities (green spaces, shopping facilities, entertainment) to include and where to put them – it may help to draw a sketch of the layout
- the practical problems people living in this environment might have (lack of fresh air, transport links) and how to solve them

3 **You can use ideas already mentioned in the texts but should explain how they would work in practice.**

---

8 Discuss your ideas with your group and come up with a plan to present to the class. Think about possible objections to your plan and how to overcome them. Use the phrases on the back cover to help you.

I think we should have a … in the centre.

On the … floor we should put a …

If we put a … here people would be able to …

9 **a** Present your design to the class. The rest of the class are the 'town planning committee'. After each presentation, question the group about their plan, referring to the brief in exercise 7b.

Yes, but have you thought about …?

Yes, but what would happen if …?

b Whose plan did you like best and why?

life changes

99

REAL TIME

INVITING AND PERSUADING

1 Discuss the questions in pairs.
- Where do you go with your friends to celebrate a birthday, the end of exams and other special occasions?
- Where are the trendiest places to go in your town?

2 a (4.33) Look at the photo, read the caption and answer the questions. Then listen and check.
1 Why do Jake, Ella and Ikram look happy?
2 What do you think Mr Douglas wants?

b (4.33) Listen again and answer the questions.
1 What is going to happen to The Ikram and Ella Student Special?
2 Where is Ikram going and for how long? What is he going to do?
3 Where are they going to celebrate? What sort of place is it?
4 What does Mr Douglas want to do? Do Ikram, Ella and Jake want that?
5 What would you have done in Ikram's situation?

3 Read *Phrases2know* and mark them as formal (F) or informal (I). The neutral phrases (N) have already been marked.

Ikram has just finished his last show. The friends are going out to celebrate.

Phrases **2** know

Inviting and persuading

Inviting
- [ ] Would you like to come with us?
- [ ] Do you fancy going for a coffee/coming with us?
- [ ] Can I invite you to the West One Bar with us?

Accepting
- [ ] Okay, why not?
- [ ] Thank you. I'd love to come.
- [N] I'd love to.

Refusing
- [ ] Not right now, thanks.
- [ ] That's very kind of you but we have other plans.
- [N] I'd love to but …

Persuading
- [N] Go on. It's my treat!
- [ ] It would mean a lot to me if you came.
- [ ] Come on. You know you'll enjoy it!

4 a Complete these extracts from the conversations with *Phrases2know*.

Ella:	Okay. That sounds nice. Jake, ^{1}_____ coming with us?
Jake:	Oh, ^{2}_____ . I've got a lot of work to do.
Ella:	Oh, ^{3}_____ , Jake. _____ enjoy it.
Jake:	Well … okay, ^{4}_____ ?
Mr Douglas:	So, ^{5}_____ for a cup of tea with me?
Ikram:	Oh, ^{6}_____ but we have other plans.
Mr Douglas:	Oh, ^{7}_____ . It's ^{8}_____ !
Ikram:	^{9}_____ to the West One Club, with us?
Mr Douglas:	Oh, well, what a surprise! ^{10}_____.

b (4.34) Listen and check your answers.

5 At the West One Club, Mr Douglas tries to persuade Ikram, Ella and Jake to go to a disco. In pairs, write the conversation then act it out. Use the dialogues and *Phrases2know* to help you.

CAN YOU DO IT IN ENGLISH?

6 a Read Ikram's blog and complete the gaps 1–4 in the photo captions.

b Look at the pictures. Would you like to visit Songo? Why? Why not?

7 STRUCTURE Read Ikram's blog again and look at the paragraph plan. In which paragraph does Ikram:

a compare Songo to a place he knows well?

b explain why he went there?

c recommend it for certain people?

d describe some particular places in Songo?

1 Introduction	basic factual information and overall impressions
2 General description and companions	first impressions and a general description
3 Specific description	the highlights
4 Summary	and your opinion

8 a LANGUAGE <u>Underline</u> phrases in Ikram's blog that are useful to describe a place.

b LANGUAGE Think of a place that you never want to go back to OR a place you can't wait to go back to. Use the phrases in *Language4writing* on the back cover to write sentences about it.

Ibiza is unlike any other place I've visited.

c In pairs, read your sentences. Guess whether your partner never wants to go back or can't wait to go back to the place they describe.

9 You are going to write a full description of a place that made a strong, positive impression on you. Follow these steps.

1 Use the paragraph plan in exercise 7 to make notes.

2 Use some of the phrases in *Language4writing* on the back cover.

10 a Write the first draft of your description then read it through or swap with a partner. Work through the checklist for writing on the back cover.

b Write the final draft of your description.

Ikram's Travel Blog

Songo in Mali

1 Mali is a landlocked country in West Africa with a population of around 14 million. Songo is located near the eastern edge of Mali. It's a small village and it sits at the top of a 150 kilometre-long cliff. I came here with a charity that builds schools and quickly realised that Songo is truly memorable and unlike any other place I've visited.

2 When you first arrive in Songo, you are immediately struck by the dry landscape and the warm smiles of the Dogon people who live in this area. It's a world away from the crowded streets of Brighton where I live. Unlike Brighton, there are no shops, no roads and no cars. Here children play freely wherever they want and many people sleep on the roof of their house. And while Brighton is on the edge of green countryside, here we are on the edge of the Sahara Desert. The heat is extraordinary and this adds to the magic of Songo.

3 One of the highlights of Songo is the waterfall area. The water runs down the cliff face and at the bottom children play and visitors like me escape from the heat. The other extraordinary place to visit is the mosque. Like all the buildings in Songo, it's built of mud and sticks and it's absolutely beautiful.

4 Songo is a unique place and well worth a visit for more adventurous travellers. Where else can you sleep on a roof, wash in a waterfall and spend the whole day outdoors?

This is Songo where the ¹_____ people live.

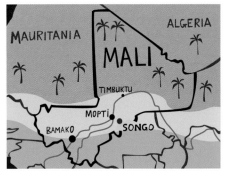

The population of Mali is ²_____. The ³_____ Desert is in the north of the country.

All the buildings are made of ⁴_____

101

Vocabulary

ACTIVE STUDY | Word formation

1 **a** Complete the sentences with the correct form of the word in brackets.

1 There isn't much _entertainment_ (entertain) where I live.

2 New York is one of the most ___ (culture) diverse cities in the world.

3 The robbers were sentenced to five years' ___ (imprison).

4 Drug addicts should be treated as ill people, not as ___ (crime).

5 The shoplifter was found guilty of ___ (thief).

6 The ___ (defend) lawyer tries to show that the accused is innocent.

b (4.35) Listen and check.

2 Match the words 1–7 to the definitions a–g.

1 [e] evidence   5 [ ] facilities
2 [ ] judge   6 [ ] scenery
3 [ ] victim   7 [ ] mortgage
4 [ ] witness

a the natural features of an area, such as mountains or forests

b buildings, rooms and equipment that serve a specific purpose, such as a sports centre or shopping mall

c someone who has suffered as a result of a crime

d someone who saw a crime committed

e information presented in court

f a bank loan taken out to buy a house

g the person who decides how a criminal will be punished

3 Complete the sentences with one preposition in each gap.

1 The murderer goes _on_ trial today.

2 The three men were charged ___ armed robbery.

3 The lady was cheated ___ of a large sum of money.

4 I wasn't taken ___ by the woman's story.

5 I was very upset when I discovered he had lied ___ me.

6 We want to put our house ___ for sale.

7 We've bought a new apartment. The sellers are moving ___ next week so we can move ___ the week after that.

Grammar

4 Complete the sentences with the gerund or infinitive form of the verb in brackets.

My parents decided [1]_to move_ (move) to the countryside [2]___ (get) away from the traffic and pollution in the city. At first, I was sad [3]___ (leave) my friends but when I saw our new house I fell in love with it. Now I know that [4]___ (live) in the countryside is my favourite way of life. Last weekend, we celebrated my mum's birthday by [5]___ (have) a picnic in the forest behind our house. After an hour, the rain forced us [6]___ (return) home so we spent the rest of the afternoon [7]___ (sit) by the open fire. I feel so lucky [8]___ (live) in this lovely place.

5 Complete the sentences with the words below.

[can't ✓   have   had   might   must   would]

1 The document _can't_ be genuine. I'm sure it's forged.

2 If only we ___ understood the situation sooner!

3 If I'd known it was a hoax, I ___ have contacted the police for sure.

4 He can't ___ pleaded guilty – he was innocent!

5 If the flat hadn't been so cramped, I ___ perhaps have bought it.

6 One of the men ___ have confessed to the crime. I'm sure that's how the truth came out.

EXAM PRACTICE | Sentence transformations

6 Complete the second sentence so that it means the same as the first.

1 I don't believe this is a family-friendly neighbourhood.
This _can't be_ a family-friendly neighbourhood.

2 I'm sure the burglars escaped.
The burglars ___ escaped.

3 Ian regrets selling his house last year.
Ian wishes ___ his house last year.

4 I'm sorry we don't have a nicer view.
If only ___ a nicer view.

5 I committed a crime and now I'm not a free man.
If I ___ a free man now.

6 There was enough evidence for the police to arrest Jones.
The police wouldn't ___ enough evidence.

7 The murderer was sent to prison for life.
The murderer was ___ imprisonment.

Reading skills

ACTIVE STUDY | Read for specific information

7 Read the article about green roofs. Tick (✓) true, cross (✗) false or write (?) if there is no information.

1 ☐ Augustenborg Botanical Garden is the best-organised park in Malmö.

2 ☐ There are more green roofs now on city houses than on cottages.

3 ☐ Ordinary roofs are an unpleasant environment because of the heat and lack of water.

4 ☐ Green roofs contribute to the 'urban heat-island effect'.

5 ☐ Green roofs help solve certain problems connected with rain in the city.

6 ☐ Large numbers of animals live on green roofs.

7 ☐ A green roof is cheaper to build than an ordinary one.

8 ☐ The aim of this text is to describe the advantages of green roofs.

Speaking skills

8 a Compare and contrast the two photos showing life in a big city.

b Answer the questions.

1 What are the good and bad sides of life in a big city for young people?

2 What could be done to improve the quality of life in big cities?

Green roofs (4.36)

1 Fresh green grass. Hundreds of colourful wild flowers. Water flowing into little ponds. Birds nesting safely in boxes. The 9,500-square metre Augustenborg Botanical Garden may look just like any other well-organised
5 park but there's a difference. It is situated on the roofs of industrial and office buildings in the city of Malmö, Sweden.

Green roofs are not a new invention. Cottages with grass on their roofs have been part of traditional
10 architecture in Scandinavia for centuries and used to be found on American prairies. Nowadays, these types of structures are becoming popular again and not just on cottages. The Waldspirale ('forest spiral') in Darmstadt, Germany, the University
15 Library in Warsaw, Poland and the Public Library in Vancouver, Canada are among the increasing number of modern buildings with gardens on top. The ordinary 'roofscape' of a modern city looks a bit like hell: endless black surfaces with no life, no water
20 and temperatures on summer days reaching sixty-five degrees centigrade. Perhaps that's why an unexpected garden on a roof feels like a little paradise.

But living roofs are not just pretty. Because they are natural ecosystems, they have a moderating, balancing
25 influence. The very high temperatures on conventional roofs in the summer can make top floor apartments uncomfortably hot. What is more, they contribute to the 'urban heat-island effect' – the tendency of cities to be hotter than the countryside around them. On a
30 green roof, however, with its soil and plants and water, temperatures change only a little, as they do in a park. This can significantly reduce heating and cooling costs in the building below.

Also, when rain falls on an ordinary roof, it pours off at
35 once into the city's drains. A living roof, on the other hand, absorbs this water, filters it and slows it down, just like a field or garden does. This can prevent street flooding and protect the city drainage system. It also means the water that flows off the roof is cleaner. A
40 green roof is alive and living creatures, such as various species of insects and birds, can make their homes on it. Thanks to this, the city may become part of the surrounding nature, rather than something completely separate from it.

45 Supporters of living roofs say the technology exists now to construct them on buildings of all kinds and sizes. While the cost of installing such a roof can still be higher than that of an ordinary one, it's likely to be cheaper in the long run thanks to energy savings. And
50 wouldn't it be wonderful to be able to walk out into a garden high above the city's noise and traffic, whether you're at school or in an office or just at home in a ten-storey block?

¹miniworkbook

✱ easy to do
✱✱ a bit harder
✱✱✱ extra challenge

Grammar

1 ✱ **Time phrases with present tenses**

Underline the correct answer. Then ask and answer the questions in pairs.

1 Are you studying more than usual *this week*/*often*?

2 What do you do *at the weekend*/*now*?

3 Have you lived here *for three years*/*at the moment*?

4 Have you been doing anything interesting *recently*/*from time to time*?

5 Are you doing anything different *this week*/*previously* from your usual routine?

6 Have you been learning English *usually*/*since you were young*?

2 ✱✱ **Present tenses**

Read the texts and choose the correct answer.

I'm a musician. I usually
¹ _a_ for about ten hours a week but at the moment
I ² ___ for a concert so I ³ ___ for three hours every day. This week, I ⁴ ___ twenty-one hours of practice!

I want to do a marathon next month. I started training two months ago and I ⁵ ___ every day since then. I think I ⁶ ___ because I've been training very hard. This isn't my first marathon (I ⁷ ___ two marathons before) but I ⁸ ___ to improve my record time.

1	a	practise ✓	b	am practising
2	a	have prepared	b	am preparing
3	a	practise	b	am practising
4	a	do	b	have done
5	a	am training	b	have been training
6	a	improve	b	am improving
7	a	have done	b	do
8	a	want	b	am wanting

3 ✱✱✱ Complete the text with the present simple, present continuous, present perfect simple or present perfect continuous form of the verb in brackets. If more than one form is possible, use the continuous form.

Serena's success story

Serena Williams ¹_is_ (be) one of the top tennis players in the world in singles and doubles. She ² ___ (play) tennis since she was very young and she started playing professionally in 1995. Since then, she ³ ___ (win) many titles. Serena always ⁴ ___ (play) doubles with her sister, Venus. They ⁵ ___ (play) together for many years and often ⁶ ___ (win) competitions – in fact, they ⁷ ___ (just win) an Open competition together. The two sisters ⁸ ___ (also play) against each other in twenty-three professional matches since 1998.

There's no doubt about her ability to play tennis but Serena also ⁹ ___ (have) the determination and vision to succeed. When she ¹⁰ ___ (get) ready for a match, she ¹¹ ___ (train) every day. Serena says she ¹² ___ (not enjoy) training. 'When I ¹³ ___ (run), I think about winning. That's the only thing that keeps me going.' However, she loves yoga and she ¹⁴ ___ (go) to classes for a few years.

4 ✱ **Past tenses**

Underline the correct answer.

Joe: ¹*Did you enjoy*/*Had you enjoyed* the film last night?

Ruth: No! I didn't see it.

Joe: What happened?

Ruth: I ²*left*/*had been leaving* the house early and went to catch the bus but the bus ³*didn't arrive*/*hadn't arrived*.

Joe: Oh dear!

Ruth: Yes, so after I ⁴*was waiting*/*had been waiting* for twenty minutes, I ⁵*decided*/*was deciding* to phone Sue. Then I discovered that my mobile ⁶*wasn't working*/*hadn't been working* so I couldn't phone. I started to walk but when I ⁷*walked*/*was walking* the bus ⁸*passed*/*was passing* me! By the time I ⁹*arrived*/*had arrived* at the cinema, the film ¹⁰*already*/*had already* started and Sue was really angry.

Joe: Oh no!

Ruth: Well, I ¹¹*explained*/*was explaining* what ¹²*had happened*/*had been happening* and Sue ¹³*had thought*/*thought* it was funny! In the end, we ¹⁴*went*/*were going* for a pizza instead.

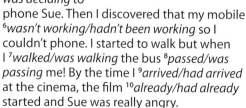

5 (✳✳) **Complete the sentences with the correct form of the verb in brackets.**

1 I _saw_ (see) the film *Precious* after I had _read_ (read) the book.

2 There ___ (be) a fire while they ___ (make) the film but everyone ___ (escape).

3 The actors ___ (work) for three hours when I ___ (arrive) at the studio.

4 Last year's Oscar ceremony ___ (be) very exciting. In the weeks before, everyone ___ (guess) who might win. Most people ___ (not guess) correctly because there ___ (be) a lot of surprises.

5 I ___ (remember) all my lines for the scene because I ___ (previously study) hard.

6 (✳✳) **Read the text and choose the correct answer.**

Sam Worthington:
DID YOU KNOW ...?

- He ¹ _a_ in his first a film in 2000.
- Most people ² ___ of him before *Avatar* came out in 2009!
- He ³ ___ in lots of Australian films and TV series before 2009.
- He was born in England but his family ⁴ ___ to Australia when he was a baby.
- Worthington ⁵ ___ school at the age of seventeen to become an actor.
- He ⁶ ___ as a builder when he got a place at the National Institute of Dramatic Art.
- He ⁷ ___ in theatre and TV in Australia before he got his first international film role.
- Worthington might be the next Bond! Producers ⁸ ___ him a few years ago but he didn't get the part then.

1	**a** starred ✓	**b** was starring	**c** had starred
2	**a** never heard	**b** had never heard	**c** had never been hearing
3	**a** appeared	**b** had been appearing	**c** was appearing
4	**a** had emigrated	**b** was emigrating	**c** emigrated
5	**a** was leaving	**b** left	**c** had been leaving
6	**a** had been working	**b** worked	**c** was working
7	**a** had worked	**b** had been working	**c** was working
8	**a** had considered	**b** considered	**c** had been considering

7 (✳✳✳) **Read *Grammar Plus*. Then <u>underline</u> the auxiliary verbs and add question tags.**

Grammar + Plus

Question tags

Use question tags to confirm something you know, to ask for another person's agreement or involve people in the conversation.

Form question tags with the auxiliary verb or *be* + pronoun which refers to the subject of the sentence:

*You're a student, **aren't you**?*

*She's been busy, **hasn't she**?*

*They've been living there since May, **haven't they**?*

*He didn't get an Oscar, **did he**?*

*She wasn't doing anything, **was she**?*

*He had already finished the film when he died, **hadn't he**?*

*They had been working hard for months, **hadn't they**?*

Use *do/does/did* for present and past simple when there is no auxiliary verb:

*Pete lives in London, **doesn't he**?*

*They went to the cinema, **didn't they**?*

Use a positive tag after a negative sentence and a negative tag after a positive sentence:

*You don't usually practise here, **do you**?*

*They haven't arrived, **have they**?*

1 Kate <u>has</u> just won an award, _hasn't she_ ?

2 The actor <u>wasn't</u> listening to the director, _was he_ ?

3 He had finished, ___ ?

4 They haven't been training recently, ___ ?

5 She plays the guitar, ___ ?

6 They aren't playing basketball now, ___ ?

7 They haven't played tennis recently, ___ ?

8 You don't like training, ___ ?

9 We weren't watching the film when you arrived, ___ ?

10 Their father told them to stop, ___ ?

11 They hadn't been working for a while, ___ ?

12 You had been preparing for the competition, ___ ?

Vocabulary

8 (＊) Going to extremes

Complete the interview with the correct form of the words in brackets.

9 (＊＊) Extreme adjectives

Read the dialogue below and put the cartoons A–E in order from 1–5. Then replace the <u>underlined</u> words with the extreme adjectives below. There are two extra adjectives.

> amazed   desperate   exhausted
> freezing   furious   hilarious   huge
> soaked   terrible ✓   terrified

Jack: I had a ¹*terrible* <u>very bad</u> day on Saturday.

Kaya: Really? What happened?

Jack: I took my dog, Rover, to the park for a walk and a ²<u>very big</u> dog chased him. Rover was ³<u>very frightened</u> and he ran away.

Kaya: Oh dear.

Jack: But that wasn't the worst thing. Rover ran into the lake and when I was trying to get him out, I fell in!

Kaya: Oh!

Jack: Yes and the water was ⁴<u>very cold</u> and I got ⁵<u>really wet</u>!

Kaya: Then what happened?

Jack: When I got home, I went inside to get a towel to dry Rover … but when I wasn't looking he ran into the house! He got water and mud everywhere – and my mum had just cleaned the house. She was ⁶<u>very angry</u>!

Kaya: Oh!

Jack: So I had to clean everything and I was ⁷<u>very tired</u> after.

Kaya: Ha ha ha!

Jack: It's not funny!

Kaya: No, it's ⁸<u>very funny</u>!

A ☐

B ☐

C ☐

D ☐

E ☐

Interviewer: Jane, you're a famous writer – tell me, what gives you your ideas?

Jane King: Where do I get my ¹*inspiration* (inspire) from? Well, from things that happen to me or things I imagine.

Interviewer: What's the most difficult part of your job?

JK: Well, you need to be ²___ (discipline) because you don't have a boss so you have to motivate and organise yourself. There's a great deal of ³___ (pressurise), too because there's a lot of ⁴___ (compete) from other writers to be the best. But I like the ⁵___ (challenging), I don't like things that are too easy! Of course, I get a lot of ⁶___ (satisfying) from my job. I love it!

Interviewer: Yes, I suppose you have to be very ⁷___ (dedicate) to be a writer because you spend such a lot of time on each book. What's your greatest ⁸___ (achieve) – have you won any prizes, for example?

JK: Yes, I won an award last year. That was very ⁹___ (satisfy).

Interviewer: Jane, thank you.

10 (＊) Active study: Extreme adjectives and intensifiers

Read the sentences and <u>underline</u> the correct intensifier. Sometimes both are possible.

1 Last winter was *absolutely/very* freezing, it was *really/very* cold all the time.

2 The news was *very/absolutely* surprising – we were all *very/absolutely* amazed.

3 This book is *really/very* brilliant and it's *absolutely/very* hilarious – I laughed a lot. I think it's *really/absolutely* outstanding.

4 We went hiking and got lost. We didn't have any food so we were *very/absolutely* starving and our parents were *really/absolutely* worried because they didn't know where we were.

5 It's *very/absolutely* hot today, in fact it's *absolutely/very* boiling!

6 The concert was very bad – actually, it was *absolutely/really* terrible!

11 (＊＊) Reaching the top

Complete the sentences with the words below.

> natural talent   determination   luck ✓
> sacrifices   support   social network

1 You need to work hard to succeed but you also need good *luck*.

2 Ian has a ___ for music, he's really outstanding.

3 I get a lot of ___ from my parents, they help me with everything.

4 She has a lot of friends, her ___ is very big.

5 When you win a competition, you know that all the ___ you made were worthwhile.

6 They never stop trying – they've got a lot of ___!

2 miniworkbook

* easy to do
** a bit harder
*** extra challenge

Grammar

1 (*) Present perfect simple and continuous

<u>Underline</u> the correct answer.

1 **A:** I really need to speak to John. I've *phoned/<u>been phoning</u>* him all morning.

   B: Have you *managed/been managing* to speak to him yet?

   A: No but I've *spoken/'ve been speaking* to his wife ten times!

2 **A:** Maggie is doing a lot of exercise at the moment.

   B: Why's that?

   A: Because she's *trained/been training* for the marathon.

3 **A:** Why are you so dirty and wet? What have you *done/been doing?*

   B: I've *run/been running.*

   A: Oh, how far have you *run/been running?*

   B: Five kilometres! It's *taken/been taking* me an hour and it's *rained/been raining* for the last twenty minutes – that's why I'm so wet!

4 **A:** Have you *finished/been finishing* your homework yet?

   B: No, I haven't *finished/been finishing* my history project. I've *read/been reading* three chapters of my history book and I've *written/been writing* notes for the project. I'll finish them after tea.

5 **A:** Mark hasn't *done/been doing* his homework for the past few weeks.

   B: Has his teacher *spoken/been speaking* to his parents about the problem?

   A: Yes, he has just *phoned/been phoning* them.

2 (**) Write sentences about what the people have been doing or what they have done.

1 copy/ten CDs <u>He has copied ten CDs</u>.

2 copy/CDs <u>She's been copying CDs</u>.

3 go out a lot/recently ___

4 go out/tonight ___

5 run ___

6 run a marathon ___

3 (***) Complete the sentences with the correct form of the verb in brackets.

How to leave home ...

Last month, Jessica Sage had to move back to her parents' house. Why? She couldn't get a job. Jessica [1]<u>has recently finished</u> (recently/finish) university. She [2]___ (try) to get a job for three months but she [3]___ (not have) any success yet.

'I [4]___ (read) hundreds of job advertisements and [5]___ (reply) to all of them but nobody [6]___ (answer) my letters. So, I designed this board and put my qualifications and experience on the back. For the past three days I [7]___ (walk) around the town centre. I [8]___ (speak) to people and [9]___ (ask) everyone about jobs.'

So, [10]___ (Jessica's plan/be) successful? Yes, it has! A company [11]___ (offer) her a job because it was impressed by her creativity. Jessica's parents were also impressed – they [12]___ (buy) her a car so that she can travel to work. Jessica [13]___ (just/find) a room in a shared flat and she is moving in next month. 'I [14]___ (live) with my parents for too long – I want my own place now,' says Jessica.

I NEED A JOB

QUALIFICATIONS ON BACK!

4 (**) Present and past habits

Toby isn't very punctual now but he was in the past. Write sentences about Toby using *always*, *keep*, *would*, *wouldn't* and *used to*.

[arrive late ✓   get up late   not get up late
forget to phone when he's late   not arrive late
get up early ✓   phone if there was a problem]

Now
1 *He keeps arriving late.*
2 _____
3 _____

In the past
4 *He used to get up early.*
5 _____
6 _____
7 _____

5 (*) Read the text and underline the correct answers. Decide where you can use both *would* and *used to* or only *used to*.

Sally is fifteen years old and she lives in the country, sixty kilometres from Manchester. She walks to school and she doesn't have to get up until 8.00 a.m. She is happy and she's got lots of friends. However, two years ago her life was very different. Sally ¹*used to*/*would* live in London. She ²*used to*/*would* get up very early because she ³*used to*/*would* catch three different buses to go to school every day. She ⁴*used to*/*would* spend hours travelling. She ⁵*used to*/*would* be unhappy because she spent so much time travelling and she ⁶*didn't use to*/*wouldn't* like her school.

6 (**) Complete the sentences about your present and past habits.

1 I keep *forgetting my homework* .
2 I used to _____ .
3 When I was younger, I would _____ .
4 I'm always _____ .
5 A few years ago, I was always _____ .
6 I didn't use to _____ .
7 When I was a child and I was tired, I would _____ .
8 When I was younger, I wouldn't _____ .

7 (**) Read *Grammar Plus*. Then underline the correct answers in the email.

Grammar + Plus

be/get used to + -ing

Use *be used to* + -ing to talk about familiar things:
I'm from Sweden so when I moved to Canada, the temperature wasn't a shock. I'm used to living in a cold county.

Use *get used to* + -ing to describe the process of becoming accustomed to something new:
I became a vegetarian a few months ago and I'm getting used to not eating meat. I got used to eating more salad very quickly but I still miss meat!

Use *be/get used to* to talk about the present or the past – unlike *used to* which is only used to talk about past habits and states.

Dear Jenny,

Do you remember I said I wanted to work as a volunteer for a few months before going to university? Well, I'm now in India working on a project! I started last week and I am slowly ¹*getting used to*/*used to* working here. I ²*am not used to*/*am not getting used to* getting up so early yet, we start at 6.30 a.m.! When I was at school I ³d*idn't use to get up*/*wasn't used to getting up* until 8.00 a.m. – now I have to get up at 5.30! The most difficult things for me are the climate and the food. I am slowly ⁴*used to living*/*getting used to living* in such a hot country – but the food is a different matter. I ⁵*used to having*/*was used to having* a lot of hot food like curries before I came here so I thought the food wouldn't be a problem. However, the curries are really HOT! I don't think I'll ever ⁶*get used to eating*/*used to eat* them!

How are you? What's your news?

Love,
Tanya

8 (***) Complete the second sentence so that it means the same as the first.

1 a John is working in Paris. He started two months ago.
  b John *has been working in Paris for two months* .

2 a When I was a child I often visited my grandparents.
  b When I was a child, I would ___ .

3 a My brother often takes my things without asking. It's really annoying.
  b My brother is always ___ .

4 a They spent this morning making cakes. They have got ten cakes now.

 b They have ___ this morning. They have got ten cakes now.

5 a I didn't live in Britain when I was younger.

 b I didn't use ___ .

6 a Caroline lives in London. She moved there in 2006.

 b Caroline has ___ .

7 a Ben started cooking three hours ago. He's still cooking.

 b Ben has ___ .

8 a They continued talking and ignored me.

 b They kept ___ .

Vocabulary

9 (**) Boomerang kids

Complete the sentences with one word in each gap.

1 I don't like arguing with people. I always avoid c*onflict* if possible.

2 If you don't treat someone with r___ they will feel bad and they probably won't treat you well either.

3 When you enjoy someone's c___ you will probably spend more time with them.

4 There is no need to get angry if everyone behaves r___ .

5 It's good to have fun and have a l___ with your friends.

6 Talking is the best way to solve problems. It's really important to communicate about i___ .

7 In my flat we always share the c___ – we take turns to do the cleaning and cooking and other things.

8 I like talking to my parents. I often have a c___ with them about what's on TV.

10 (*) Behaviour and relationships

Choose the correct answer.

Kate: My brother always leaves ¹ *a* in the bathroom, it drives me crazy. When he goes out with his girlfriend, he ² ___ ages to get ready. I always have to wait for him.

Melanie: But you get on with your brother!

Kate: I suppose he's okay really.

Melanie: I'm having real problems with my friend Paula.

Kate: Why?

Melanie: Well, I get annoyed when she ³ ___ what I'm saying and continues talking – and I can never finish what I'm saying when I talk to her because she always ⁴ ___ me. The thing is, she loves talking about other people and what they're doing, she's always ⁵ ___ about someone.

Kate: You should tell her you don't want to hear stories about other people.

Melanie: I've tried but then she says I'm ⁶ ___ her and tells me to stop!

Kate: Well, you should try speaking to her again.

Melanie: Okay, I'll try!

1	a a mess ✓	b a drama
2	a takes	b makes
3	a nags	b ignores
4	a ignores	b interrupts
5	a gossiping	b showing off
6	a mislaying	b nagging

11 (**) Happily ever after

Match the words and expressions below to the definitions 1–8.

full-time housewife ✓   settle down
breadwinner   inherit property
arranged marriage   head of the household
divorce rate   ask someone out

1 a woman who stays at home and looks after the children – *full-time housewife*

2 invite a boy or girl to go out with you on a date

3 get a house after someone in the family dies and gives it to you

4 the number of people who legally end marriages every year

5 stay in a relationship or place permanently

6 the person in a household who earns the money to support the family

7 the most important person in the family

8 when parents choose a husband or wife for their son or daughter

12 (*) Active study: Phrasal verbs (1)

Underline the correct answer. In some cases, both are possible.

1 My aunt *brought up me/brought me up*.

2 Jeff's got my book. I hope he *gives back my book/gives my book back* soon. Do you think he will *give back it/give it back*?

3 Jackie *gave her job up/gave up her job* when she had her children.

4 I don't understand the question. I can't *work out the answer/work the answer out*. Can you *work out it/work it out*?

5 Alison *asked Steve out/asked out Steve* – I think it's great!

6 Who usually *looks after the children/looks the children after* in your country? In the UK, the mother usually *looks after them/looks them after*.

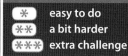

* easy to do
** a bit harder
*** extra challenge

Grammar

1 (**) Future forms

Underline the correct answer.

1 Look at those black clouds. It *will rain/is going to rain.*

2 There's someone at the door. Don't worry, I'm *opening/'ll open* it.

3 What time *does the train leave/is the train leaving?*

4 I've spoken to Jim. We'*ll meet/'re meeting* at six o'clock tonight.

5 In the future I think perhaps I'*ll travel/'m going to travel* a lot, although I haven't got any plans yet.

6 I failed two exams last year. I'*ll work/'m going to work* harder at school this year because I want to go to university.

7 The football team has lost most of their matches this season. However, I think they'*ll win/'re going to win* the game tomorrow because the other team is terrible.

8 I'll be back in five minutes. I'*ll phone/'m going to phone* my friend.

2 (**) Complete the conversation with the correct form of the verb in brackets.

Sam: Mike and Ruby have been together for ages. I think they ¹*'ll get married* (get married) soon.

Ann: I saw Mike in the jeweller's shop last week. He was buying a ring. He ²___ (ask) Ruby to marry him.

Pete: Mike and Ruby? Haven't you heard? Mike asked Ruby to marry him yesterday. They ³___ (get married) next May or June.

Ann: That's wonderful! I ⁴___ (meet) Ruby tonight so I'm sure she ⁵___ (tell) me all about it.

Sam: I ⁶___ (phone) Mike now to congratulate him.

Pete: Okay but hurry. We've got to go or we ⁷___ (be) late for the cinema. The film ⁸___ (start) in ten minutes.

3 (**) Read *Grammar Plus*. Then rewrite the <u>underlined</u> phrases so the meaning is the same.

> **Grammar + Plus**
>
> ***be about to, be on the point of, be likely to*** **and *be unlikely* to**
>
> Use *be about to* (+ infinitive) and *be on the point of* (+ *-ing*) to say something is going to happen in the immediate future:
>
> *Look at the sky, it's **about to** snow. Yes, it's starting now.*
>
> *They **are on the point of** leaving so ask them before they go.*
>
> Use *likely to* and *unlikely to* to talk about the probability of something happening in the future:
>
> *Mark is often late so he's **unlikely to** arrive on time tonight. He's **likely to** be late.*

1 Jane is coming to my house at 6.00 p.m. and it's 5.55 p.m. now. <u>She's going to arrive very soon</u>.

 She's about to arrive/She's on the point of arriving.

2 They haven't sold many tickets. <u>They'll probably cancel</u> the concert.

 They are likely to cancel the concert.

3 <u>I'm going to leave the house in a few seconds</u> or I'll be late for school.

4 I've been doing my homework for hours. <u>I'm going to stop right now.</u>

5 Mark doesn't like Indian food, <u>he probably won't come</u> to the restaurant.

6 They love comedy films so <u>it's very possible they'll come</u> to the cinema with us.

7 Scientists are investigating the problem now. <u>They are going to find a solution very soon.</u>

8 They have no idea how to solve the problem. <u>They probably won't find</u> a solution soon.

4 (＊) Second conditional

Match the two parts of the sentences. Add commas (,) where necessary.

1 If we had a high-speed connection,   a you could go anywhere in the world?
2 What gadget would you buy if   b they could!
3 Where would you go if   c I would update it.
4 If you didn't have to go to school   d I would use the internet more.
5 They would chat online all day if   e you had some money?
6 If I had an old profile   f what would you do all day?

5 (＊＊＊) Complete the second conditional sentences using the correct form of the verb in brackets.

1 I _would move_ (move) to London if my parents _allowed_ (allow) me to go.
2 Where ___ (you/live) if you ___ (not live) in your town or city?
3 If they ___ (not have) to work so hard, they ___ (not complain) so much.
4 I ___ (use) the new printer if I ___ (know) how it ___ (work).
5 If she ___ (have) a lot of money, what ___ (she/buy)?
6 John ___ (use) his mobile in the car if he ___ (have) a hands-free phone.

6 (＊＊＊) Ryan isn't very happy with his life. Look at his problems and complete the second conditional sentences. Then write sentences using the cues.

1 I can't get a job because I haven't got any experience.

2 I don't go out because I haven't got any money.

3 I want to ask Sandra out but I don't know if she'll accept.

4 I argue with my parents all the time because I have to live at home.

5 I play computer games all day because I haven't got anything to do.

1 If _he had some experience, he could get a job_.
   get a job/provided that/have some experience
   He would get a job provided that he had some experience.

2 If he _____ .
   supposing/he/have some money/he/come out with us?
   _____ .

3 If he _____ .
   he/ask Sandra out/provided that/he/know/she/accept
   _____ .

4 He _____ .
   he/get on better with his parents/provided that/he/live in his own flat
   _____ .

5 He _____ .
   supposing/he/have a job/he/not play computer games all day
   _____ .

Vocabulary

7 (✱✱) Talking about technology

Complete the crossword.

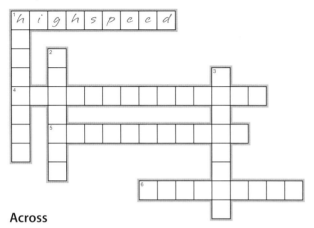

Across

1 My internet connection is really slow. I want to get a *high-speed* internet connection.

4 The picture on this ___ TV is excellent – it's really clear.

5 Ruth has got a ___ computer. You don't have to use the mouse – you can access things directly with your fingers.

6 I use a ___ phone in the car when I'm driving so I don't need to hold the phone.

Down

1 I often play games on my ___ games console when I'm travelling. It's small enough to go in my pocket.

2 I've got all the pictures from my last holiday in my ___ photo frame.

3 I've got a ___ mouse – you don't have to plug it in so it's easy to move.

8 (✱✱) Unscramble the letters to complete the conversation.

A: Are you a member of a ¹*social networking* (ciosla entngkiowr) site?

B: Yes … actually, I need to update my ²___ (lofipre), the information is months old.

A: Could I use your laptop when you finish? I want to ³___ (lwadnodo) some new music but my internet ⁴___ (noconctine) isn't working properly.

B: Maybe it's a problem with the ⁵___ (dhra ridev). Anyway, of course you can use my laptop. You might have to plug it in or recharge it because the ⁶___ (abteytr ifle) is very short.

A: Okay. Can I also use it to ⁷___ (frus het tne) to find information about internet service providers?

B: Sure.

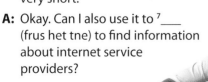

9 (✱) Active study: Compound words

Complete the sentences with a suitable compound word. Use a word from column A and a word from B.

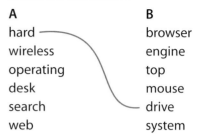

A	B
hard	browser
wireless	engine
operating	top
desk	mouse
search	drive
web	system

1 All the information on a computer is stored on the *hard drive*.

2 I've got a new ___. It's very easy to use because you can move it anywhere.

3 ___s like Google are very useful to help you find information.

4 Which ___ do you use, Internet Explorer, Firefox or another one?

5 My new laptop is more powerful than my old ___ computer.

6 I've got a new computer with the latest ___ .

10 (✱✱) Slang and informal English

Read the quiz and choose the answers that mean the same as the underlined words and phrases.

Do you know your slang and informal English?

How much do you know about slang and informal English? Take our quiz and find out!

1 **You look very stressed. You should <u>chill out</u>.**
  a relax ✓   b sleep

2 **Have you ever <u>nicked</u> anything?**
  a hidden   b stolen

3 **It's not serious. Don't <u>blow your top</u>.**
  a joke   b get angry

4 **Lucy really <u>fancies</u> Daniel.**
  a finds him attractive
  b thinks he's a terrible person

5 **I bought that CD. It was <u>a rip off</u>.**
  a really good   b too expensive

6 **Stop <u>messing around</u> and help me.**
  a behaving in a silly way   b relaxing

7 **Jonathan is really <u>fit</u>!**
  a stupid   b attractive

8 **Olivia and Sarah are <u>mates</u>.**
  a in the same class   b friends

Score

0–2 Oh dear! You need to brush up on your slang and informal English.

3–5 Not bad. Try talking to a few teenagers and you'll soon learn some more slang and informal English!

6–8 You're totally up-to-date on your slang and informal English. Well done!

4 miniworkbook

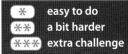

* easy to do
** a bit harder
*** extra challenge

Grammar

1 (*) Modals of obligation and advice

Complete the school leaflet with the correct form of *have (got) to*, *must*, *should* or *needn't* and the words in brackets.

BRAMPTON SCHOOL

the school where students come first

Where is the school?

It's in Kent, near Maidenhead.

[1]*Do I have to wear a uniform?* **(I/wear)**
No, you [2]___ (not wear) a uniform. Students can choose what they want to wear. However, you [3]___ (wear) smart clothes – other than that it's up to you!

What subjects [4]___ **(I/study)?**

Unlike most schools where you [5]___ (study) many compulsory subjects, we believe students [6]___ (choose) most of the subjects they want to study. We only have two compulsory subjects, English and Maths – all students [7]___ (study) those two subjects.

What if I don't want to study a foreign language?

You [8]___ (not study) a foreign language if you don't want to! However, it's a good idea to try one – we offer over ten different languages so you're sure to find one that interests you. You [9]___ (choose) a good variety of subjects. We believe that all students [10]___ (talk) to the tutors before choosing.

What about sport – [11]___ **(I/do) sport?**

Yes, you [12]___ (do) at least one physical activity but you choose what you want to do! It could be dance, horse-riding or windsurfing or one of the many other exciting activities we offer.

2 (**) Complete the sentences with *should, shouldn't* or *needn't* and the correct form of the verb in brackets.

1 I *shouldn't have watched* (watch) TV all night. I ___ (go) to bed earlier.

3 I wrote a few extra pages for my English homework but it wasn't necessary. I ___ (write) them.

5 Oh, you're asleep! Perhaps I ___ (talk) for so long, I ___ (stop) earlier.

2 I took some books to school that I didn't use. I ___ (take) the books.

4 I decided to study Geography but I'm not very good at it. I ___ (study) History instead and I ___ (become) an explorer!

3 (✱✱✱) Complete Matthew's blog with *must*, *have (got) to*, *should*, *needn't* and the correct form of the verb in brackets.

Matthew goes to uni!

End of term update

This is my first year at university and I've had some problems. For one thing, I've got no money left. I ¹*shouldn't have spent* (not spend) so much on clothes but I had no idea how to organise my money. I think schools ² ___ (teach) students how to manage their personal finances – that would be really useful. My advice to avoid money problems is that you ³ ___ (divide) the money you have by the number of weeks in the term. That's what I'll do next term. Now I know that I absolutely ⁴ ___ (keep) to my weekly limit. I've just failed two exams as well. I ⁵ ___ (not go out) so much and I ⁶ ___ (study) more. Now, I ⁷ ___ (take) the exams again in January and I ⁸ ___ (have a meeting) with all my teachers (I got a letter telling me it's obligatory). Also, I've got too much stuff in my room – I brought lots of unnecessary things, I ⁹ ___ (not bring) them, then I'd have more space. I definitely ¹⁰ ___ (bring) my TV – that was a big mistake because I watch too much TV. Oh well, I'm sure next term will be better because of everything I've learned about being a student!

posted by Matthew at 10.04 p.m. 2 comments

4 (✱✱) Read *Grammar Plus*. Then complete the conversations with *ought to* or *ought to have* and the correct form of the verb in brackets.

Grammar + Plus

ought to

We spmetimes use *ought to* instead of *should*. Use *ought to* + infinitive to talk about doing something that is a good idea and to give advice:

We **ought to go** now, it's getting late.

You **ought to talk** to your parents about the problem.

The past form is *ought to* + *have* + past participle:

I didn't say I was sorry for being late. I **ought to have apologised**.

---

1 Amy: My best friend isn't speaking to me and I don't know why.

Bob: You ¹*ought to speak* (speak) to her and find out what the problem is.

Amy: I asked her but she didn't tell me. I think she ²*ought to have explained* (explain) what was wrong.

2 Colin: The government doesn't spend enough money on education.

Donna: Yes, they ³ ___ (spend) more.

3 Emma: I took my sister's jacket without asking her. She was really angry with me.

Fiona: You ⁴ ___ (ask) her first.

4 Gerry: I got home really late last night after the party and my parents weren't at all happy. I didn't apologise.

Hal: You ⁵ ___ (arrive) home on time and you ⁶ ___ (apologise) to your parents tonight.

5 Mum: Jo and Sam didn't work very hard at school last year and they failed all their exams.

Dad: They ⁷ ___ (work) harder and they ⁸ ___ (study) more in future.

Mum: Yes, I think they ⁹ ___ (talk) to their teacher now and ask her advice.

5 (✱) Future continuous and future perfect

Rewrite the sentences putting the adverbs in brackets in the correct place.

1 They will have applied for some jobs by then. (also)
They will also have applied for some jobs by then.

2 We won't be working there in five years time. (definitely)

3 He will have updated his CV by tomorrow. (certainly)

4 She will be working in the new office this time next week. (definitely)

5 She won't have started her new job before then. (probably)

6 We will have got our exam results by then. (hopefully)

6 (✱✱) Complete the sentences with the correct form of the verb in brackets.

1 I'm working on my project now. I *will have finished* (finish) it by the weekend.

2 This time tomorrow I ___ (take) my English exam.

3 I've got a summer job. In July and August I ___ (work) in an office.

4 By the end of the month I ___ (apply) for over thirty jobs!

5 This time next year they ___ (study) at university.

6 I hope that by the time I'm forty I ___ (become) a famous scientist.

7 (***) Kate has just finished studying Fashion Design at university. Read her career plan and write sentences using the future perfect and future continuous.

- find a job with a clothes design company (by the end of this year)
- work in London for one of the big fashion companies (this time next year)
- get lots of experience (by the time I'm twenty-eight)
- start my own fashion company (by the time I'm twenty-nine)
- work for myself (when I'm thirty)
- employ at least fifty people (in ten years time)
- retire (by the end of 2040)

1 *By the end of this year, I'll have found a job with a clothes design company.*

2 _____

3 _____

4 _____

5 _____

6 _____

7 _____

Vocabulary

8 (*) Skills and ambitions

Match the words 1–5 to a–e to make expressions.

1 sound   a in a team
2 positive   b attitude
3 proven   c experience
4 highly-   d IT skills
5 work   e motivated

9 (**) Complete the job advert with the expressions from exercise 8.

Office manager

A well-known company is looking for a new office manager. You should have ¹*sound IT skills* and be familiar with different computer programmes. You should also have at least three years ²____ in a position of responsibility in an office. You should be a ³____ individual who wants to succeed. We are looking for someone with a ⁴____ who always wants to improve in their job. You should be able to ⁵____ as well as manage tasks on your own.

10 (**) Read what two candidates said in the job interview and complete the interviewer's notes. Who do you think will get the job?

Amanda

I prefer working alone.

Has little ¹a*bility* to work in a ²t___ .

Yes, I've got a lot of experience with computers.

Has sound IT ³s___ .

I've got a university degree in Business Studies and I've done several management courses.

Is ⁴w___ -q___ .

No … I don't think I need any further training!

Isn't ⁵w___ to learn.

Diana

I've got good qualifications and I'd be happy to go on any courses that you offer. It's good to learn new things. I think I could bring some new ideas to the job. I'd love to try!

Is very ⁶e___ .

Yes, I think I'm very good at communicating and I enjoy working with different people.

Has good ⁷i___ s___ .

5 mini workbook

* easy to do
** a bit harder
*** extra challenge

Grammar

1 (*) Passives

Complete the sentences with the passive form of the verb in brackets.

Gig cancelled

The Stormy Sand gig in Bristol [1]*was cancelled* (cancel) last night because the lead singer, Annie James, suddenly became ill. It [2]___ (organise) as part of a tour to promote the band's new album, *Backdrop*, which [3]___ (just/release). Fans [4]___ (send) new tickets next week for the next gig on the tour, taking place in Bath.

TEENAGER GIVES RING BACK TO CHARITY SHOP

When sixteen-year-old Maddy Jackson bought a ring for five pounds at a charity shop, she had no idea it was actually worth a lot more. The ring [5]___ (give) to the charity shop by an elderly lady a few months earlier but the staff thought it was costume jewellery. However, Maddy's mother thought the jewels might be real diamonds so they took it to a jewellery shop. 'The ring [6]___ (value) at the moment. They think it might be worth about £10,000 but that [7]___ (not confirm) yet,' said Maddy. 'I'm going to give it back to the charity shop and it [8]___ (sold) later this month. I think the money should go to charity.'

Police catch art thieves

The police arrived just in time as priceless Japanese vases [9]___ (remove) from the National Gallery. The thieves [10]___ (arrest) immediately and they [11]___ (send) to prison for up to five years under a new law. 'Fortunately, the vases [12]___ (not damage),' said an art expert.

It [13]___ (believe) that the thieves [14]___ (help) by someone who works at the museum and it is possible that all staff [15]___ (investigate).

2 (*) **Underline** the correct form of the verb, active or passive.

A man [1]*has banned/has been banned* from the Tate Britain art gallery after a sculpture [2]*damaged/was damaged*. The man [3]*was looking/ was being looked* at the sculpture when he suddenly [4]*took out/was taken out* a pencil and started drawing on it. The man [5]*had previously warned/had previously been warned* by staff not to stand too near the works of art. The man [6]*has taken/has been taken* to the police station where he [7]*will charge/will be charged* with criminal damage. He [8]*may spend/may be spent* the night in prison. The sculpture [9]*is cleaning/is being cleaned* at the moment. It [10]*says/is said* that the gallery is considering introducing new security measures.

3 (***) **Complete the text with the active or passive form of the verb in brackets.**

The *Mona Lisa* [1]*is* (be) one of the most famous paintings in the world. It [2]___ (see) by millions of people every year. It is not on display at the moment because it [3]___ (clean) but it [4]___ (put back) on display again next week. There is a possibility that it [5]___ (move) to a bigger room in the museum but the curators [6]___ (not confirm) that yet. It [7]___ (paint) by Leonardo da Vinci – he [8]___ (start) in 1503 and finished it in 1507. Throughout the period it [9]___ (paint), da Vinci refused to say who the model was so today nobody [10]___ (know) for sure. Since then, the painting [11]___ (copy) or reworked in different styles by many artists. There is no doubt it [12]___ (still/be) famous in many years time.

4 (✳✳✳) Read *Grammar Plus*. Then circle the object and underline the verb in the sentences below. Write sentences using the correct form of *get* so the meaning is the same.

Grammar + Plus

get something done

We use *get something done* when we pay someone, usually a professional, to do something for us:

I **got my hair cut** last week. (I went to the hairdresser's and paid someone to cut my hair)

We're **getting the house painted** soon. (We're going to pay some decorators to paint our house)

Form: subject + the correct tense of *get* + object + past participle

Notice: do not put the person who does the job (this is understood):

He **got his motorbike repaired** ~~by a mechanic~~ last week.

This is similar to *have something done* but a little more informal. We can also use it instead of the passive:

I **had my mp3 player repaired** by a specialist.

I **got my mp3 player repaired**.

1 I paid a carpenter to <u>make</u> a (table.)
   I got a table made.

2 I'm going to ask someone to decorate my bedroom.

3 She pays a beautician to paint her nails.

4 They were paying a graphic designer to design a website.

5 My dress was made by a professional.

6 Mark is paying someone to pierce his ear.

5 (✳) More complex question forms

Order the words to make questions. Make negative questions into contractions.

1 not/you/enjoy/listening/their new album/to/do/?
   Don't you enjoy listening to their new album?

2 me/can/you/lives/the artist/where/tell/?

3 they/what/music/kind/play/of/do/?

4 wonder/what/be like/their next album/I/will/.

5 know/coming/do/when/out/is/you/the album/?

6 they/do/usually/release/their new songs/not/on the internet/?

6 (✳✳) Complete the questions.

1 Who *do you go to concerts with*?
   I go to concerts with my best friend.

2 How _____ ?
   I go to concerts every month.

3 Do you know _____ ?
   I think Gorillaz wrote that song.

4 Don't _____ ?
   Yes, I download most of my music.

5 Which _____ ?
   I listen to all of their albums.

6 Doesn't _____ ?
   Yes, Lily Allen lives in London.

7 How _____ ?
   It feels great to have a hit single!

8 Who _____ ?
   I want to work with good musicians.

Vocabulary

7 (✳✳) Performance arts

Complete the description with the correct form of the word in brackets.

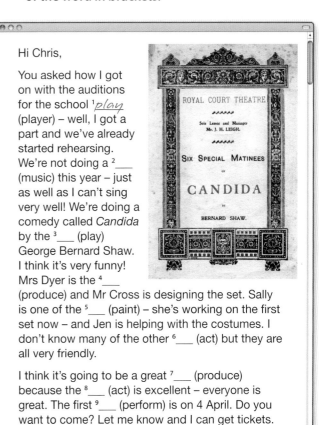

Hi Chris,

You asked how I got on with the auditions for the school ¹*play* (player) – well, I got a part and we've already started rehearsing. We're not doing a ²___ (music) this year – just as well as I can't sing very well! We're doing a comedy called *Candida* by the ³___ (play) George Bernard Shaw. I think it's very funny! Mrs Dyer is the ⁴___ (produce) and Mr Cross is designing the set. Sally is one of the ⁵___ (paint) – she's working on the first set now – and Jen is helping with the costumes. I don't know many of the other ⁶___ (act) but they are all very friendly.

I think it's going to be a great ⁷___ (produce) because the ⁸___ (act) is excellent – everyone is great. The first ⁹___ (perform) is on 4 April. Do you want to come? Let me know and I can get tickets.

Love,
Petra x

ROYAL COURT THEATRE

Sole Lessee and Manager
Mr. J. H. LEIGH.

SIX SPECIAL MATINEES

of

CANDIDA

by

BERNARD SHAW.

8 (✱✱) The new overnight sensation

Choose the correct answer.

| GIG | GUIDE | REVIEWS | NEW MUSIC | NEWS |

Grace and Glory are the sensational new band of the year. They started off by ¹ b music on the internet and all their songs got a lot of ² ___ . They started playing in small ³ ___ and then became an overnight sensation after they won a ⁴ ___ . Soon after that, they ⁵ ___ with a record label and ⁶ ___ their first album. Since then, they have had three ⁷ ___ singles.

Grace and Glory are ⁸ ___ on a world tour next month. Tickets are available from buytickets.com

1	**a** getting	**b** posting ✓	**c** having
2	**a** hits	**b** gigs	**c** clicks
3	**a** posts	**b** venues	**c** albums
4	**a** venue	**b** number one	**c** talent contest
5	**a** wrote up	**b** made up	**c** signed up
6	**a** released	**b** went	**c** got
7	**a** number one	**b** gigs	**c** venues
8	**a** releasing	**b** going	**c** getting

9 (✱✱✱) Making it alone

Write the missing letters to complete the text.

Advice for authors

- Think of an original ¹a*ngle* for the book and ²t___ the story from one or more points of ³v___ .

- Don't make the ⁴p___ too complicated or people won't understand the story.

- Always do plenty of ⁵r___ on the topic so your facts are correct.

- Send the first chapter to different people to get some constructive ⁶f___ .

- After you've written the book, look for an ⁷a___ who can find a publisher. Then you can get a good publishing ⁸d___ .

10 (✱✱✱) Active study: Phrasal verbs (2)

Rewrite the sentences replacing the underlined verbs with the correct form of a phrasal verb below. You will need to use some verbs more than once. Make any other necessary changes.

> talk (somebody) into   sign up
> come up with ✓   come out
> bring up   work out   make up

1 How did you <u>think of</u> the plot for the film?
How did you come up with the plot for the film?

2 They <u>persuaded me</u> to write a new book.

3 I read all the information about the club and then I <u>joined</u>.

4 My book <u>is being published</u> next month.

5 The actor is very strong because he <u>does exercise</u> every day.

6 I can't <u>logically solve</u> the puzzle.

7 He <u>invented</u> every bit of the story – he's got such a good imagination!

8 They <u>started discussing</u> the problem to try and find a solution.

11 (✱✱) A review

Complete the text with the words below.

> acting   cast   dialogue
> soundtrack   special effects
> storyline ✓   suspense   twists

Discussion topic:

What did you think of *Iron Man 2*?

I thought there was a good ¹*storyline* and I really liked the ² ___ – there were some funny lines.
Olga, Moscow

I loved the music! The ³ ___ is excellent.
Kate, London

Some great ⁴ ___ , especially Robert Downey Jr! The director managed to create a lot of ⁵ ___ because of the ⁶ ___ in the plot.
Marek, Warsaw

It was an all-star ⁷ ___ and I thought the ⁸ ___ were stunning but overall it was a bit disappointing.
Nick, San Diego

see earlier thread

6 miniworkbook

* easy to do
** a bit harder
*** extra challenge

Grammar

1 (*) Quantifiers

<u>Underline</u> the correct answers.

Q. My friend eats ¹*plenty of/loads of* fast food and ²*hardly any/very few* fruit. Isn't that very bad for you?

Mark

A. It's okay to eat ³*a little/few* fast food but not too much. ⁴*Very few/Very little* people have a perfect diet but it sounds like your friend has an unhealthy diet. Talk to him about it!

Q. I love hot, spicy food but my boyfriend doesn't want to try it. He loves vegetables though. What should I do?

Debbie

A. Try making a curry with only ⁵*very few/a bit of* curry powder in it and ⁶*a great deal of/a large number of* vegetables. If he likes that, then you could try something spicier.

Q. We eat ⁷*a great deal of/a number of* bread – we love it. Is that okay?

Jenny and Andy

A. That's okay as long as you eat ⁸*a large number of/plenty of* fresh fruit and vegetables. Remember, having a balanced diet is important. A diet with ⁹*hardly any/a little* fresh food isn't good for you.

Q. I don't eat very much processed food and I don't drink ¹⁰*a lot of/plenty of* fizzy drinks. But I enjoy having ¹¹*hardly any/a couple of* cakes and a cola now and then. Do you think I should stop having cakes and fizzy drinks?

Naomi

A. Don't worry, Naomi. If you only have these things occasionally that's fine. It sounds like you eat ¹²*quite a lot of/a large number of* fresh food so that's fine.

2 (**) Read the dialogue and order the pictures. Then complete the dialogue with the words below.

[a couple of   a few   a large   loads of   quite a lot of ✓   very little]

Olivia: What are you cooking?

Chloe: I'm making up a new recipe!

Olivia: Oh right, what are you putting in it?

Chloe: Oh, everything I can find! There are ¹*quite a lot of* prawns and there are ²___ tuna … and there's ³___ tin of tomatoes. There's ⁴___ salt but that doesn't matter because I'm putting in some garlic. Oh and curry powder and chilli. And chicken.

Olivia: Oh! Chicken and seafood?

Chloe: Yes, it should be interesting. I couldn't find many vegetables, only ⁵___ carrots so I'm putting in some fruit instead. There are ⁶___ apples, a bit of watermelon and three mangoes. Do you think I should put these muffins in too? Olivia? Where are you going?

Olivia: To phone for a pizza!

3 (***) Look at the pictures again and write as many sentences as you can about the quantity of the food items.

1 watermelon
   There's hardly any watermelon. There's very little watermelon. There's a bit of watermelon.

2 garlic

3 muffins

4 mangoes

5 water

6 chicken drumsticks

4 (✲) Relative clauses

Underline the correct relative pronoun.

1 Aubergines, _which/that_ are easy to find, are the main ingredient of moussaka.

2 That's the shop _that/where_ I buy all my vegetables.

3 The weekend is the time _when/where_ I usually do all my cooking.

4 Garlic, _which/where_ is supposed to be good for you, gives a wonderful flavour to food.

5 Watermelon, _who/which_ is cheap at the moment, is wonderful in a fruit salad.

6 The market _where/which_ I go has lots of fresh fruit and vegetables.

7 Jane, _who/that_ is coming for tea, loves muffins so I'll make some this morning.

8 My garden, _where/which_ I often sit, has lots of fruit trees.

5 (✲✲) Complete the sentences with the correct relative pronouns. Add commas where necessary.

1 Those are the potatoes ○ _which/ that_ ○ I cooked yesterday.

2 The potatoes ○ _which_ I roasted ○ will be fine to eat tonight.

3 My grandmother ○ ___ is a good cook ○ loves getting the family together. Mother's Day is the time ○ ___ I see all my family. We go to my grandparents' house ○ ___ the kitchen is big.

4 That's the cook ○ ___ has just won an award. The award ○ ___ is given annually ○ is for best new chef.

5 Christmas is the time ○ ___ turkey is traditionally eaten in the UK. My sister ○ ___ is a vegetarian ○ eats a nut roast instead. Many vegetarians eat nut roast ○ ___ doesn't contain any meat. Nut roast ○ ___ is easy to prepare ○ is one of my favourite dishes.

6 That's the woman ○ ___ presents that new TV cooking programme. The programme ○ ___ is watched by thousands of people every week ○ is very successful. Unfortunately, it's on TV on Wednesdays ○ ___ I go to French classes.

6 (✲✲✲) Rewrite the sentences changing the information in brackets into relative clauses. Add commas where necessary.

1 They use a lot of chilli sauce in Mexico. (It makes the food hotter.)

They use a lot of chilli sauce in Mexico, which makes the food hotter.

2 My fruit salad looked wonderful. (It contained lots of exotic fruits.)

3 That's the restaurant. (They serve roast pigeon there.)

4 We had chicken drumsticks for lunch. (They were delicious.)

5 Tuna is a healthy fish to eat. (It contains omega 3 oils.)

6 The chef at that restaurant is very famous. (My brother knows him.)

7 (✲✲) Read _Grammar Plus_. Then **underline** the correct participle.

Grammar + Plus

Reduced relative clauses

Instead of a full relative clause we can sometimes use a participle clause with a present or past participle:

The people ~~who are~~ **sitting** over there are Swedish.

We didn't see the car ~~which was~~ **coming** towards us.

Applications ~~which are~~ **sent** after the deadline will be ignored.

Let's talk about some of the problems ~~that have been~~ **discussed** today.

In these cases, the relative pronoun and auxiliary verbs are understood.

1 Australians eat sausages _making/made_ from kangaroo meat.

2 There are people in the UK _cooking/cooked_ interesting new dishes.

3 _Auld Lang Syne_ is the song _singing/sung_ in Scotland on New Year's Eve.

4 The cook _making/made_ the dish is famous in the UK.

5 Paella is a Spanish dish _making/made_ from rice and seafood.

6 I didn't recognise the man _waiting/waited_ in the restaurant.

8 (✲✲✲) Add the full relative clause to the sentences in exercise 7.

                    which/that are
1 _Australians eat sausages|made from kangaroo meat._

2 _____

3 _____

4 _____

5 _____

6 _____

Vocabulary

9 (✱✱) **Complete the sentences with words from unit 6.**

1 In Indian cooking they use a lot of
   curry powder .

2 My favourite fruits are ___ and ___ .

3 I don't like seafood so I never eat ___
   or ___ .

4 I really love vegetables, especially ___ .
   I don't like turnip, though.

5 I don't eat many sweet things but I do
   like ___ .

6 I'm vegetarian so I never eat ___ or ___ .

10 (✱) **Describing dishes**

Choose the correct answer to complete the set menu.

Starters

Salad with ¹___ goat's cheese
Chicken drumsticks with a ²___ sauce - very hot!

Main courses

³___ pigeon with ⁴___ potatoes and ⁵___ cabbage
⁶___ chicken with chips ~ a dish full of ⁷___ !
⁸___ fish and salad

Chef's special

Ciabatta with spinach and eggs on top - they're soft
and ⁹___ - and delicious!

Desserts

¹⁰___ fruit salad
Ice cream

1	a pickled	b grilled ✓	
2	a spicy	b raw	
3	a raw	b roast	
4	a mashed	b lean	
5	a pickled	b runny	
6	a mashed	b lean	
7	a tender	b protein	
8	a grilled	b soft	
9	a runny	b disgusting	
10	a exotic	b flavour	

11 (✱✱) **Discussing holiday options**

Complete the texts with words from the boxes. There is one extra word in each box.

> sunbathing   beach resort ✓
> package holiday   hiring   chilling out

Do you want to relax this summer?

Come to our world-famous ¹_beach resort_ in Mexico.
It's perfect for ²___ (you'll be beautifully sun-tanned
after a week) and ³___ – you don't have to do anything.
Everything is included in the price – it's a fantastic ⁴___ !
You won't get a better deal than this!

> backpack   beaten track   guide   hiking
> hitch-hike   self-catering   roughing it

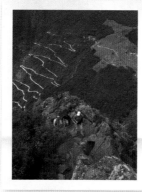

Do you want to get off the ⁵___?

Then try a ⁶___ holiday this year.
All you need is a ⁷___ to carry your
things. Our ⁸___ will take you to all
the best places. But be warned:
you will be ⁹___ because there are
no luxury hotels! Accommodation
is all ¹⁰___ . A great holiday that
everyone can afford!

> alone   the locals   five-star   city break
> guided tour   landmarks   room service

Do you want a short luxury holiday?

Try our ¹¹___ in Amsterdam. You can take a ¹²___ of the
city and see the famous local ¹³___ or simply walk round
and meet ¹⁴___ . There are plenty of restaurants or you
can stay in your ¹⁵___ hotel and order ¹⁶___ .

7 miniworkbook

⁑ easy to do
⁑⁑ a bit harder
⁑⁑⁑ extra challenge

Grammar

1 ⁑ Articles

<u>Underline</u> the correct article or (ø) if an article is not needed.

Michel Lioto is ¹*the*/<u>*a*</u> French entertainer. He is called 'Monsieur Mangetout' (Mr Eat-it-all) because he eats objects made of ²*the*/*ø* glass, metal or rubber! He began eating unusual objects when he was ³*a*/*ø* child. In the past he has eaten ⁴*a*/*the* bicycle and ⁵*a*/*the* TV! He cuts up ⁶*the*/*ø* objects into pieces and then eats them. Once, he even ate ⁷*a*/*the* whole plane. It took him two years but he ate every single piece of ⁸*a*/*the* aircraft! How does he do it? Experts aren't sure but they think ⁹*the*/*an* inside of his stomach is thicker than in ordinary ¹⁰*the*/*ø* people. Luckily, Lioto's strange diet doesn't cause him any problems. You can watch ¹¹*a*/*ø* video of Lioto on ¹²*a*/*the* internet – it's amazing!

2 ⁑⁑ Complete the gaps with *a, an, the* or write (ø) for no article.

¹*The* brain is ²___ amazing thing – it tells us what we see. However, it can be fooled by ³___ optical illusion. ⁴___ optical illusions use ⁵___ colour, light and patterns to create images that can deceive our brains into seeing things which may or may not be real. For example, if you look at ⁶___ picture A, ⁷___ purple lines appear to be curved. However, if you use ⁸___ ruler, you see that ⁹___ lines are in fact straight. In picture B there's ¹⁰___ red box and ¹¹___ orange dot but where is ¹²___ dot? Is it in front of ¹³___ box or behind it? ¹⁴___ people who think it's in front don't believe ¹⁵___ people who say it's behind. Of course, both are possible! If you want to create ¹⁶___ optical illusion, you can look on the internet for ¹⁷___ information on how to do so. Then you can create your own illusions to confuse your friends!

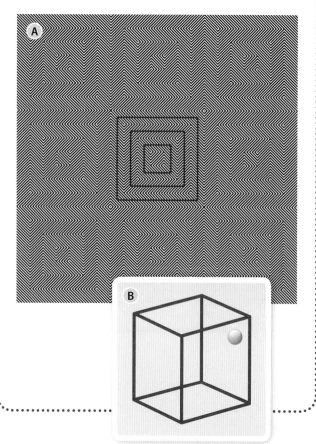

3 (⁕⁕) Read *Grammar Plus*. Then complete the sentences with *the* or write (ø) for no article.

Articles with geographical features

Use *the* with names of oceans, rivers and seas but not with lakes:

*We sailed up **the Nile** and then we visited **Lake Victoria**.*

*Have you swum in **the Mediterranean** or **the Atlantic**?*

Names of mountains don't usually have articles (except *the Matterhorn, the Eiger*) but we use *the* with mountain ranges:

*She's climbed **K2** and now she's in **the Alps**.*

1 **A:** Have you been to ¹*the* Amazon?

   B: No but I've been to ² ___ Lake Titicaca. It's amazing.

2 **A:** Many people have died trying to climb ³ ___ Everest.

   B: Yes but it's ⁴ ___ mountain that everyone wants to climb. I prefer ⁵ ___ Carpathian Mountains.

3 **A:** Last year we sailed across ⁶ ___ Atlantic.

   B: I bet it took a long time to cross ⁷ ___ ocean!

4 **A:** Did you know, ⁸ ___ Thames is one of the most famous rivers in the UK?

   B: Yes, I took a boat trip down part of ⁹ ___ river last year. And I went canoeing on ¹⁰ ___ Loch Ness but I didn't see the monster!

4 (⁕) Modals of ability

<u>Underline</u> the correct answer.

1 After trying for many hours, he finally *managed to/could* solve the puzzle.

2 When I was only two years old I *can/could* swim. I *was able to/succeeded in* swim the length of the pool by the time I was four.

3 John *managed to/was able to* pick me up at the airport so I didn't have to get a taxi.

4 We *aren't able to/weren't able to* climb the mountain yesterday because the weather was bad.

5 *Could you/Were you able* understand what he was saying?

6 I hope that I will *be able to/can* speak Chinese in the future. I *can/managed to* already speak four other languages.

5 (⁕⁕⁕) Complete the text with *can, could, able to, managed to* or *succeeded in* and the correct form of the verb in brackets. In some cases, more than one answer is possible.

The Magnetic Man
(Liew Thow Lin)

Liew Thow Lin has an amazing ability – he ¹*can make/is able to make* (make) metal objects stick to his body. He was in the news recently because he ² ___ (pull) a car twenty metres using a metal hook that was attached to some metal on his stomach! Lin discovered that he ³ ___ (make) metal objects stick to him 'magnetically' after reading an article about a whole family in Taiwan who ⁴ ___ (do) it. He tried it and found that he ⁵ ___ (get) many different types of metal to stick. Once, he even ⁶ ___ (get) an iron to stick to him – not only that, he ⁷ ___ (put) three bricks on top of it! Nobody knows how he ⁸ ___ (do) it but three of his sons and two of his grandchildren ⁹ ___ (do) it too! Perhaps in the future everyone ¹⁰ ___ (do) it but it's unlikely!

Vocabulary

6 (✻) Qualities of mind

Unscramble the letters to complete the sentences.

1 People who can understand other people's feelings and emotions are _empathetic_ (pecihtetma).

2 I can't understand John's notes. The information is very ___ (labyd-goresidna).

3 Kate likes to think for herself; she's very ___ (dendneptein).

4 Mark is very good at ___ (rsenigscop) information and understanding the most important ideas.

5 Leanne is very good at planning and making decisions; she's very ___ (ratalicpc).

6 Writers have to be creative and ___ (amgeitanivi) to think of ideas for their stories.

7 (✻✻) Match the quiz questions and answers.

THE BRAIN CHALLENGE!

How well do you know your brain?

1 [d] Can you understand how someone feels because you can imagine what it is like to be them?

2 [ ] Can you explain your ideas clearly when you're speaking to someone?

3 [ ] Do you make decisions quickly without thinking about the consequences?

4 [ ] Are you good at solving puzzles where you have to put geometric shapes in the correct place?

5 [ ] Can you think of ideas fast and solve problems without taking too much time?

6 [ ] Are you good at doing more than one thing at the same time and doing them all well?

7 [ ] Are you good at examining things in detail to understand them?

8 [ ] Are you good at painting, drawing or sculpture?

a Yes? Then you're analytical.

b Yes? Then you're artistic.

c Yes? Then you have good spatial skills.

d Yes? Then you're strongly empathetic.

e Yes? Then you've got good verbal skills.

f Yes? Then you're quick-thinking

g Yes? Then you're impulsive.

h Yes? Then you're good at multi-tasking.

8 (✻✻) Health

Complete the crossword.

Across

1 Is the _healthcare_ in your country state funded?

5 His illness isn't serious; doctors think they can ___ him easily.

7 You shouldn't ___ your health by eating too much junk food and not sleeping enough.

9 He needs to go to hospital to have ___ on his knee. The operation is tomorrow.

10 What ___ is your doctor giving you for your illness?

11 My kidneys don't work properly so I'm going to have a ___ next week. That means I'll be able to lead a normal life again!

12 Many cancer patients are given ___ to treat the disease.

Down

2 He was in a serious accident. Doctors are using machines to keep him ___ at the moment but they hope he'll recover completely.

3 He is extremely overweight. He's 150 kilos! He's ___ .

4 Do you ___ from any serious illnesses?

6 His liver has stopped working completely so he has liver ___ .

8 When I die I want someone to have my liver and my kidneys, that's why I'm an ___ .

8 miniworkbook

* easy to do
** a bit harder
*** extra challenge

Grammar

1 (**) **Reported speech**

Look at the cartoon and write the reported questions.

1 Do you like this song?

2 Would you like to dance?

3 Have you been here before?

4 What's your name?

5 Who did you come with tonight?

6 Will you be here next week?

7 What are you thinking about?

8 Do you always ask so many questions?

1 He asked *if she liked the song* .
2 He asked _____ .
3 He asked _____ .
4 He asked _____ .
5 He asked _____ .
6 He asked _____ .
7 He asked _____ .
8 She asked _____ .

2 (**) **Match the answers a–h to the questions 1–8 in exercise 1. Then write the answers in reported speech. Delete any unnecessary words.**

a [2] 'Yes, I'd love to dance. I enjoy dancing,' she told him.

She told him she'd love to dance and that she loves dancing.

b [ ] 'My name's Izabelle, but everyone calls me 'Izzy',' she said.

c [ ] 'I don't know. I might come next week but I'm not sure,' she said.

d [ ] 'I came with my friends. They were sitting over there but they had to leave early,' she told him.

e [ ] 'I'm not thinking about anything, I'm just resting,' she said.

f [ ] 'Yes, I really love it,' she said.

g [ ] 'No, I don't usually ask so many questions but I'm a bit nervous!' he told her.

h [ ] 'No, it's the first time I've ever been here,' she said.

3 (*) **Reporting verbs**

Choose the correct answer.

1 He refused *a* it.
  a to do ✓   b doing

2 He insisted ___ ten new albums.
  a to buy   b on buying

3 She warned me ___ the site.
  a not to use   b not using

4 Max ___ he wouldn't spend any more money.
  a promised to his parents   b promised his parents that

5 They denied ___ fake designer goods.
  a to buy   b buying

6 The bank manager ___ of stealing some money.
  a accused   b accused them

7 He explained ___ in cash.
  a that he had paid   b paying

8 Roxy admitted ___ her bank statement.
  a that she hadn't checked   b not to check

4 (✷✷) Rewrite the sentences using the people and verbs in brackets. Remember, you don't always need to report every word.

1 'I bought the jeans online without checking the size properly!'
(Sally/admit)
Sally admitted that she had bought the jeans online without checking the size.

2 'I put my credit card somewhere safe and now I can't find it!'
(Mark/explain)

3 'That was stupid, Jim! You shouldn't have bought another phone!'
(Celia/criticise)

4 'I'll lend you the money, you can repay me later.'
(Layla/offer/her friend)

5 'I'm sorry Sasha, I won't borrow your clothes again.'
(Holly/apologise for)

6 'Why don't you get a bank loan?'
(the salesman/suggest/Daniel)

5 (✷✷✷) Match the verbs to the sentences. Then rewrite the sentences in reported speech. Remember, you don't always need to report every word.

> advise   congratulate   refuse ✓
> persuade   remind   accuse

1 'I won't tell you what I spent the money on and that's final!' he said to me. *refuse*
He refused to tell me what he had spent the money on and said that was final.

2 'Go on! Buy the computer game, it's on special offer!' Mark said to his friend.

3 'You should always check your bank statements,' Kate's mum said to her.

4 'Don't forget to keep the receipt after you buy something,' Mike's dad said to him.

5 'You've bought some fake designer clothes, haven't you?!' Felix said to Sam.

6 'Well done! You've repaid all your debts, that's fantastic,' Rachel said to Tanya.

6 (✷✷✷) Read *Grammar Plus*. Then rewrite the sentences using two different structures.

Grammar + Plus

Reporting verbs

Some reporting verbs can take more than one structure:

'I used the credit card.' → He admitted **using/that he had used** the credit card.

'Let's go to the park.' → She suggested **going/that we go** to the park.

'Yes, I'll help you.' → He offered **to help** me/He offered **(me) his help.**

'Don't buy anything from that website, it's not safe.' → She warned me **not to buy** anything from the site./She warned me **that it wasn't safe to buy** anything from that website.

'Yes, I'll do it.' → He agreed **to do/that he would do** it.

'Don't forget to buy bread.' → She reminded **me to buy/that I should buy** bread.

1 'Remember you have to buy Kate's birthday present tomorrow,' Lucy said to Steve.
Lucy reminded Steve to buy Kate's birthday present.
Lucy reminded Steve that he had to buy Kate's birthday present.

2 'Why don't we buy a new TV?' Matt said to his wife.

3 'I'll lend you my car,' Simon said to Amanda.

4 'Stop it! I'll tell Mum and Dad,' Maeve said to her brother.

5 'Actually, I spend too much money and now I've got an overdraft,' Nathan said.

6 'Don't forget to check your bank statement,' Martin said to me.

Vocabulary

7 (✱✱) Advertising

Complete the web posts with the words below.

[aimed   brand   campaigns   jingle
  logos   promote ✓   slogan   target]

Advertising – love it or hate it, it's here to stay. Tell us your opinion!

Alexia, Glasgow on 14 June, 4.38 p.m.

Why do companies need to
¹*promote* products with advertising?
If the product's good, then it will sell
by itself!

Reply

Simon, Manchester on 14 June, 5.16 p.m.

I think most advertising ²___ are a
waste of time. You might read the ³___
but do you remember the name of the
⁴___ ? Most people don't!

Reply

Joanne, London on 15 June, 8.33 a.m.

@Simon, I don't agree! I think there
are some really clever campaigns.
They know who their ⁵___ audience is
and they design an advert to appeal
to them. Do you remember the Fanta
advert? It was clearly ⁶___ at young
people. They used a popular song for
the ⁷___ and changed the words. For
a few weeks everyone was singing it.
Now everyone associates that song
with the drink and with being happy.

Reply

Pete, Leeds on 15 June, 9.12 a.m.

I don't think advertising is very
successful. I see ⁸___ all the time.
I recognise them but I've no idea
what company they are — I can just
about remember the yellow 'M' for
McDonald's but that's all!

Reply

8 (✱) Shopping

Underline the correct answer.

Tips for shopping

🪝 When you buy something, always keep
the ¹*receipt*/*refund* – you will need it if the
product is ²*funny*/*faulty* and you have to take
it back for an exchange or a ³*refund*/*return*.

🪝 If you ⁴*order*/*charge* something online, check
if it is in ⁵*stock*/*store* first – you don't want to
have to wait weeks for them to deliver it. Also,
make sure you use a ⁶*sure*/*secure* website –
don't give your credit card ⁷*details*/*statement*
on sites that aren't safe. Always check
your credit card ⁸*statement*/*note* after
to make sure you have been charged
the correct amount.

🪝 Be careful with bargains!
Sometimes things are on
special ⁹*offer*/*order* because
they are not good quality.

🪝 If you pay in cash, check
your ¹⁰*change*/*charge*
immediately – you can't go
back to the shop later and
say they didn't give you
the correct money.

9 (✱✱) Generation debt

Write the missing letters to complete the sentences.

1 I haven't got much money. I can't a*fford* to buy a new phone.

2 I opened my first b___ a___ when I went to university. I haven't got much money in it, though!

3 I have to go and see the bank manager because I'm o___ . I took more money out of the bank than I had in my account.

4 We got a b___ l___ of £5,000 to buy our car. We have to pay it back over the next five years.

5 If you are in serious d___ and owe a lot of money, you can talk to financial advisers about the best way to r___ the money.

6 If you owe money to a credit card company, don't i___ the problem. Credit card companies charge a lot of interest.

miniworkbook

✳ easy to do
✳✳ a bit harder
✳✳✳ extra challenge

Grammar

1 ✳ **Gerunds and infinitives**

Read the prisoner's confession and <u>underline</u> correct answers.

I tried ¹*to get/getting* a job many times but I couldn't. I thought about ²*to ask/asking* for help but the people I had asked before refused ³*to help/helping* so I gave up. Because I wasn't able ⁴*to get/getting* a job, I became a criminal. ⁵*Stealing/To steal* things is wrong, I know but I didn't have any choice. I stole things ⁶*to get/getting* money for food. I never enjoyed ⁷*to steal/stealing* anything, in fact I regretted ⁸*to take/taking* every single thing. Circumstances forced ⁹*me to do/to do* it. I avoided ¹⁰*to get caught/getting caught* for months but then the police managed ¹¹*to catch/catching* me. I'm planning ¹²*to apologise/apologising* to everyone.

2 ✳✳ **Complete the sentences with the gerund or infinitive form of the verb in brackets.**

1 The police were waiting <u>*to catch*</u> (catch) the robbers. The police allowed them ___ (think) they were alone and then they arrested them.

2 The criminals spent a lot of time ___ (plan) the robbery. However they couldn't avoid ___ (be/arrest) because they made so many mistakes.

3 The gang wore disguises ___ (prevent) anyone from recognising them. They were unlucky ___ (get/catch) because someone recognised their shoes!

4 Judges are looking into ___ (give) more severe sentences. They want ___ (increase) the sentences for armed robbery.

5 During the trial, the accused decided ___ (plead) guilty ___ (get) a shorter sentence.

3 ✳✳ **Modals of deduction**

Rewrite the sentences using present modals of deduction.

1 I'm sure the criminals are from London.
The criminals <u>*must be from London*</u> .

2 I'm sure they aren't very intelligent because they made a lot of mistakes.
They _____ .

3 Perhaps they stole money because they're poor.
They _____ .

4 It's possible they are unemployed.
They _____ .

5 They know the area well, I'm sure.
They _____ .

6 They definitely don't care about the victims.
They _____ .

4 ✳✳ **Complete the article with past modals of deduction and the correct form of the verb in brackets.**

Surprise for car thieves!

Car thieves who stole a truck and trailer two days ago ¹<u>*must have thought*</u> (think) they had done well when they managed to get away. However, the truck and trailer belonged to a zoo and the thieves ²___ (get) a shock when they discovered the contents of the trailer – a tiger! They ³___ (know) what was in the trailer when they stole the truck or they wouldn't have stolen it. The police think the thieves ⁴___ (steal) the truck because it looks expensive or perhaps they ⁵___ (take) it because it was parked in a quiet place. The police got an anonymous phone call about the truck so the thieves ⁶___ (panic) when they realised they had stolen a tiger, too. Zoo staff say the tiger ⁷___ (be) hungry because it hadn't been fed for hours. The tiger ⁸___ (be) aggressive because it was hungry. Police found some meat near the abandoned trailer so the thieves ⁹___ (try) to feed it but they obviously ¹⁰___ (be) successful.

5 (✳✳✳) Read the start of a newspaper story and complete the reporter's notes using present or past modal verbs.

FAKE ATM USED BY THIEVES

Thieves in Beijing, China, set up a fake ATM★ machine. The device looked exactly like a normal ATM machine but it recorded the bank details of anyone who used it. The thieves then used the information to rob people's accounts and steal thousands of yuan …

★ an ATM (automated teller machine) is a machine that dispenses cash from your bank account when you insert your bank card and enter your personal identification number (PIN)

- The thieves ¹*must know* (know) a lot about technology.

- They ² ___ (research) the location carefully because a lot of people used the machine. They ³ ___ (choose) the location because it's near a lot of offices – it's possible … perhaps they thought business people would use it.

- The people who used the machine ⁴ ___ (suspect) anything or they wouldn't have used it. I'm sure the machines looked authentic – they ⁵ ___ (seem) totally convincing.

- The thieves only stole money from accounts with a lot of money. All the victims ⁶ ___ (be) rich.

- The thieves knew a lot about banking – they ⁷ ___ (work) in a bank before, that's possible.

- The police have arrested the thieves. The thieves ⁸ ___ (be) in prison now.

6 (✳✳) Read *Grammar Plus*. Then complete the conversation between two policemen with a modal of deduction and the correct form of the verb in brackets.

Grammar + Plus

Modals of deduction

Use modals of deduction with continuous tenses to make deductions about the present.

Form: modal + *be* + *-ing*:

*It's late and John isn't answering his phone. He **must be sleeping**.*

*Jackie isn't at home. She often plays basketball. She **could be playing** basketball now.*

We can also use modals of deduction with continuous tenses to make deductions about the past.

Form: modal + *have* + *been* + *-ing*:

*I don't know what Mike was doing at 5.00 p.m. He **can't have been playing** football because he never plays then. I suppose he **might have been studying**.*

Jones: So, what do we know about the crime?

Smith: Well, it happened last night. The victim ¹*must have been watching* (watch) TV because it's still on.

Jones: Yes, she ² ___ (sit) in this chair, it's right in front of the TV.

Smith: And there are footprints outside the window. I think the burglar ³ ___ (watch) the woman.

Jones: Yes, that's possible. He ⁴ ___ (wait) for the right moment to break in. I wonder why the woman didn't hear him … the TV sound is off.

Smith: Perhaps she fell asleep.

Jones: Yes, she ⁵ ___ (sleep) when he came in. I'm sure that's why she didn't hear him. I wonder where the burglar is now.

Smith: Look, the jewellery box is almost empty. He ⁶ ___ (try) to sell the jewellery. It's possible.

Jones: Yes, he ⁷ ___ (try) to make some money to escape.

Smith: You might be right. It's possible he ⁸ ___ (leave) the country right now! Let's phone the airports.

Vocabulary

7 (✱✱) Crime and justice

Complete the word puzzle. What is the mystery crime word?

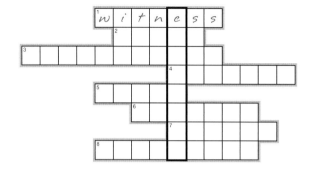

1 The _witness_ saw exactly what happened during the crime.
2 The lawyers managed to ___ that the gang members were guilty.
3 The ___ lawyer tries to show that someone is guilty.
4 The ___ lawyer tries to show that someone on trial is innocent.
5 The ___ decides how to punish criminals at the end of a trial.
6 Some criminals ___ that they have committed crimes.
7 How many people ___ crimes every year?
8 The guilty criminals were ___ to ten years in prison.

8 (✱✱) Truth and lies

Complete the sentences with the words below.

> admitted   cheating   conned ✓   forged
> fraud   pretended   taken in

1 The hoaxers _conned_ a lot of people. However, they got a long prison sentence for ___ people out of their money.
2 The hoax was very convincing and many people were ___ by it – they totally believed it.
3 They ___ documents to make their claims seem genuine.
4 The thieves ___ their car had broken down and robbed the people who stopped to help them.
5 During the court case, they ___ the truth about the hoax and they were sent to prison for committing ___ .

9 (✱✱) Crime

Complete the definitions with the correct crime words below.

> community service   life imprisonment ✓
> imprisonment   fined   parole
> sentenced to death   suspended sentence

1 _Life imprisonment_ is a punishment where someone is sent to prison for the rest of their life.

2 A ___ is time that someone will have to spend in prison only if they commit another crime within a certain period of time.

3 ___ is work that someone does as punishment instead of going to prison.

4 ___ is permission to leave prison early on the condition that you obey particular rules.

5 If you are ___ you have to pay the court a certain amount of money.

6 ___ is the punishment of being put in prison.

7 If you are ___ , you will be killed by the state for the crime you committed.

10 (✱) Active study: Word families

Complete the sentences with the correct form of the words in brackets.

1 Police caught the _robber_ (rob) while he was committing a ___ (rob). The man had previously been in prison for ___ (burgle).
2 The ___ (kidnap) hid the child in his van. It was the first case of ___ (kidnap) in the area.
3 The teenagers were arrested for ___ (shoplift). The shop owners decided to ___ (prosecute) them.
4 The ___ (fraud) was sentenced to five years in prison because he had committed ___ (fraud).
5 The ___ (prosecute) lawyer and the ___ (defend) lawyer both talked to the judge about the case.

10 miniworkbook

* easy to do
** a bit harder
*** extra challenge

Grammar

1 (*) *wish* and *if only*

Read the texts and <u>underline</u> the correct answer.

I'm from a village in Scotland but I moved to London last year. I'm not happy here. I wish I [1]*don't move/didn't move/<u>hadn't moved</u>* here. If only I still [2]*live/lived/had lived* in Scotland! I live in a flat in the city but I don't like it. I wish I [3]*live/didn't live/don't live* in a flat. I can't have pets in the flat but I'd love to get a cat. If only I [4]*can/can't/could* have a cat. I wish I [5]*live/lived/had lived* in a house with a garden.

I live in a really quiet village. I wish it [6]*was/wasn't/isn't* so boring. My friends have all gone to university this year but I failed my exams. If only I [7]*failed/didn't fail/hadn't failed* my exams. I wish I [8]*didn't study/hadn't studied/had studied* more!

2 (***) Look at the pictures and write two sentences using *wish* and *if only* for each problem.

1 I lost my job. I can't find another one.

2 I can't pay the rent. I haven't got any money.

3 I left the nightclub late last night and I missed the last bus.

4 I didn't learn to drive. It's hard to get around without a car.

5 There aren't any good facilities where I live. The nightlife is terrible.

6 I've got a big bill for my mobile phone. I phone my friends all the time.

7 I haven't seen my son very often this year. The transport links here are bad.

8 I can't afford to move. I want to live nearer my son.

1 I wish *I hadn't lost my job* .
  If only *I could find another job* .

2 I wish _____ .
  If only _____ .

3 I wish _____ .
  If only _____ .

4 I wish _____ .
  If only _____ .

5 I wish _____ .
  If only _____ .

6 I wish _____ .
  If only _____ .

7 I wish _____ .
  If only _____ .

8 I wish _____ .
  If only _____ .

3 (✲✲) Read *Grammar Plus*. Then complete the sentences using the correct form of the verb in brackets.

Grammar **+** Plus

We use *it's time* + person + past simple to say we think something should happen now:

You aren't in bed yet. **It's time you went** to bed.

They don't work hard at school. **It's time they started** to study more.

We use *I'd rather* + person + past simple to express our desire for another person to do or not do something:

I don't want you here. **I'd rather you left**.

Why are you doing that? **I'd rather you didn't do** it.

Jake wants to talk to Karris about the problem. **I'd rather he talked** to me about it.

Mark: Have you heard? Steve and Kelly are moving to London.

Paula: What? But Kelly's my best friend! I'd rather ¹*they didn't move* (they/not move) to another city.

Mark: Please don't tell Kelly I told you. I'd rather ² ___ (you/not tell) her. She wants to tell you herself.

Paula: Well, she hasn't returned any of my messages. It's time ³ ___ (she/get) in touch!

Mark: I'll ask her to call you.

Paula: No, I'd rather ⁴ ___ (you/not do) that. I'd rather ⁵ ___ (she/ring) me when she's ready.

Mark: Okay. Listen, it's getting late … It's time ⁶ ___ (I/leave). I'm going to miss the bus.

Paula: Okay, see you tomorrow.

Mark: Bye.

4 (✲) Third conditional

Underline the correct answer.

When Kate MacDonald bought her new house she didn't know it was going to change her life! The house had a garden so Kate started gardening. She discovered she loved it. If she ¹*wouldn't have bought*/**hadn't bought** the house she ²*might not have discovered*/*hadn't discovered* her love of gardening. Two of the neighbours were so impressed by Kate's garden that they asked her to do theirs. The neighbours ³*hadn't asked*/*wouldn't have asked* her to do their gardens if they ⁴*hadn't seen*/*wouldn't have seen* hers. If Kate ⁵*hadn't started*/*wouldn't have started* to do other people's gardens, she ⁶*might not have decided*/*hadn't decided* to leave her job and start a business. Now Kate has a successful business and she loves her life. If she ⁷*had stayed*/*hadn't stayed* in her old job, she ⁸*might not have become*/*might have become* so successful.

5 (✲✲✲) Mixed conditional

Join the sentences to make mixed conditional sentences. Add commas and make any other changes if necessary.

1 Kate started gardening. She has a beautiful garden now.
   If Kate hadn't started gardening, she wouldn't have a beautiful garden now.

2 Kate read as much as she could about gardening. She knows a lot about it now.

3 Kate's neighbours saw her garden. Kate does their gardening now.

4 Kate started gardening. She has a successful gardening business now.

5 Kate started her own business. She doesn't work in an office now.

6 (✲✲) Read the article and complete the text with the correct form of the verbs in brackets. Use *might* if you think it's appropriate.

WEDDING WITH A DIFFERENCE!

When most people get married, they choose a church or a hall or even their home for the wedding – not Connor Robson and Lindsey Turner. They chose a supermarket! Why? Connor was working at the supermarket when Lindsey came in one day. If ¹*he hadn't been* (not be) at work that day, he ² ___ (not meet) Lindsey. Lindsey doesn't normally shop there but that day she went to visit a friend and the supermarket was nearby. If she ³ ___ (not visit) her friend, she ⁴ ___ (not go) to the supermarket. She ⁵ ___ (not meet) Connor if she ⁶ ___ (go) to her usual supermarket.

In the supermarket, Lindsey asked Connor a question and they started chatting. If she ⁷ ___ (not ask) Connor a question, they ⁸ ___ (not start) chatting. Connor ⁹ ___ (ask) Lindsey out if they ¹⁰ ___ (start) chatting. If they ¹¹ ___ (not start) going out, then they ¹² ___ (not fall) in love and decided to get married. They chose the supermarket for their wedding because if they ¹³ ___ (not be) there that day, they ¹⁴ ___ (not get) married. Where are they going to live? Near the supermarket, of course!

Vocabulary

7 (✱✱) Home and environment

Complete the descriptions with the words below. There are two extra words.

> transport links   cramped
> culturally diverse   family-friendly
> spaces ✓   lively atmosphere   traffic
> views   scenery   local facilities

Location	Property	Energy-rating

Cottage for sale

If you love green ¹spaces and beautiful ²____ , then this could be your ideal home! It's in a small village and has fantastic ³____ of the mountains. The village is very ⁴____ so it's a great place to live if you have children. There's a train station in the village, you can be in the city in just thirty minutes and there are regular buses – the ⁵____ are excellent.

£190,000

Two bedroom flat for rent

The flat is in the city centre in a ⁶____ area with people of many different nationalities. There are plenty of places to go out and there is a ⁷____ ! There are also good ⁸____ such as a supermarket and sports centre.

£1,100 a month

8 (✱✱) Unscramble the letters to complete the description.

I live in a small town in the country. The ¹scenery (sreycen) around the town is wonderful. Because it's a small town, there's a great ²____ (sseen fo momuytcin) and people help each other. Some people complain that there's ³____ (tonignh) to do at night but I think if you want ⁴____ (nefitlihg) or ⁵____ (nteaentnimret) then you can easily go into the big town nearby. What are the benefits for me? Well, there's very little noise, there's no ⁶____ (ertilt) on the ground (no papers or other rubbish). There aren't many cars so the ⁷____ (firtcaf) isn't a problem and there isn't much ⁸____ (luonipolt) so the air's clean. And I live in a big house with a lot of space, not in a small ⁹____ (rapcmde) flat.

9 (✱) Buying and selling houses

Choose the correct answer.

Sarah put her house ¹b . Sam saw the sign and arranged to ²____ .

Sam ³____ an offer but Sarah ⁴____ it.

Then Sam and Sarah ⁵____ until they agreed a ⁶____ .

The sale went ⁷____ and Sam ⁸____ yesterday. Now he's a happy ⁹____ and he's looking for a ¹⁰____ for his old house.

1 a for sale	b up for sale ✓
2 a look round	b look into
3 a made	b moved
4 a returned	b rejected
5 a negotiated	b argued
6 a cost	b price
7 a up	b through
8 a moved in	b moved into
9 a estate agent	b homeowner
10 a buyer	b mortgage

Unit 2, page 21, exercise 5 (Student A)

You are a newspaper journalist. You are writing an article about a new EasyBuy supermarket that is being built on a school sports field. Try to get through to the PR manager.

Unit 8, page 79, exercise 6

What is the problem?

- A has recently left home and is managing his/her own finances for the first time. He/She is finding it very difficult and is borrowing a lot of money from friends.
- A was offered a credit card by his/her bank a few months ago and now has a very large bill which he/she can't pay.

How did the person get into this situation?

- He/She is very badly organised and doesn't open letters from the bank, etc.
- He/She has rich friends and is trying to do everything that they do.
- He/She can't resist adverts/expensive shops/designer goods, etc.

Who has he/she spoken to about the problem?

- the people he/she borrowed from
- family
- no one – he/she is too scared/embarrassed

What did the people above say?

- They were very angry.
- They wouldn't help.
- They offered to lend him/her even more money.

What advice can B give?

(See tips in exercise 7 plus your own ideas.)

Unit 6, page 59, exercise 7a (Student A)

Holiday option 1
Beach holiday in Cornwall, UK

Accommodation: A self-catering apartment in Newquay, a large beach resort, popular with surfers and teenagers.

Things to do: Surfing, mountain biking, chilling out on the beach with other young people and loads of good nightlife! And if you like hiking, there are a large number of coastal walks and beautiful beaches.

Weather in May: The British weather is never reliable! If you're lucky you'll be sunbathing on the beach but it can be cold and there's always the risk of rain.

Cost and length of stay: The UK is quite expensive. The apartment costs £80 per night and you'll need about £20 a day for food. You can afford to stay for a week.

Unit 9 page 84, exercise 1

Word List

achievement (n)	/əˈtʃiːvmənt/
all of a sudden (adv)	/ɔːl əv eɪ ˈsʌdn/
amazed (adj)	/əˈmeɪzd//
amazingly (adv)	/əˈmeɪzɪŋli/
boiling (adj)	/ˈbɔɪlɪŋ/
boxer (n)	/ˈbɒksə/
brilliant (adj)	/ˈbrɪljənt/
challenge (n)	/ˈtʃæləndʒ/
coach (n)	/kəʊtʃ/
compete (v)	/kəmˈpiːt/
competition (n)	/ˌkɒmpəˈtɪʃən/
competitor (n)	/kəmˈpetɪtə/
dedication (n)	/ˌdedɪˈkeɪʃən/
desperate (adj)	/ˈdespərət/
determination (n)	/dɪˌtɜːməˈneɪʃən/
discipline (n)	/ˈdɪsɪplɪn/
event (n)	/ɪˈvent/
eventually (adv)	/ɪˈventʃuəli, -tʃəli/
exhausted (adj)	/ɪɡˈzɔːstɪd/
finishing line (n)	/ˈfɪnɪʃɪŋ laɪn/
fortunately (adv)	/ˈfɔːtʃənətli/
freezing (adj)	/ˈfriːzɪŋ/
furious (adj)	/ˈfjʊəriəs/
goalkeeper (n)	/ˈɡəʊlˌkiːpə/
gradually (adv)	/ˈɡrædʒuəli/
hard work (n)	/hɑːd wɜːk/
hike (v)	/haɪk/
hiking (n)	/ˈhaɪkɪŋ/
hilarious (adj)	/hɪˈleəriəs/
hockey (n)	/ˈhɒki/
huge (adj)	/hjuːdʒ/
inspiration (n)	/ˌɪnspəˈreɪʃən/
luck (n)	/lʌk/
match (n)	/mætʃ/
motivation (n)	/ˌməʊtəˈveɪʃən/
natural talent (n)	/ˈnætʃərəl ˈtælənt/
outstanding (adj)	/aʊtˈstændɪŋ/
play (v)	/pleɪ/
pressure (n)	/ˈpreʃə/
race (n)	/reɪs/
respect (n)	/rɪˈspekt/
sacrifice (n)	/ˈsækrəfaɪs/
sadly (adv)	/ˈsædli/
satisfaction (n)	/ˌsætəsˈfækʃən/
self-confidence (n)	/ˌself ˈkɒnfɪdənts/
skill (n)	/skɪl/
soaked (adj)	/səʊkt/
social network (n)	/ˈsəʊʃəl ˈnetwɜːk/
sportsman (n)	/ˈspɔːtsmən/
starving (adj)	/ˈstɑːvɪŋ/
strangely (adv)	/ˈstreɪndʒli/
suddenly (adv)	/ˈsʌdnli/
support (n)	/səˈpɔːt/
surfing (n)	/ˈsɜːfɪŋ/
surprisingly (adv)	/səˈpraɪzɪŋli/
swimmer (n)	/ˈswɪmə/
team (n)	/tiːm/
terrible (adj)	/ˈterəbəl/
terrifying (adj)	/ˈterəfaɪ-ɪŋ, ˈterɪfaɪ-ɪŋ/
thankfully (adv)	/ˈθæŋkfəli/
to my horror (adv)	/tə maɪ ˈhɒrə/
train (v)	/treɪn/
training (n)	/ˈtreɪnɪŋ/
unfortunately (adv)	/ʌnˈfɔːtʃənətli/
win (v)	/wɪn/

arranged marriage (n)	/əˈreɪndʒd ˈmærɪdʒ/
ask out (phr v)	/ɑːsk aʊt/
avoid (v)	/əˈvɔɪd/
behave (v)	/bɪˈheɪv/
breadwinner (n)	/ˈbredˌwɪnə/
bring up (phr v)	/brɪŋ ʌp/
child (n)	/tʃaɪld/
chore (n)	/tʃɔː/
communicate (v)	/kəˈmjuːnɪkeɪt/
company (n)	/ˈkʌmpəni/
conflict (n)	/ˈkɒnflɪkt/
custom (n)	/ˈkʌstəm/
dad (n)	/dæd/
date (v)	/deɪt/
divorce rate (n)	/dəˈvɔːs reɪt/
drive mad (phr v)	/draɪv mæd/
enjoy company (v)	/ɪnˈdʒɔɪ ˈkʌmpəni/
family (n)	/ˈfæməli/
finances (n)	/ˈfaɪnænsɪz/
forget (v)	/fəˈget/
full-time (adj)	/ˌfʊl ˈtaɪm /
generation (n)	/ˌdʒenəˈreɪʃən/
get married (v)	/get ˈmærid/
get on nerves (phr v)	/get ɒn nɜːvz/
give back (phr v)	/gɪv bæk/
give up (phr v)	/gɪv ʌp/
go up (phr v)	/gəʊ ʌp/
gossip (v)	/ˈgɒsɪp/
habit (n)	/ˈhæbɪt/
hand over (phr v)	/hænd ˈəʊvə/
happily ever after (adv)	/ˈhæpəli ˈevə ˈɑːftə/
have a chat (adv)	/hæv ə tʃæt/
have a laugh (v)	/hæv ə lɑːf/
head of the household (n)	/hed əv ðə ˈhaʊshəʊld/
household (n)	/ˈhaʊshəʊld/
househusband (n)	/ˈhaʊsˌhʌzbənd/
housewife (n)	/ˈhaʊswaɪf/
housework (n)	/ˈhaʊswɜːk/
husband (n)	/ˈhʌzbənd/
in charge of (v)	/ɪn tʃɑːdʒ əv/
inherit (v)	/ɪnˈherɪt/
interrupt (v)	/ˌɪntəˈrʌpt/
issue (n)	/ˈɪʃuː, ˈɪsjuː/
kid (n)	/kɪd/
leave a mess (v)	/liːv eɪ mes/
leave home (v)	/liːv həʊm/
live with (n)	/lɪv wɪð/
look after (phr v)	/lʊk ˈɑːftə/
make a drama (v)	/meɪk ə ˈdrɑːmə/
marry (v)	/ˈmæri/
matriarchal (n)	/ˌmeɪtriˈɑːkl/
mislay (v)	/ˌmɪsˈleɪ/
mother (n)	/ˈmʌðə/
move back (v)	/muːv bæk/
mum (n)	/mʌm/
nag (v)	/næg/
nest (n)	/nest/
one-parent family (n)	/ˌwʌn ˈpeərənt ˈfæməli/
parent (n)	/ˈpeərənt/
partner (n)	/ˈpɑːtnə/
pay for (phr v)	/peɪ fə/
property (n)	/ˈprɒpəti/
reasonable (adj)	/ˈriːzənəbəl/
reasonably (adv)	/ˈriːzənəbli/
relationship (n)	/rɪˈleɪʃənʃɪp/

135

responsibility (n)	/rɪˌspɒnsəˈbɪləti/
row (n)	/rəʊ/
rule (n)	/ruːl/
settle down (phr v)	/ˈsetl daʊn/
share (v)	/ʃeə/
show off (v)	/ʃəʊ ɒf/
stay-at-home-dad (n)	/steɪ ət həʊm dæd/
take ages (v)	/teɪk ˈeɪdʒɪz/
tie the knot (v)	/taɪ ðə nɒt/
treat with respect (v)	/triːt wɪð rɪˈspekt/
wife (n)	/waɪf/
wind up (phr v)	/wɪnd ʌp/
work out (phr v)	/wɜːk aʊt/

Unit 3
Pages 24-33

3D (adj)	/θriː ˈdiː/
app (n)	/æp/
battery life (n)	/ˈbætəri laɪf/
billion (n)	/ˈbɪljən/
blog (n)	/blɒg/
blogger (n)	/ˈblɒgə/
boyfriend (n)	/ˈbɔɪfrend/
character (n)	/ˈkærəktə/
communicate (v)	/kəˈmjuːnɪkeɪt/
communication technology (n)	/kəˌmjuːnɪˈkeɪʃən tekˈnɒlədʒi/
computer virus (n)	/kəmˈpjuːtə ˈvaɪərəs/
crazy (adj)	/ˈkreɪzi/
desktop (n)	/ˈdesktɒp/
digital (adj)	/ˈdɪdʒətl/
download (v)	/ˌdaʊnˈləʊd/
dump (v)	/dʌmp/
dunno (contraction)	/ˈdʌnəʊ/
email (n)	/ˈiːmeɪl/
figure (n)	/ˈfɪgə/
gadget (n)	/ˈgædʒɪt/
games console (n)	/geɪmz kənˈsəʊl/
Globish (n)	/ˈgləʊbɪʃ/
go off with (v)	/gəʊ ɒf wɪð/
go out with (phr v)	/gəʊ aʊt wɪð/
gossip (n)	/ˈgɒsɪp/
handheld (adj)	/ˈhændheld/
handset (n)	/ˈhændset/
hands-free (adj)	/ˌhændz ˈfriː/
hard drive (n)	/hɑːd draɪv/
high-definition (adj)	/ˌhaɪ defəˈnɪʃən/
high-speed (adj)	/ˌhaɪ ˈspiːd/
innit (contraction)	/ˈɪnɪt/
internet connection (n)	/ˈɪntənet kəˈnekʃən/
internet-enabled (adj)	/ˈɪntənet ɪˈneɪbəld/
landline (adj)	/ˈlændˌlaɪn/
laptop (n)	/ˈlæptɒp/
lol (contraction)	/ˈel əʊ el/
media player (n)	/ˈmiːdiə ˈpleɪə/
million (n)	/ˈmɪljən/
mini projector (n)	/ˈmɪni prəˈdʒektə/
mobile phone network (n)	/ˈməʊbaɪl fəʊn ˈnetwɜːk/
non-native (adj)	/nɒn ˈneɪtɪv/
online (adj)	/ˌɒnˈlaɪn/
operating system (n)	/ˈɒpəreɪtɪŋ sɪstɪm/
percent (adv)	/pəˈsent/
percentage (n)	/pəˈsentɪdʒ/
phishing (n)	/ˈfɪʃɪŋ/
profile (n)	/ˈprəʊfaɪl/
refusnik (n)	/rɪˈfjuːznɪk/
search engine (n)	/sɜːtʃ ˈendʒɪn/

sick (adj)	/sɪk/
slang (n)	/slæŋ/
smartphone (n)	/ˈsmɑːtfəʊn/
social networking site (n)	/ˈsəʊʃəl ˈnetwɜːkɪŋ saɪt/
state-of-the-art (adj)	/ˌsteɪt əv ðɪ ˈɑːt /
techie (adj)	/ˈteki/
technology (n)	/tekˈnɒlədʒi/
technophobe (n)	/ˈteknəfəʊb/
text message (n)	/tekst ˈmesɪdʒ/
texting (n)	/ˈtekstɪŋ/
touch-screen (adj)	/tʌtʃ skriːn/
transfer (v)	/trænsˈfɜː/
trust (v)	/trʌst/
update (v)	/ʌpˈdeɪt/
upload (v)	/ʌpˈləʊd/
upset (adj)	/ˌʌpˈset/
video (n)	/ˈvɪdiəʊ/
wassup (contraction)	/wɒˈsʌp/
web browser (n)	/web ˈbraʊzə/
web page (n)	/web peɪdʒ/
wind-up (adj)	/ˈwaɪnd ʌp/
wireless (adj)	/ˈwaɪələs/
World Wide Web (n)	/wɜːld waɪd web/
YouTube (n)	/ˈjuːtjuːb/

Unit 4
Pages 34-43

ability (n)	/əˈbɪləti/
achieve (v)	/əˈtʃiːv/
A-levels (n)	/ˈeɪ ˌlevəlz/
assess (v)	/əˈses/
basic (n)	/ˈbeɪsɪk/
career (n)	/kəˈrɪə/
chemistry (n)	/ˈkeməstri/
confident (adj)	/ˈkɒnfɪdənt/
correspondent (n)	/ˌkɒrəˈspɒndənt/
course (n)	/kɔːs/
curriculum (n)	/kəˈrɪkjələm/
degree (n)	/dɪˈgriː/
develop (v)	/dɪˈveləp/
education (n)	/ˌedjuˈkeɪʃən/
employer (n)	/ɪmˈplɔɪə/
enthusiastic (adj)	/ɪnˌθjuːziˈæstɪk/
experience (n)	/ɪkˈspɪəriəns/
happiness (n)	/ˈhæpinəs/
highly-motivated (adj)	/ˈhaɪli ˈməʊtəveɪtəd/
History (n)	/ˈhɪstəri/
hospital porter (n)	/ˈhɒspɪtl ˈpɔːtə/
ICT (n)	/ˌaɪ siː ˈtiː/
interpersonal (adj)	/ˌɪntəˈpɜːsənəl/
job (n)	/dʒɒb/
job offer (n)	/dʒɒb ˈɒfə/
journalism (n)	/ˈdʒɜːnəlɪzəm/
journalist (n)	/ˈdʒɜːnəlɪst/
kitchen porter (n)	/ˈkɪtʃɪn ˈpɔːtə/
learn (v)	/lɜːn/
lesson (n)	/ˈlesən/
life skill (n)	/laɪf skɪl/
lifestyle (n)	/ˈlaɪfstaɪl/
literacy (n)	/ˈlɪtərəsi/
low-paid (adj)	/ˌləʊ ˈpeɪd /
manager (n)	/ˈmænɪdʒə/
miner (n)	/ˈmaɪnə/
music (n)	/ˈmjuːzɪk/
numeracy (n)	/ˈnjuːmərəsi/
nurse (n)	/nɜːs/

politics (n)	/ˈpɒlətɪks/
positive attitude (n)	/ˈpɒzətɪv ˈætɪtjuːd/
proven (adj)	/ˈpruːvən, ˈprəʊvən/
pupil (n)	/ˈpjuːpəl/
report (v)	/rɪˈpɔːt/
senior (adj)	/ˈsiːnɪə/
sound IT skills (adj)	/saʊnd ˌaɪ ˈtiː skɪlz/
study (v)	/ˈstʌdi/
subject (n)	/ˈsʌbdʒɪkt/
teach (v)	/tiːtʃ/
teacher (n)	/ˈtiːtʃə/
telesales worker (n)	/ˈteliseɪlz ˈwɜːkə/
travel rep (n)	/ˈtrævəl rep/
well-being (n)	/wel ˈbiːɪŋ/
well-paid (adj)	/ˌwel ˈpeɪd /
well-qualified (adj)	/ˌwel ˈkwɒlɪfaɪd /
willing (adj)	/ˈwɪlɪŋ/
work in a team (v)	/wɜːk ɪn eɪ tiːm/

Unit 5
Pages 44-53

acting (n)	/ˈæktɪŋ/
album (n)	/ˈælbəm/
angle (n)	/ˈæŋgəl/
art collector (n)	/ɑːt kəˈlektə/
artist (n)	/ˈɑːtɪst/
auction house (n)	/ˈɔːkʃən haʊs/
audience (n)	/ˈɔːdiəns/
backstage (n)	/ˌbækˈsteɪdʒ/
band (n)	/bænd/
base on (v)	/beɪs ɒn/
baton (n)	/ˈbætɒn, -tn/
be set (v)	/bi set/
blockbuster (n)	/ˈblɒkˌbʌstə/
bow (v)	/baʊ/
budget (n)	/ˈbʌdʒɪt/
camcorder (n)	/ˈkæmˌkɔːdə/
cast (n)	/kɑːst/
centre on (v)	/ˈsentə ɒn/
cheer (v)	/tʃɪə/
cinema (n)	/ˈsɪnəmə/
circle (n)	/ˈsɜːkəl/
clap (v)	/klæp/
climax (n)	/ˈklaɪmæks/
club (n)	/klʌb/
come out (v)	/kʌm aʊt/
come up with (phr v)	/kʌm ʌp wɪð/
concert (n)	/ˈkɒnsət/
conduct (v)	/kənˈdʌkt/
conductor (n)	/kənˈdʌktə/
constructive (adj)	/kənˈstrʌktɪv/
costume (n)	/ˈkɒstjʊm/
criticism (n)	/ˈkrɪtɪsɪzəm/
curtain (n)	/ˈkɜːtn/
direct (v)	/dəˈrekt, daɪˈrekt/
do research (v)	/duː rɪˈsɜːtʃ/
dressing room (n)	/ˈdresɪŋ ruːm/
DVD (n)	/ˌdiː viː ˈdiː/
edit (v)	/ˈedɪt/
end up (phr v)	/end ʌp/
exhibition (n)	/ˌeksəˈbɪʃən/
extra (n)	/ˈekstrə/
fail (v)	/feɪl/
fan (n)	/fæn/
fantasy (adj)	/ˈfæntəsi/
fault (n)	/fɔːlt/
feedback (n)	/ˈfiːdbæk/

festival (n)	/ˈfestəvəl/
film (n)	/fɪlm/
film studio (n)	/fɪlm ˈstjuːdiəʊ/
filmmaker (n)	/ˈfɪlmeɪkə/
first act (n)	/fɜːst ækt/
get hits (v)	/get hɪts/
gig (n)	/gɪg/
go up (v)	/gəʊ ʌp/
good point (n)	/gʊd pɔɪnt/
interval (n)	/ˈɪntəvəl/
literary agent (n)	/ˈlɪtərəri ˈeɪdʒənt/
make-up (n)	/ˈmeɪkʌp/
movie (n)	/ˈmuːvi/
museum (n)	/mjuːˈziəm/
music (n)	/ˈmjuːzɪk/
musical (n)	/ˈmjuːzɪkəl/
number one single (n)	/ˈnʌmbə wʌn ˈsɪŋgəl/
on location (prep phr)	/ɒn ləʊˈkeɪʃən/
on stage (prep phr)	/ɒn steɪdʒ/
opening night (n)	/ˈəʊpənɪŋ naɪt/
orchestra (n)	/ˈɔːkəstrə/
original (adj)	/əˈrɪdʒɪnəl, -dʒənəl/
overnight sensation (n)	/ˌəʊvəˈnaɪt senˈseɪʃən/
painting (n)	/ˈpeɪntɪŋ/
performance (n)	/pəˈfɔːməns/
pick up (phr v)	/pɪk ʌp/
play (v)	/pleɪ/
plot (n)	/plɒt/
point of view (n)	/pɔɪnt əv vjuː/
pop star (n)	/pɒp stɑː/
post (v)	/pəʊst/
producer (n)	/prəˈdjuːsə/
production (n)	/prəˈdʌkʃən/
publish (v)	/ˈpʌblɪʃ/
publisher (n)	/ˈpʌblɪʃə/
publishing deal (n)	/ˈpʌblɪʃɪŋ diːl/
put on (v)	/pʊt ɒn/
reader (n)	/ˈriːdə/
recommend (v)	/ˌrekəˈmend/
record label (n)	/ˈrekɔːd ˈleɪbəl/
recording deal (n)	/rɪˈkɔːdɪŋ diːl/
refreshments (n)	/rɪˈfreʃmənts/
refund (v)	/rɪˈfʌnd/
release (v)	/rɪˈliːs/
restore (v)	/rɪˈstɔː/
review (n)	/rɪˈvjuː/
review (v)	/rɪˈvjuː/
romance (n)	/rəʊˈmæns, ˈrəʊmæns/
rope in (phr v)	/rəʊp ɪn/
schoolboy (n)	/ˈskuːlbɔɪ/
script (n)	/skrɪpt/
set (n)	/set/
shoot a scene (v)	/ʃuːt ə siːn/
show appreciation (v)	/ʃəʊ əˌpriːʃiˈeɪʃən/
sign (v)	/saɪn/
singer (n)	/ˈsɪŋə/
special effect (n)	/ˈspeʃəl ɪˈfekt/
special feature (n)	/ˈspeʃəl ˈfiːtʃə/
stalls (n)	/stɔːlz/
storyline (n)	/ˈstɔːriːlaɪn/
succeed (v)	/səkˈsiːd/
suspense (n)	/səˈspens/
take a seat (v)	/teɪk eɪ siːt/
take place (v)	/teɪk pleɪs/
talent (n)	/ˈtælənt/
talent contest (n)	/ˈtælənt ˈkɒntest/
talk into (phr v)	/tɔːk ˈɪntə/

137

tell the story (v)	/tel ðə ˈstɔːri/
theatre (n)	/ˈθɪətə/
thriller (n)	/ˈθrɪlə/
ticket (n)	/ˈtɪkɪt/
turning point (n)	/ˈtɜːnɪŋ pɔɪnt/
twist (n)	/twɪst/
venue (n)	/ˈvenjuː/
walk around (phr v)	/wɔːk əˈraʊnd/
well-rounded (adj)	/ˌwel ˈraʊndɪd /
world tour (n)	/wɜːld tʊə/
worldwide (adj)	/ˌwɜːldˈwaɪd/
writer (n)	/ˈraɪtə/

Unit 6
Pages 54-63

abroad (n)	/əˈbrɔːd/
aubergine (n)	/ˈəʊbəʒiːn/
backpack (n)	/ˈbækpæk/
barbecue (v)	/ˈbɑːbɪkjuː/
beach resort (n)	/biːtʃ rɪˈzɔːt/
bean (n)	/biːn/
boiled (adj)	/bɔɪld/
bread (n)	/bred/
cabbage (n)	/ˈkæbɪdʒ/
cheese (n)	/tʃiːz/
chef (n)	/ʃef/
chicken drumstick (n)	/ˈtʃɪkɪn ˈdrʌmˈstɪk/
chilli (n)	/ˈtʃɪli/
chilling out (n)	/ˈtʃɪlɪŋ aʊt/
couch surfing (n)	/kaʊtʃ ˈsɜːfɪŋ/
country (n)	/ˈkʌntri/
cuisine (n)	/kwɪˈziːn/
culture (n)	/ˈkʌltʃə/
curry powder (n)	/ˈkʌri ˈpaʊdə/
delicious (adj)	/dɪˈlɪʃəs/
dessert (n)	/dɪˈzɜːt/
dinner (n)	/ˈdɪnə/
disgusting (adj)	/dɪsˈgʌstɪŋ, dɪz-/
dish (n)	/dɪʃ/
drink (n)	/drɪŋk/
eating out (n)	/ˈiːtɪŋ aʊt/
feed (v)	/fiːd/
fish (n)	/fɪʃ/
fizzy (adj)	/ˈfɪzi/
flavouring (n)	/ˈfleɪvərɪŋ/
fried (adj)	/fraɪd/
fruit (n)	/fruːt/
fruit salad (n)	/fruːt ˈsæləd/
full board (n)	/fʊl bɔːd/
garlic (n)	/ˈgɑːlɪk/
grilled (adj)	/grɪld/
guided tour (n)	/ˈgaɪdɪd tʊə/
haggis (n)	/ˈhægəs, ˈhægɪs/
herb (n)	/hɜːb/
hiking holiday (n)	/ˈhaɪkɪŋ ˈhɒlədeɪ/
hire (v)	/haɪə/
hitch-hike (v)	/hɪtʃ haɪk/
host (n)	/həʊst/
kangaroo (n)	/ˌkæŋgəˈruː/
kitchen (n)	/ˈkɪtʃɪn/
kiwi (n)	/ˈkiːwiː/
lamb (n)	/læm/
landmark (n)	/ˈlændmɑːk/

lean (adj)	/liːn/
liver (n)	/ˈlɪvə/
main course (n)	/meɪn kɔːs/
mango (n)	/ˈmæŋgəʊ/
mashed (adj)	/mæʃt/
meal (n)	/miːl/
meat (n)	/miːt/
menu (n)	/ˈmenjuː/
muffin (n)	/ˈmʌfɪn/
nightlife (n)	/ˈnaɪtlaɪf/
nut (n)	/nʌt/
nutritious (adj)	/njuːˈtrɪʃəs/
oatmeal (n)	/ˈəʊtmiːl/
off the beaten track (prep phr)	/ɒf ðə ˈbiːtn træk/
package holiday (n)	/ˈpækɪdʒ ˈhɒlədeɪ/
packaged food (n)	/ˈpækɪdʒ fuːd/
pickled (adj)	/ˈpɪkəld/
pigeon (n)	/ˈpɪdʒɪn/
pizza (n)	/ˈpiːtsə/
potato (n)	/pəˈteɪtəʊ/
prawn (n)	/prɔːn/
processed (adj)	/ˈprəʊsest/
protein (n)	/ˈprəʊtiːn/
raw (adj)	/rɔː/
ready meal (n)	/ˈredi miːl/
recipe (n)	/ˈresəpi/
restaurant (n)	/ˈrestərɒnt/
rice (n)	/raɪs/
rich (adj)	/rɪtʃ/
roast (adj)	/rəʊst/
room service (n)	/ruːm ˈsɜːvɪs/
runny (adj)	/ˈrʌni/
salad (n)	/ˈsæləd/
sauce (n)	/sɔːs/
sausage (n)	/ˈsɒsɪdʒ/
seafood (n)	/ˈsiːfuːd/
self-catering (adj)	/ˌself ˈkeɪtərɪŋ/
soft (adj)	/sɒft/
soup (n)	/suːp/
special offer (n)	/ˈspeʃəl ˈɒfə/
speciality (n)	/ˌspeʃiˈæləti/
spice (n)	/spaɪs/
spicy (adj)	/ˈspaɪsi/
starter (n)	/ˈstɑːtə/
steak (n)	/steɪk/
strong (adj)	/strɒŋ/
sunbathing (n)	/ˈsʌnbeɪðɪŋ/
sweet (adj)	/swiːt/
tender (adj)	/ˈtendə/
the locals (n)	/ðə ˈləʊkəlz/
three-course meal (n)	/θriː kɔːs miːl/
toast (v)	/təʊst/
tour guide (n)	/tʊə gaɪd/
tourist (n)	/ˈtʊərɪst/
travel (v)	/ˈtrævəl/
travel rep (n)	/ˈtrævəl rep/
traveller (n)	/ˈtrævələ/
tuna (n)	/ˈtjuːnə/
turnip (n)	/ˈtɜːnɪp/
vegetable (n)	/ˈvedʒtəbəl/
vegetarian (n)	/ˌvedʒəˈteəriən/
watermelon (n)	/ˈwɔːtəˌmelən/
wine (n)	/waɪn/

Unit 7
Pages 64-73

achieve (v)	/əˈtʃiːv/
admire (v)	/ədˈmaɪə/
analytical (adj)	/ˌænəlˈɪtɪkəl/
antibiotic (n)	/ˌæntɪbaɪˈɒtɪk/
artistic (adj)	/ɑːˈtɪstɪk/
attitude (n)	/ˈætɪtjuːd/
bacteria (n)	/bækˈtɪəriə/
badly organised (adj)	/ˈbædli ˈɔːgənaɪzd/
behave (v)	/bɪˈheɪv/
body (n)	/ˈbɒdi/
chemotherapy (n)	/ˌkiːməʊˈθerəpi, ˌkem-/
colourful (adj)	/ˈkʌləfəl/
confidence (n)	/ˈkɒnfɪdəns/
cure someone (v)	/kjʊə ˈsʌmwʌn/
damage your health (v)	/ˈdæmɪdʒ jə helθ/
depressed (adj)	/dɪˈprest/
description (n)	/dɪˈskrɪpʃən/
dialysis (n)	/daɪˈæləsəs, daɪˈælɪsəs/
empathetic (adj)	/ˌempəˈθetɪk/
energetic (adj)	/ˌenəˈdʒetɪk/
ethical (adj)	/ˈeθɪkəl/
famous (adj)	/ˈfeɪməs/
good for you (adj)	/gʊd fə jə/
have surgery (v)	/hæv ˈsɜːdʒəri/
healthcare (n)	/ˈhelθkeə/
hospital (n)	/ˈhɒspɪtl/
huge (adj)	/hjuːdʒ/
ill (adj)	/ɪl/
illness (n)	/ˈɪlnəs/
imaginative (adj)	/ɪˈmædʒənətɪv/
impulsive (adj)	/ɪmˈpʌlsɪv/
independent (adj)	/ˌɪndəˈpendənt/
infection (n)	/ɪnˈfekʃən/
inspiration (n)	/ˌɪnspəˈreɪʃən/
inspire (v)	/ɪnˈspaɪə/
keep alive (v)	/kiːp əˈlaɪv/
liver failure (n)	/ˈlɪvə ˈfeɪljə/
lung cancer (n)	/lʌŋ ˈkænsə/
make an impression (v)	/meɪk ən ɪmˈpreʃən/
medical (adj)	/ˈmedɪkəl/
medicine (n)	/ˈmedɪsən/
memorable (adj)	/ˈmemərəbəl/
motor-neuron disease (n)	/ˈməʊtə ˈnjʊərɒn dɪˈziːz/
multi-tasking (n)	/ˈmʌlti ˌtɑːsk ɪŋ/
nose (n)	/nəʊz/
obese (adj)	/əʊˈbiːs/
obsess (v)	/əbˈses/
operation (n)	/ˌɒpəˈreɪʃən/
organ donor (n)	/ˈɔːgən ˈdəʊnə/
paralysed (adj)	/ˈpærəlaɪzd/
personality (n)	/ˌpɜːsəˈnæləti/
petite (adj)	/pəˈtiːt/
physical (adj)	/ˈfɪzɪkəl/
possible (adv)	/ˈpɒsəbəl/
practical (adj)	/ˈpræktɪkəl/
process information (v)	/ˈprəʊses ˌɪnfəˈmeɪʃən/
quick-thinking (adj)	/kwɪk ˈθɪŋkɪŋ/
risk your health (v)	/rɪsk jə helθ/
role model (n)	/rəʊl ˈmɒdl/
self-confidence (n)	/ˌself ˈkɒnfɪdəns/
sick (adj)	/sɪk/
slender (adj)	/ˈslendə/
spatial skills (n)	/ˈspeɪʃəl skɪlz/

suffer from an illness (v)	/ˈsʌfə frəm ən ˈɪlnəs/
take care of (v)	/teɪk keə əv/
therapy (n)	/ˈθerəpi/
transplant (n)	/ˈtrænsplɑːnt/
treatment (n)	/ˈtriːtmənt/
unpredictable (adj)	/ˌʌnprɪˈdɪktəbəl/
unusual (adj)	/ʌnˈjuːʒuəl, -ʒəl/
verbal skills (n)	/ˈvɜːbəl skɪlz/
virus (n)	/ˈvaɪərəs/
wheelchair (n)	/ˈwiːltʃeə/
wild (adj)	/waɪld/

Unit 8
Pages 74-83

accuse (v)	/əˈkjuːz/
admit (v)	/ədˈmɪt/
advert (n)	/ˈædvɜːt/
advertising agency (n)	/ˈædvətaɪzɪŋ ˈeɪdʒənsi/
advertising campaign (n)	/ˈædvətaɪzɪŋ kæmˈpeɪn/
advise (v)	/ədˈvaɪz/
afford (v)	/əˈfɔːd/
agree (v)	/əˈgriː/
aim at (v)	/eɪm ət/
apologise (v)	/əˈpɒlədʒaɪz/
bank (n)	/bæŋk/
bank account (n)	/bæŋk əˈkaʊnt/
bank loan (n)	/bæŋk ləʊn/
bargain (n)	/ˈbɑːgɪn/
bill (n)	/bɪl/
billboard (n)	/ˈbɪlbɔːd/
borrow (v)	/ˈbɒrəʊ/
brand (n)	/brænd/
buy (v)	/baɪ/
cash (n)	/kæʃ/
chain store (n)	/ˈtʃeɪn stɔː/
change (n)	/tʃeɪndʒ/
charge (v)	/tʃɑːdʒ/
cheap (adj)	/tʃiːp/
consumer (adj)	/kənˈsjuːmə/
consumer (n)	/kənˈsjuːmə/
cough up (phr v)	/kɒf ʌp/
credit card (n)	/ˈkredɪt kɑːd/
debt (n)	/det/
deny (v)	/dɪˈnaɪ/
department store (n)	/dɪˈpɑːtmənt stɔː/
designer (adj)	/dɪˈzaɪnə/
details (n)	/ˈdiːteɪlz/
expensive (adj)	/ɪkˈspensɪv/
explain (v)	/ɪkˈspleɪn/
fake (adj)	/feɪk/
faulty (adj)	/ˈfɔːlti/
fly poster (n)	/flaɪ ˈpəʊstə/
free (adj)	/friː/
ignore (v)	/ɪgˈnɔː/
in credit (prep phr)	/ɪn ˈkredɪt/
in debt (prep phr)	/ɪn det/
in stock (prep phr)	/ɪn stɒk/
in the red (prep phr)	/ɪn ðə red/
insist (v)	/ɪnˈsɪst/
jingle (n)	/ˈdʒɪŋgəl/
leaflet (n)	/ˈliːflɪt/
live the high life (v)	/lɪv ðə haɪ laɪf/
loan (n)	/ləʊn/
logo (n)	/ˈləʊgəʊ/
market (n)	/ˈmɑːkɪt/

139

on special offer (prep phr)	/ɒn ˈspeʃəl ˈɒfə/	deception (n)	/dɪˈsepʃən/
order (v)	/ˈɔːdə/	defence (n)	/dɪˈfens/
overdraft (n)	/ˈəʊvədrɑːft/	defend (v)	/dɪˈfend/
overdrawn (adj)	/ˌəʊvəˈdrɔːn/	deterrent (n)	/dɪˈterənt/
owe (v)	/əʊ/	escape (v)	/ɪˈskeɪp/
packaging (n)	/ˈpækɪdʒɪŋ/	evidence (n)	/ˈevɪdəns/
pay (v)	/peɪ/	execute (v)	/ˈeksəkjuːt/
pay back (phr v)	/peɪ bæk/	execution (n)	/ˌeksəˈkjuːʃən/
payment (n)	/ˈpeɪmənt/	fine (v)	/faɪn/
pop-up (adj)	/ˈpɒp ʌp/	fine (n)	/faɪn/
price (n)	/praɪs/	fool (v)	/fuːl/
product (n)	/ˈprɒdʌkt/	forged (adj)	/fɔːdʒd/
promise (v)	/ˈprɒmɪs/	fraud (n)	/frɔːd/
promote (v)	/prəˈməʊt/	fraudster (n)	/ˈfrɔːdstə/
promotional (adj)	/prəˈməʊʃənəl/	gang (n)	/gæŋ/
receipt (n)	/rɪˈsiːt/	genuine (adj)	/ˈdʒenjuɪn/
refund (n)	/ˈriːfʌnd/	guilty (adj)	/ˈgɪlti/
refuse (v)	/rɪˈfjuːz/	hoax (n)	/həʊks/
repay (v)	/rɪˈpeɪ/	illegally (adv)	/ɪˈliːgəli/
retailer (n)	/ˈriːteɪlə/	in prison (prep phr)	/ɪn ˈprɪzən/
save up (phr v)	/seɪv ʌp/	innocent (adj)	/ˈɪnəsənt/
second-hand (adj)	/ˌsekəndˈhænd/	jail (v)	/dʒeɪl/
secure (adj)	/sɪˈkʊə/	judge (n)	/dʒʌdʒ/
shop assistant (n)	/ʃɒp əˈsɪstənt/	judge (v)	/dʒʌdʒ/
shopper (n)	/ˈʃɒpə/	judgement (n)	/ˈdʒʌdʒmənt/
slogan (n)	/ˈsləʊgən/	judgemental (adj)	/dʒʌdʒˈmentl/
spend (v)	/spend/	jury (n)	/ˈdʒʊəri/
statement (n)	/ˈsteɪtmənt/	kidnap (v)	/ˈkɪdnæp/
steal (v)	/stiːl/	lawyer (n)	/ˈlɔːjə/
stealth marketing (n)	/stelθ ˈmɑːkətɪŋ/	lie to (v)	/laɪ tə/
stock (v)	/stɒk/	life imprisonment (n)	/laɪf ɪmˈprɪzənmənt/
supermarket (n)	/ˈsuːpəˌmɑːkɪt/	murder (v)	/ˈmɜːdə/
target audience (n)	/ˈtɑːgɪt ˈɔːdiəns/	parole (n)	/pəˈrəʊl/
warn (v)	/wɔːn/	plead (v)	/pliːd/
word-of-mouth (n)	/wɜːd əv maʊθ/	police (n)	/pəˈliːs/
wrap up (v)	/ræp ʌp/	possession of drugs (n)	/pəˈzeʃən əv drʌgz/
		pretend (v)	/prɪˈtend/
Unit 9		prosecute (v)	/ˈprɒsɪkjuːt/
Pages 84-93		prosecution (n)	/ˌprɒsɪˈkjuːʃən/
abolish (v)	/əˈbɒlɪʃ/	prove (v)	/pruːv/
accuse (v)	/əˈkjuːz/	punishment (n)	/ˈpʌnɪʃmənt/
admit (v)	/ədˈmɪt/	reform (v)	/rɪˈfɔːm/
arrest (v)	/əˈrest/	release (v)	/rɪˈliːs/
attack (v)	/əˈtæk/	rob (v)	/rɒb/
break the law (v)	/breɪk ðə lɔː/	robber (n)	/ˈrɒbə/
burglary (n)	/ˈbɜːgləri/	robbery (n)	/ˈrɒbəri/
burgle (v)	/ˈbɜːgəl/	sentence (v)	/ˈsentəns/
case (n)	/keɪs/	sentence (n)	/ˈsentəns/
charge with (phr v)	/tʃɑːdʒ wɪð/	shoot (v)	/ʃuːt/
cheat out of (phr v)	/tʃiːt aʊt əv/	shoplift (v)	/ˈʃɒpˌlɪft/
claim (v)	/kleɪm/	shoplifter (n)	/ˈʃɒpˌlɪftə/
commit (v)	/kəˈmɪt/	shoplifting (n)	/ˈʃɒpˌlɪftɪŋ/
community service (n)	/kəˈmjuːnəti ˈsɜːvɪs/	steal (v)	/stiːl/
con (v)	/kɒn/	suspect (v)	/səˈspekt/
confess (v)	/kənˈfes/	take in (phr v)	/teɪk ɪn/
convict (v)	/kənˈvɪkt/	terrorism (n)	/ˈterərɪzəm/
conviction (n)	/kənˈvɪkʃən/	theft (n)	/θeft/
copyright (n)	/ˈkɒpiraɪt/	thief (n)	/θiːf/
court (n)	/kɔːt/	trial (n)	/ˈtraɪəl/
crime (n)	/kraɪm/	truth (n)	/truːθ/
criminal (n)	/ˈkrɪmɪnəl/	victim (n)	/ˈvɪktɪm/
death penalty (n)	/deθ ˈpenlti/	witness (n)	/ˈwɪtnəs/
deceive (v)	/dɪˈsiːv/	wound (v)	/wuːnd/

accommodation (n) /əˌkɒməˈdeɪʃən/
agree a price (v) /əˈgriː eɪ praɪs/
apartment (n) /əˈpɑːtmənt/
architect (n) /ˈɑːkətekt/
atmosphere (n) /ˈætməsfɪə/
build (v) /bɪld/
building (n) /ˈbɪldɪŋ/
buyer (n) /ˈbaɪə/
cave (n) /keɪv/
city centre (n) /ˈsɪti ˈsentə/
cliff face (n) /klɪf feɪs/
climate (n) /ˈklaɪmət/
colonise (v) /ˈkɒlənaɪz/
colony (n) /ˈkɒləni/
conventional (adj) /kənˈvenʃənəl/
countryside (n) /ˈkʌntrisaɪd/
cramped (adj) /kræmpt/
crowded (adj) /ˈkraʊdɪd/
culturally diverse (adj) /ˈkʌltʃərəli daɪˈvɜːs/
demolish (v) /dɪˈmɒlɪʃ/
desert (n) /ˈdezət/
energy (n) /ˈenədʒi/
environment (n) /ɪnˈvaɪrənmənt/
estate agent (n) /ɪˈsteɪt ˈeɪdʒənt/
family-friendly (adj) /ˈfæməli ˈfrendli/
floating city (n) /ˈfləʊtɪŋ ˈsɪti/
glacier (n) /ˈglæsɪə/
global warming (n) /ˈgləʊbəl ˈwɔːmɪŋ/
go through (phr v) /gəʊ θruː/
green space (n) /griːn speɪs/
grow crops (v) /grəʊ krɒps/
habitable (adj) /ˈhæbətəbəl/
homeowner (n) /ˈhəʊmˌəʊnə/
ice cap (n) /aɪs kæp/
island (n) /ˈaɪlənd/
landscape (n) /ˈlændskeɪp/
litter (n) /ˈlɪtə/
local facilities (n) /ˈləʊkəl fasɪlɪtiːz/

locate (v) /ləʊˈkeɪt/
look round (phr v) /lʊk ˈraʊnd/
make an offer (v) /meɪk ən ˈɒfə/
make room for (phr v) /meɪk ruːm fə/
melt (v) /melt/
mine (v) /maɪn/
mineral (n) /ˈmɪnərəl/
mortgage (v) /ˈmɔːgɪdʒ/
move house (v) /muːv haʊs/
move in (phr v) /muːv ɪn/
move out (n) /muːv aʊt/
natural resource (n) /ˈnætʃərəl rɪˈzɔːs/
negotiate (v) /nɪˈgəʊʃieɪt/
nothing to do (phrase) /ˈnʌθɪŋ tə duː/
oil (n) /ɔɪl/
pollution (n) /pəˈluːʃən/
population (n) /ˌpɒpjəˈleɪʃən/
purify (v) /ˈpjʊərɪfaɪ/
rainwater (n) /ˈreɪnwɔːtə/
raise animals (v) /reɪz ˈænɪməlz/
reject an offer (v) /rɪˈdʒekt ən ˈɒfə/
renewable (adj) /rɪˈnjuːəbəl/
rent (n) /rent/
rise (v) /raɪz/
roof (n) /ruːf/
scenery (n) /ˈsiːnəri/
sea level (n) /siː ˈlevəl/
sense of community (phrase) /sens əv kəˈmjuːnəti/
skyscraper (n) /ˈskaɪˌskreɪpə/
structure (n) /ˈstrʌktʃə/
town (n) /taʊn/
traffic (n) /ˈtræfɪk/
transport links (n) /ˈtrænspɔːt lɪŋks/
tree house (n) /triː haʊs/
uninhabitable (adj) /ˌʌnɪnˈhæbətəbəl/
up for sale (prep phr) /ʌp fə seɪl/
village (n) /ˈvɪlɪdʒ/
waterfall (n) /ˈwɔːtəfɔːl/

Unit 2, page 21, exercise 5 (Student B)

You are a receptionist at EasyBuy supermarket head office. The PR manager is Ms. Price. She is in the office but she's very busy and doesn't want to talk to anyone on the phone. Try to take a message or recommend that the caller sends a letter.

Unit 6, page 59, exercise 7a (Student B)

Holiday option 2
Sightseeing package tour in New York, US

Accommodation: The package includes full board in a luxury hotel near the centre of New York. Guided tours and the services of an experienced travel rep are also included and the hotel has twenty-four-hour room service.

Things to do: Sightseeing, obviously. Think of all those famous New York landmarks. Plus, there's the shopping of course!

Weather in May: Usually great. It's warm enough to spend all your time outside but not too hot for walking around the city.

Cost and length of stay: All accommodation and travel are included in the package but of course New York is an expensive city – you will need plenty of pocket money. Four days is the maximum you can afford!

Unit 9, page 87, exercise 9a and 9b

A bank was robbed by a single robber and man A was identified as the robber by several witnesses. When the case was brought to court, man A called his twin brother, twin B, as a witness. Twin B then confessed to committing the robbery.

Twin A was released and twin B was then tried for the crime. Twin B called twin A as witness and twin A confessed to the crime. Twin B had to be released as he could not be found guilty 'beyond reasonable doubt'. Twin A could not be tried again because by law, a person cannot be tried for the same crime twice.

a Did twin A rob the bank?

He might have committed the crime because witnesses identified him.

He can't have committed the crime because his brother confessed.

b Did twin B rob the bank?
c Did one of them the bank?
d Did both twins rob the bank?
e Are both twins guilty of committing a crime?
f Do you think the police knew that A had an identical twin?
g Are the twins identical?
h What do you think the police did about the case after the end of the second trial?

Unit 9, page 88, exercise 4a and 4b

1f 2a 3d 4c 5b e = extra sentence

Unit 5, page 49, exercise 4a

Case study 2: The crime writer

Melinda Scott, twenty-six, has just published her first novel, *Murderland*, a thriller about a teenager who is wrongly accused of a gang killing. Melinda is one of the new 'internet generation' writers. So, what role did the Net play?

'I've always been fascinated by the criminal justice system, maybe because my aunt's a lawyer. She used to tell me stories about cases,' says Melinda, who has wanted to be a writer since childhood. As a teenager she posted stories on a website called FanFiction.net 'My stories were always about kids solving mysteries,' she recalls. 'Those sites are read by thousands of people so I got used to having readers and getting reviews.'

Later, she joined an online community called WriteCrime.net, which was an enormous help. 'When you sign up, you agree to edit and review other people's work as well as posting stories yourself. So everyone gets feedback.' Melinda found the constructive criticism very useful. 'People helped me with things like working out the plot, as well as practical stuff like researching what type of poison your killer should use!'

Murderland was posted on the website in instalments and soon had several thousand regular readers. Other writers on the website also provided tips about how to get published. Melinda followed their advice and eventually found a literary agent and got a publishing deal. So, what kind of story is *Murderland*? 'It's partly a mystery but it's also about how the investigation affects the suspect's family,' explains Melinda. 'I'm so excited that it's finally coming out!'

Unit 6, page 59, exercise 7a (Student C)

Holiday option 3
Couch surfing in the Loire Valley, France

Accommodation: A farmhouse in rural France owned by a friendly middle-aged couple.

Things to do: There are loads of beautiful walks in the countryside nearby and some amazing castles to visit. There are also some beautiful villages to explore. Public transport is good. Plus you will meet the locals, eat in local restaurants, etc.

Weather in May: It's usually beautiful. It's warm enough to swim in the rivers but not so hot that you can't travel around.

Cost and length of stay: You will have to pay for your own transport and food but as you are couch surfing, accommodation will be free. You have plenty of money for two to three weeks in France.

Irregular verbs

Infinitive	2nd Form (Past Simple)	3rd Form (Past Participle)
be	was/were	been
become	became	become
begin	began	begun
break	broke	broken
bring	brought	brought
build	built	built
burn	burned/burnt	burned/burnt
buy	bought	bought
catch	caught	caught
choose	chose	chosen
come	came	come
cost	cost	cost
cut	cut	cut
dig	dug	dug
do	did	done
draw	drew	drawn
dream	dreamed/dreamt	dreamed/dreamt
drink	drank	drunk
drive	drove	driven
eat	ate	eaten
fall	fell	fallen
feed	fed	fed
feel	felt	felt
fight	fought	fought
find	found	found
fly	flew	flown
forget	forgot	forgotten
forgive	forgave	forgiven
get	got	got
give	gave	given
go	went	gone
grow	grew	grown
have	had	had
hear	heard	heard
hide	hid	hidden
hit	hit	hit
hold	held	held
hurt	hurt	hurt
keep	kept	kept
know	knew	known
lead	led	led
learn	learned/learnt	learned/learnt
leave	left	left

Infinitive	2nd Form (Past Simple)	3rd Form (Past Participle)
let	let	let
lie	lay	lain
light	lit	lit
lose	lost	lost
make	made	made
mean	meant	meant
meet	met	met
pay	paid	paid
put	put	put
read	read	read
ride	rode	ridden
ring	rang	rung
run	ran	run
say	said	said
see	saw	seen
sell	sold	sold
send	sent	sent
set	set	set
shine	shone	shone
show	showed	shown
shut	shut	shut
sing	sang	sung
sit	sat	sat
sleep	slept	slept
smell	smelled/smelt	smelled/smelt
speak	spoke	spoken
spend	spent	spent
spill	spilled/spilt	spilled/spilt
stand	stood	stood
steal	stole	stolen
swim	swam	swum
take	took	taken
teach	taught	taught
tear	tore	torn
tell	told	told
think	thought	thought
throw	threw	thrown
understand	understood	understood
wake	woke	woken
wear	wore	worn
win	won	won
write	wrote	written